Essential

A2 Physics

for OCR

Jim Breithaupt

SOUTH DEVON COLLEGE LIBRARY

D0352537

WITHDRAWN

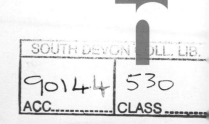

SOUTH DEVON COLL. Lib.	
90144	530
ACC	CLASS

Text © Jim Breithaupt 2004
Original illustrations © Nelson Thornes 2004

The right of Jim Breithaupt to be identified as the author of this work has been
asserted by him in accordance with the Copyright, Designs and Patents Act 1988.

All rights reserved. No part of this publication may be reproduced or transmitted in
any form or by any means, electronic or mechanical, including photocopy,
recording or any information storage and retrieval system, without permission in
writing from the publisher or under licence from the Copyright Licensing Agency
Limited, of 90 Tottenham Court Road, London W1T 4LP.

Any person who commits any unauthorised act in relation to this publication may be
liable to criminal prosecution and civil claims for damages.

Published in 2004 by:
Nelson Thornes Ltd
Delta Place
27 Bath Road
CHELTENHAM
GL53 7TH
United Kingdom

04   05   06   07   08   /   10   9   8   7   6   5   4   3   2   1

A catalogue record for this book is available from the British Library

ISBN 0 7487 8508 6

Illustrations by IFA Design
Page make-up by Tech-Set Ltd

Printed and bound in Croatia by Zrinski

Contents

Introduction

About A2 Physics

This book is for A2 Physics students who are following, or are about to follow the A2 part of OCR Physics (Specification A). This book covers all the compulsory content of the A2 course. The companion book, Essential AS Physics for OCR (Specification A), covers all the AS specification. The A2 specification consists of three modules which take the study of physics beyond AS level in both depth and breadth. In addition, students are expected to be able to synthesise (i.e. bring together) knowledge, understanding and skills from different areas of physics in the AS course and A2 module 2824, Forces, Fields and Energy, which is the central part of the A2 course. Assessment of this additional feature is called **synoptic assessment** and accounts for 20% of the total A level award through the other two A2 modules (2825 and 2826), as explained below.

Chapters 1–13 of this book cover the content of A2 module 2824, Forces, Fields and Energy, in detail and provide the background for synoptic features where appropriate. A set of short questions is provided at the end of every topic as well as examination-style questions at the end of each chapter. Chapter 14, Mathematical skills for A2 physics, provides detailed knowledge of the mathematical skills needed in the A2 physics course as well as further synoptic support. A set of short questions is provided at the end of each topic in this chapter. Chapter 15, Synoptic assessment, provides detailed guidance on synoptic assessment. The reference section at the end of the book includes data and formulae, a glossary, answers to numerical questions and a comprehensive index.

The A2 course accounts for 50% of the total A level mark and is not certificated separately. The three A2 modules are:

Module 2824 Forces, Fields and Energy This module is tested by means of a written paper of duration 1 hour 30 minutes. All the questions on the written paper must be answered. The paper accounts for 15% of the total A level mark. The content of this module is covered in detail in chapters 1–13 of this book. In-depth knowledge and understanding of this module is essential to succeed in synoptic assessment in modules 2825 and 2826.

Module 2825 Options in Physics One optional topic is studied, from Cosmology, Health Physics, Materials, Nuclear and Particle Physics, and Telecommunications. Each option is tested by means of a written paper of duration 1 hour 30 minutes which accounts for 15% of the total A level mark. Synoptic assessment accounts for one-third of the total marks for this written paper (i.e. 5% of the total A level mark) and is based on the bringing together of data analysis and comprehension skills developed in the AS course, in module 2824 of the A2 course and in practical work in the A2 course. Guidance on the assessment of data analysis and comprehension is provided in Topic 15.1 Data analysis and comprehension.

Module 2826 Unifying Concepts in Physics/ Experimental Skills 2 Candidates take component 01 of this module, Unifying Concepts in Physics, and either component 02, Coursework 2, or component 03, Practical Examination 2. Each component is worth 10% of the total A level mark. The total mark for this module therefore accounts for 20% of the total A level mark.

- **Unifying Concepts in Physics (component 01)** tests the synthesis of knowledge and understanding of facts, principles and concepts developed in the AS course and module 2824 of the A2 course. Guidance on assessment of synoptic knowledge, understanding and skills for this component is provided in Topic 15.2 Unifying concepts in physics.

- **Experimental Skills 2 (components 02 and 03)** extends the assessment of two of the four skill areas to include synoptic knowledge and understanding in planning experimental and investigative work (skill P) and in analysing evidence and drawing conclusions (skill A). Such synoptic assessment accounts for half the mark awarded for this component and is therefore worth 5% of the total A level award. Guidance on assessment of synoptic knowledge, understanding and skills for component 02 and 03 is provided in Topic 15.3 Synoptic practical skills.

This book is written to help you to do well on the A2 course and to complete the A level physics course successfully. More importantly, I hope it will give you a lasting interest in physics, a real awareness of its importance as a subject that shapes the future, and an on-going enthusiasm for this fascinating subject.

Jim Breithaupt

1 Work and energy

1.1 Conservation of energy

1.1.1 Fact file

Here are some reminders from your AS course about energy. As you read through these points, don't think there isn't much more to learn about energy. For example, energy transfer to an object causes the object to gain mass in accordance with Einstein's famous equation $E = mc^2$, where c is the speed of light in free space, m is the gain of mass of an object when energy E is transferred to it due to energy transfer E. You will learn more about this on p. 144. Why does energy transfer cause the mass of an object to change? $E = mc^2$ tells us how much it changes by but not why. Unfortunately, you won't find the answer to this question in this book – or in any other book at present. Scientists presently working on high energy colliders like the one at CERN in Geneva hope to come up with the answer. So here's what you should know now about energy.

Fig 1.1 *Investigating mass and energy*

- Energy is needed to make stationary objects move or to lift an object or to change its shape or to warm it up.

- Objects can possess energy in different forms, including:
  - potential energy which is energy due to position,
  - kinetic energy which is energy due to motion,
  - thermal energy which is energy due to the temperature of an object,
  - chemical or nuclear energy which is energy associated with chemical or nuclear reactions,
  - electrical energy which is energy of electrically charged objects,
  - elastic energy which is energy stored in an object when it is stretched or compressed.

- Energy can be changed from one form into other forms. In any change, the total amount of energy after the change is always equal to the total amount of energy before the change. The total amount of energy is unchanged. In other words,

Energy cannot be created or destroyed.

This statement is known as the **Principle of Conservation of Energy**.

1.1.2 Energy transfer experiments

1 The falling ball

a A ball released from rest in air gains speed as it descends. It loses gravitational potential energy and gains kinetic energy as it falls. Provided air resistance is negligible, its gain of kinetic energy between any two points is equal to its loss of gravitational potential energy.

b A ball released in a fluid in which drag is not negligible loses gravitational potential energy as it descends. However, the fluid gains thermal energy due to drag force. The drag force increases with speed until it is equal and opposite to the force of gravity less the 'upthrust' on the ball. The upthrust is the upward force on the ball caused by the pressure of the fluid. At terminal speed, gravitational potential energy is transferred to thermal energy of the fluid.

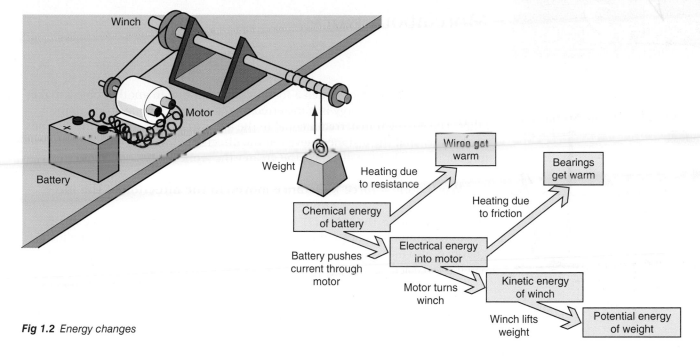

Fig 1.2 *Energy changes*

2 Joule's experiments

James Joule carried out very precise experiments to find out what happens to the energy lost by an object when it descends at constant speed. He devised ingenious methods of making an object falling in air turn a paddle wheel in a fluid at steady speed. He measured the temperature rise for different amounts of fluid when the object lost a certain amount of gravitational potential energy. He showed that the fluid gained the same amount of thermal energy each time the test was carried out, provided the loss of gravitational potential energy of the object was the same each time. He concluded that energy is conserved when it changes from one form into any other form.

An energy puzzle

Radioactive substances emit ionising radiation in the form of alpha particles or beta particles or gamma photons. An unstable nucleus becomes stable or less unstable as a result of emitting an alpha or a beta particle or a gamma photon. Alpha particles from a radioactive isotope are emitted with a certain amount of kinetic energy. Gamma photons are also emitted with a certain amount of energy that depends on the source. However, beta particles from a radioactive isotope are emitted with a range of speeds and, therefore, kinetic energies. When this discovery was first made in the 1930s, scientists faced a puzzle because each nucleus that releases a beta particle loses a certain amount of energy in the process but the emitted beta particle carries away a variable proportion of this energy. Scientists had to consider the possibility that energy may not be conserved on a nuclear scale. To avoid this possibility, a hypothetical particle called the 'neutrino' was invented to carry away the energy released by the nucleus not carried away by the beta particle. The only problem was that the neutrino could not be detected. Two decades later and after many more experiments, the neutrino was at last detected. Now we know that millions of these tiny elusive particles from the Sun sweep through our bodies every second. Yet for two decades, the failure to discover neutrinos called conservation of energy into question. The discovery of the neutrino strengthened the principle of conservation of energy.

QUESTIONS

1 Describe the energy changes that take place when a rubber ball is released from a certain height above a concrete floor and rebounds to a lesser height.

2 A simple pendulum consists of a metal bob on a thread. The bob is displaced from equilibrium with the thread taut then released. Describe the energy changes of the bob as it swings across to maximum displacement on the other side of equilibrium.

3 A parachutist jumps from a plane and falls at increasing speed until she opens her parachute. After her parachute opens, she descends at constant speed. Describe, without calculations, the energy changes of the parachutist from the moment she jumps from the plane to when she is descending at steady speed.

4 A child on a bicycle accelerates from rest down a hill and then brakes to a standstill at the bottom of the hill. Describe the energy changes that take place from start to finish.

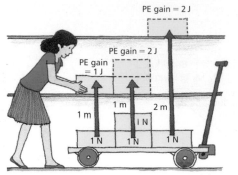

Fig 1.3 *Using joules*

Work is done on an object when a force acting on it due to another object makes it move. As a result, energy is transferred by the force from one object to the other. The energy transferred is equal to the amount of work done. This depends on the force and the distance moved in the direction of the force. The greater the force or the further the distance, the greater the work done.

Work done = force × distance moved in the direction of the force

The unit of work is the **joule** (J), equal to the work done when a force of 1 N moves its point of application by a distance of 1 m in the direction of the force. Energy is also measured in joules because the energy transferred to an object when a force acts on it is equal to the work done on it by the force. For example, a force of 2 N needs to be applied to an object of weight 2 N to raise the object steadily. If the object is raised by 1.5 m, the work done by the force is 3 J (= 2 N × 1.5 m). Therefore, the gain of potential energy of the object is 3 J.

1.2.1 Force and displacement

Imagine a yacht acted on by a wind force F at an angle θ to the direction in which the yacht moves. The wind force has a component $F \cos \theta$ in the direction of motion of the yacht and a component $F \sin \theta$ at right angles to the direction of motion. If the yacht is moved a distance s by the wind, the work done on it is equal to the component of force in the direction of motion × the distance moved.

$$W = Fs \cos \theta$$

Note that if $\theta = 90°$, the force is perpendicular to the direction of motion. Because $\cos 90° = 0$, the work done is zero.

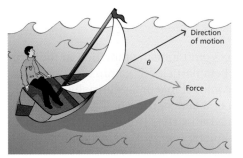

Fig 1.4 *Force and displacement*

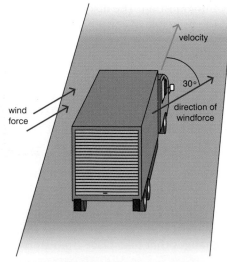

Fig 1.5 *Wind force and work*

Worked example

A horizontal force of 250 N due to the wind acts on a vehicle travelling at a constant velocity of 27 m s^{-1} due North on a straight motorway. The wind force acts in a direction 30° east of due North, as shown in Figure 1.5. Calculate the work done in 100 s by the wind force on the vehicle.

Solution
Distance moved in 100 s, $s = 27$ m s^{-1} × 100 s = 2700 m

$\theta = 30°$, $F = 250$ N

∴ $W = F s \cos \theta = 250$ N × 2700 m × $\cos 30° = 580$ kJ

QUESTIONS

1 Calculate the work done when a force of 15 N displaces an object by a distance of 8.0 m

   a in the direction of the force,

   b in a direction at 30° to the direction of the force.

2 A yacht moves due North at a constant velocity of 3.0 m s^{-1} when it is acted on by a constant force of 170 N acting in a direction 60° east of due North.

Calculate:

   a the distance moved by the yacht in 600 s,

   b the work done by the wind on the yacht in this time.

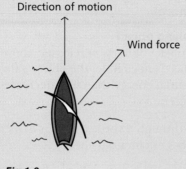

Fig 1.6

3 A parachutist of total weight 950 N descending at a constant velocity is acted on by a horizontal force of 250 N due to a cross-wind. The parachutist loses height at a rate of 2.4 m each second.

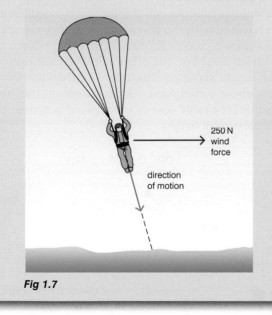

Fig 1.7

   a Calculate the work done by gravity on the parachutist each second.

   b (i) Show that the size of the resultant force on the parachutist is 980 N.

      (ii) Calculate the work done per second on the parachutist by the cross-wind.

4 A ship is towed at a steady speed of 7.5 m s^{-1} by two tug boats, each pulling on the ship with a force of 5.2 kN, as shown in Figure 1.8. The angle between each cable and the direction of motion of the boat is 25°.

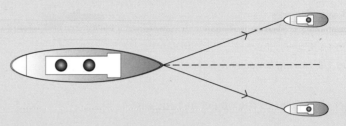

Fig 1.8

   a Show that the resultant force acting on the ship due to the tugboats is 9.4 kN.

   b Calculate the work done by the tugboats on the ship in 300 s.

1.3   Kinetic energy and potential energy

1.3.1 Kinetic energy

Kinetic energy is the energy of an object due to its motion. The faster an object moves, the more kinetic energy it has. To see the exact link between kinetic energy and speed, consider an object of mass m, initially at rest, acted on by a constant force F for a time t.

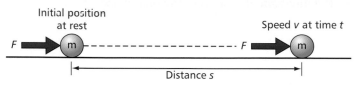

Fig 1.9 *Gaining kinetic energy*

Let the speed of the object at time t be v.

$\therefore$ distance travelled, $s = \frac{1}{2}(u + v)t$

$$= \frac{1}{2}vt \text{ because } u = 0$$

$$\text{acceleration, } a = \frac{(v - u)}{t} = \frac{v}{t}$$

Using Newton's 2nd Law, $F = ma = \dfrac{mv}{t}$

$\therefore$ the work done by force F to move the object through distance s,

$$W = Fs = \frac{mv}{t} \times \frac{vt}{2} = \frac{1}{2}mv^2$$

Because the gain of kinetic energy is due to the work done, then

$$\textbf{kinetic energy, } E_K = \tfrac{1}{2}mv^2$$

Note The formula does not hold at speeds approaching the speed of light. Einstein's theory of special relativity tells us that the mass of an object increases with speed and that the energy of an object can be worked out from the equation $E = mc^2$, where c is the speed of light in free space and m is the mass of the object.

1.3.2 Potential energy

Potential energy is the energy of an object due to its position.

If an object of mass m is raised through a vertical height h at steady speed, the force needed to raise it is equal and opposite to its weight, mg. Therefore, the work done to raise the object = force $\times$ distance moved = mgh. The work done on the object increases its gravitational potential energy.

Change of gravitational potential energy $\Delta E_P = mgh$

At the Earth's surface, $g = 9.8 \text{ m s}^{-2}$

Note The formula does not hold unless the change of height h is much smaller than the Earth's radius. If height h is not insignificant compared with the Earth's radius, the value of g is not the same over height h. The force of gravity on an object decreases with increased distance from the Earth.

1.3.3 Energy changes involving kinetic and potential energy

1 A freely falling object

Consider an object of mass m released above the ground. If air resistance is negligible, the object gains speed as it falls. Its potential energy therefore decreases and its kinetic energy increases.

After falling through a vertical height h, its kinetic energy is equal to its loss of potential energy.

In other words,

$$\tfrac{1}{2}mv^2 = mgh$$

2 The pendulum bob

Consider a pendulum bob displaced from equilibrium and then released with the thread taut. The bob passes through equilibrium at maximum speed then slows down to reach maximum height on the other side of equilibrium. If its initial height above equilibrium $= h_0$, then whenever its height above equilibrium $= h$, its speed v at this height is such that its kinetic energy = its loss of potential energy from maximum height

$$\tfrac{1}{2}mv^2 = mgh_0 - mgh$$

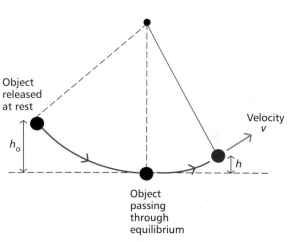

Fig 1.10 *A pendulum in motion*

3 A fairground ride

Consider a fairground vehicle of mass m on a downward track, as in Figure 1.11.

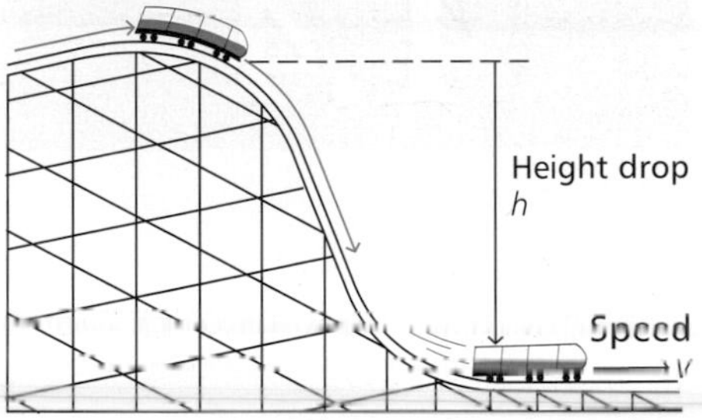

If it was initially at rest at the top of the track and its speed is v at the bottom of the track, then at the bottom of the track:

- its kinetic energy $= \frac{1}{2}mv^2$, and its loss of potential energy $= mgh$, where h is the vertical distance between the top and the bottom of the track,
- the work done to overcome friction and air resistance $= mgh - \frac{1}{2}mv^2$

If F represents the average value of the force due to friction and air resistance, then

$$Fs = mgh - \tfrac{1}{2}mv^2$$

where s is the total distance travelled by the vehicle.

Fig 1.11 *At the fairground*

Worked example $\quad g = 9.8 \, \text{m s}^{-2}$

On a fairground ride, the track descends by a vertical drop of 55 m over a distance of 120 m along the track. A train of mass 2500 kg on the track reaches a speed of 30 m s^{-1} at the bottom of the descent after being at rest at the top. Calculate

a the loss of potential energy of the train,

b its gain of kinetic energy,

c the average frictional force during the descent.

Solution

a Loss of potential energy $= mgh = 2500 \times 9.8 \times 55 = 1.35 \times 10^6$ J

b Its gain of kinetic energy $= \frac{1}{2}mv^2 = 0.5 \times 2500 \times 30^2 = 1.13 \times 10^6$ J

c Work done to overcome friction $= mgh - \frac{1}{2}mv^2 = 1.35 \times 10^6 - 1.13 \times 10^6$
$= 2.2 \times 10^5$ J

Because the work done to overcome friction = frictional force × distance moved along track,

$$\text{the frictional force} = \frac{\text{work done to overcome friction}}{\text{distance moved}} = \frac{2.2 \times 10^5 \text{ J}}{120 \text{ m}} = 1850 \text{ N}$$

QUESTIONS

1 A ball of mass 0.80 kg was thrown directly up at a speed of 7.0 m s^{-1}. Calculate:

  a its kinetic energy at 7.0 m s^{-1},

  b its maximum gain of potential energy,

  c its maximum height gain.

2 A ball of mass 0.25 kg at a height of 1.6 m above a table is released from rest and it rebounds to a height of 1.1 m above the table. Calculate:

  a (i) the loss of potential energy on descent,
     (ii) its kinetic energy and speed just before impact.

  b (i) its gain of potential energy when it rises to maximum height from the floor,
     (ii) its kinetic energy and speed just after it loses contact with the floor.

3 A car of mass 850 kg travels on a downhill road that is 180 m lower at the bottom of the hill than at the top.

The car takes 250 s to travel at a steady speed of 28 m s^{-1} from the top to the bottom. Calculate:

  a the loss of potential energy of the car in this descent,

  b (i) the work done against friction and air resistance during the descent,
     (ii) the average resistive force during the descent.

4 A fairground vehicle of total mass 1500 kg moving at an initial speed of 2 m s^{-1} descends through a height of 70 m to reach a speed of 36 m s^{-1} after travelling a distance of 120 m along the track.

  a Calculate:
    (i) its loss of potential energy,
    (ii) its gain of kinetic energy.

  b Show that the average frictional force on it during the descent was 500 N.

1.4.1 Power and energy

In any energy transfer process, the more energy transferred per second, the greater the power of the transfer process. For example, in a tall building where there are two lifts of the same total weight, the more powerful lift is the one that can reach the top floor faster. In other words, its motor transfers energy from electricity at a faster rate than the motor of the other elevator. The energy transferred per second is the **power** of the motor.

Power is defined as the rate of transfer of energy.

The unit of power is the watt (W), equal to an energy transfer rate of 1 joule per second. Note that 1 kilowatt (kW) = 1000 W, and 1 megawatt (MW) = 10^6 W.

If energy E is transferred steadily in time t,

$$\text{the power } P = \frac{E}{t}$$

1.4.2 Engine power

Vehicle engines, marine engines and aircraft engines are all designed to make objects move. When a powered object moves at constant velocity at constant height, the resistive forces (e.g. friction, air resistance, drag) are equal and opposite to the engine force. The work done by the engine is converted to thermal energy of the surroundings by the resistive forces.

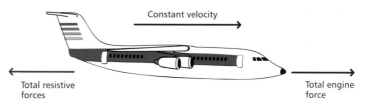

Constant velocity

Total resistive forces

Total engine force

Fig 1.12 *Engine power*

For a powered vehicle driven by a constant force F moving at speed v in the direction in which the force acts,

the work done per second = force × distance moved per second

∴ the output power of the engine $P = Fv$

Worked example

An aircraft powered by engines that exert a force of 40 kN is in level flight at a constant velocity of 80 m s⁻¹. Calculate the output power of the engine at this speed.

Solution

Output power = force × velocity = 40 000 N × 80 m s⁻¹ = 3.2×10^6 W

Notes

1 If a vehicle speeds up at constant height, the engine force must increase the kinetic energy of the vehicle and overcome resistive forces. At any instant, the rate of increase of kinetic energy is equal to the output power of the engine – the work done per second to overcome the resistive forces.

2 When the velocity is not in the same direction as the driving force (e.g. an aircraft acted on by a cross-wind), the work done per second by the driving force, F, (i.e. the output power of the engine) = $Fv \cos \theta$ because the component of the driving force F in the direction of the velocity v is $F \cos \theta$.

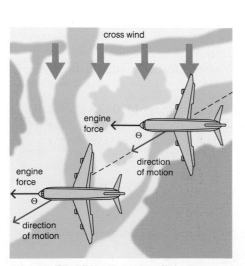

cross wind

engine force

direction of motion

engine force

direction of motion

Fig 1.13 *The effect of a cross-wind*

1.4.3 Efficiency

Useful energy is energy transferred for a purpose. In any machine where friction is present, some of the energy transferred by the machine is wasted. In other words, not all the energy supplied to the machine is transferred for the intended purpose. For example, suppose a 500 W electric winch raises a weight of 150 N by 6.0 m in 10 s.

- The electrical energy supplied to the winch
  = 500 W × 10 s = 5000 J
- The useful energy transferred by the machine
  = potential energy gain of the load = 150 N × 6.0 m = 900 J.

Therefore, in this example, 4100 J of energy is wasted.

The efficiency of a machine

$$= \frac{\text{useful energy transferred by the machine}}{\text{energy supplied to the machine}}$$

$$= \frac{\text{work done by the machine}}{\text{energy supplied to the machine}}$$

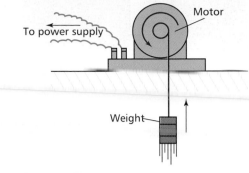

Fig 1.14 Efficiency

> **NOTES**
>
> 1 Percentage efficiency = efficiency × 100 %. In the above example, the efficiency of the machine is therefore 0.18 or 18%.
>
> 2 Efficiency can also be expressed as
>
> $$\frac{\textbf{the output power of a machine}}{\textbf{the input power to the machine}}$$

QUESTIONS

1 Calculate the power of the engines of an aircraft if the total engine thrust is 2.0 MN when the velocity is 250 m s^{-1}

   a in the same direction as the thrust,

   b in a direction at 50° to the direction of the thrust.

2 A train of total mass 45 000 kg is powered by a 1.2 MW electric motor. On a certain section of track inclined at 2° to the horizontal, the train moves up the incline at a steady speed of 24 m s^{-1} with its motor operating at full power.

   a Calculate:
   (i) the distance moved along the track by the train in 100 s,
   (ii) its height gain and its gain of potential energy in this time.

   b Calculate the efficiency of its motor during this time.

3 A road vehicle of mass 8800 kg accelerates from rest to a speed of 15 m s^{-1} in 25 s on a level road.

   a Calculate its gain of kinetic energy.

   b The vehicle's engine has a constant power output of 55 kW. Calculate:
   (i) the energy wasted due to friction and air resistance,
   (ii) the average force of friction and air resistance.

4 A 50 W electric pump is used to raise water from an underground reservoir through a height of 15 m to ground level at a flow rate of 0.025 kg s^{-1}. Calculate:

   a the gain of potential energy per second of the water,

   b the efficiency of the motor.

CHAPTER SUMMARY

- The Principle of Conservation of Energy states that energy cannot be created or destroyed.
- In any change, the total amount of energy after the change is always equal to the total amount of energy before the change.
- Work done by a force = $Fs \cos \theta$
- Kinetic energy, $E_K = \frac{1}{2}mv^2$

- Change of gravitational potential energy, $\Delta E_P = mg\,\Delta h$
- Power = $\dfrac{\text{energy transferred}}{\text{time taken}}$
- Engine power = force × speed
- Efficiency = $\dfrac{\text{useful energy transferred}}{\text{total energy supplied}}$

$g = 9.8\,\text{m s}^{-2}$

1 A metal ball was released from rest above a bed of sand. Discuss the energy changes of the ball from the moment it was released to when it is at rest in the sand.

2 a Calculate the kinetic energy of a ball of mass 0.80 kg moving at a speed of $14\,\text{m s}^{-1}$.

   b Calculate the height gain of the ball if it was thrown vertically upwards with a speed of $14\,\text{m s}^{-1}$.

3 A swimmer of mass 63 kg dives from a diving board which is 5.4 m above the water level of a swimming pool.

   a Describe the energy changes from the moment the swimmer jumps off the diving board to when he surfaces in the pool.

   b Calculate:
      (i) the loss of potential energy of the diver due to a vertical descent of 5.4 m,
      (ii) the kinetic energy and speed of the diver just before entering the water.

4 A ball of mass 0.25 kg was released from rest at a height of 1.2 m above a level floor. It rebounded to a height of 0.8 m above the floor.

   a Calculate:
      (i) its loss of potential energy between being released and hitting the floor,
      (ii) its gain of potential energy between losing contact with the floor and reaching its maximum rebound height.

   b Assuming air resistance was negligible, calculate:
      (i) its kinetic energy just before impact,
      (ii) its loss of kinetic energy due to the impact.

5 A train of total mass 65 000 kg was moving along a level track at a speed of $36\,\text{m s}^{-1}$ when the brakes were applied, causing the train to come to a standstill 1200 m further along the track.

   a Calculate:
      (i) the initial kinetic energy of the train,
      (ii) the average braking force, assuming air resistance was negligible.

   b Describe the energy changes that occur as a result of the brakes being applied.

6 A cyclist of mass 53 kg started off from rest at the top of a hill and reached a speed of $12\,\text{m s}^{-1}$ at the bottom of the hill 67 m lower where the road becomes level. She stopped pedalling and came to a standstill 450 m after she stopped pedalling.

   a Calculate:
      (i) the loss of potential energy,
      (ii) the gain of kinetic energy of the cyclist from the top to the bottom of the hill.

   b (i) Discuss the energy changes of the cyclist from the moment she stopped pedalling to when she came to a standstill.
      (ii) Calculate the average force of friction and air resistance opposing the motion of the cyclist on the level road.

7 A skier of mass 72 kg, initially at rest, reached a speed of $32\,\text{m s}^{-1}$ at the bottom of a ski run of length 1500 m that was 120 m lower at the bottom than at the top.

   a Calculate:
      (i) the loss of potential energy,
      (ii) the gain of kinetic energy of the skier.

   b Calculate:
      (i) the work done against friction and air resistance,
      (ii) the average force opposing the motion of the skier.

8 At a fairground, a train of total mass 8700 kg was pulled by a cable to the top of a track. Its speed at the top of the track was $1.5\,\text{m s}^{-1}$. It then descended through a height of 55 m along a steep section of the track reaching a speed of $24\,\text{m s}^{-1}$ at the start of a level section of the track where its brakes were applied.

   a Calculate:
      (i) the loss of potential energy of the train,
      (ii) its gain of kinetic energy due to the descent,
      (iii) the work done by friction and air resistance during the descent.

   b When the brakes were applied, the train came to a standstill on the level section in a distance of 170 m. Calculate:
      (i) the braking force on the train,
      (ii) its deceleration.

Force and momentum

2

Momentum

2.1

If you have ever run into someone on the sports field, you will know something about momentum. If the person you ran into is more massive than you, then you probably came off worse than the other person. When two bodies collide, the effect they have on each other depends not only on their initial velocities but also on the mass of each object. You can easily test the ideas using coins, as shown in Figure 2.1. You might already have developed your skill in this area! It's not too difficult to show that when a large coin and a small coin collide, the motion of the small coin is affected more.

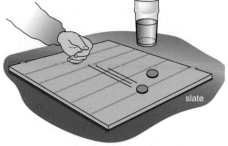

Fig 2.1 A momentum game

Sir Isaac Newton was the first person to realise that a force was needed to change the velocity of an object. He realised that the effect of a force on an object depended on its mass as well as on the amount of force. He defined the momentum of a moving object as its mass multiplied by its velocity and showed how the momentum of an object changes when a force acts on it. In the AS course, you learned that the force needed to give an object a certain acceleration can be calculated from the equation 'force = mass × acceleration'. In the A2 course, we consider the ideas that Newton established in full.

Although Newton put forward his ideas over 300 years ago, his laws continue to provide the essential mathematical rules for predicting the motion of objects in any situation except inside the atom (where the rules of quantum physics apply) or at speeds approaching the speed of light (where Einstein's theory of relativity applies). For example, the launch of a satellite into orbit is carefully planned using Newton's laws of motion.

The **momentum** of an object is defined as its **mass × its velocity**.

- The unit of momentum is kg m s^{-1}. The symbol for momentum is p.
- Momentum is a vector quantity. Its direction is the same as the direction of the object's velocity.
- For an object of mass m moving at velocity v, its momentum $p = mv$.

For example, a ball of mass 2.0 kg moving at a velocity of 10 m s^{-1} has the same amount of momentum as a person of mass 50 kg moving at a velocity of 0.4 m s^{-1}.

2.1.1 Momentum and Newton's laws of motion

Newton's 1st law of motion: An object remains at rest or in uniform motion unless acted on by a force.

In effect, Newton's 1st law tells us that a force is needed to change the momentum of an object. If the momentum of an object is constant, there is no resultant force acting on it. Clearly, if the mass of an object is constant and the object has constant momentum, it follows that the velocity of the object is also constant. However, if a moving object with constant momentum gains or loses mass, its velocity would change to keep its momentum constant. For example, a cyclist in a race who collects a water bottle as he or she speeds past a 'service' point gains mass (i.e. the water bottle) and therefore loses velocity.

15

Newton's 2nd law of motion: The rate of change of momentum of an object is proportional to the resultant force on it. In other words, the resultant force is proportional to the change of momentum per second.

At AS level, Newton's 2nd law was presented in the form 'force = mass × acceleration'. At A2, we look at how this equation is derived from Newton's 2nd law in its general form as stated above.

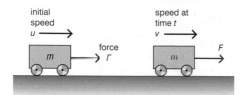

initial speed u

speed at time t v

force F

Fig 2.2 Force and momentum

Consider an object of constant mass m acted on by a constant force F. Its acceleration causes a change of its speed from initial speed u to speed v in time t without change of direction.

- its initial momentum = mu, and its final momentum = mv
- its change of momentum = its final momentum (mv) − its initial momentum (mu).

According to Newton's 2nd law, the force is proportional to the change of momentum per second.

Therefore, force $F \propto \dfrac{\text{change of momentum}}{\text{time taken}} = \dfrac{mv - mu}{t} = \dfrac{m(v-u)}{t} = ma$

where $a = \dfrac{v-u}{t} = $ the acceleration of the object.

This proportionality relationship (i.e. $F \propto ma$) can be written as $F = kma$, where k is a constant of proportionality.

The value of k is made equal to 1 by defining the unit of force, **the newton**, as the amount of force that gives an object of mass 1 kg an acceleration of 1 m s^{-2} (i.e. force $F = 1$ N, mass $m = 1$ kg, acceleration, $a = 1 \text{ m s}^{-2}$ so k = 1).

Therefore, with k = 1, the equation $F = ma$ follows from Newton's 2nd law provided the mass of the object is constant.

In general, the change of momentum of an object may be written as $\Delta(mv)$, where the symbol Δ means 'change of'. Therefore, if the momentum of an object changes by $\Delta(mv)$ in time Δt, the force F on the object is given by the equation

$$F = \frac{\Delta(mv)}{\Delta t}$$

1 **If m is constant**, then $\Delta(mv) = m\,\Delta v$, where Δv is the change of velocity of the object.

$$\therefore \quad F = m\frac{\Delta v}{\Delta t} = ma \text{ where acceleration } a = \frac{\Delta v}{\Delta t}$$

2 **If m changes at a constant rate** as a result of mass being transferred at constant velocity, then $\Delta(mv) = v\,\Delta m$, where Δm is the change of mass of the object.

$$\therefore \quad F = v\frac{\Delta m}{\Delta t} \text{ where } \frac{\Delta m}{\Delta t} = \text{change of mass per second.}$$

This form of Newton's 2nd law is used in any situation where an object gains or loses mass continuously. For example, if a hosepipe ejects water at speed v, the force F needed to eject the water is given by $F = v\dfrac{\Delta m}{\Delta t}$ where $\dfrac{\Delta m}{\Delta t} = $ mass of water lost per second. An equal and opposite reaction force acts on the hosepipe due to the water.

Note The A2 specification does not include force due to continuous change of mass. Inclusion here is to reinforce the point that '$F = ma$' is an application of Newton's 2nd law to situations where the mass is constant.

2.1.2 Force v. time graphs

Suppose an object of constant mass m is acted on by a constant force F which changes its velocity from initial velocity u to velocity v in time t. As explained on p. 16, Newton's 2nd law gives

$$F = \frac{mv - mu}{t}$$

Rearranging this equation gives $Ft = mv - mu$

Figure 2.3 is a graph of force v. time for this situation. Because force F is constant for time t, the area under the line represents Ft which is equal to $mv - mu$. In other words, the area under the line of a force v. time graph represents the change of momentum.

Note The unit of momentum can be given as the newton second (N s) or the kilogram metre per second (kg m s^{-1}).

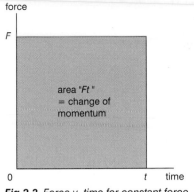
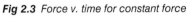

Fig 2.3 Force v. time for constant force

Worked example

A force of 10 N acts for 20 s on an object of mass 50 kg which is initially at rest. Calculate:

a the change of momentum of the object,

b the velocity of the object at 20 s.

Solution

a Change of momentum = Ft = 10 N $\times$ 20 s = 200 N s.

b Momentum at 20 s = 200 N s as the object was initially at rest.

$$\therefore \quad \text{Velocity} = \frac{\text{momentum}}{\text{mass}} = \frac{200 \text{ N s}}{50 \text{ kg}} = 4.0 \text{ m s}^{-1}$$

QUESTIONS

1 a Calculate the momentum of
   (i) an atom of mass 4.0×10^{-25} kg moving at a velocity of 3.0×10^{6} m s^{-1},
   (ii) a pellet of mass 4.2×10^{-4} kg moving at a velocity of 120 m s^{-1},
   (iii) a bird of mass 0.56 kg moving at a velocity of 25 m s^{-1}.

  b Calculate:
   (i) the mass of an object moving at a velocity of 16 m s^{-1} with momentum of 96 kg m s^{-1},
   (ii) the velocity of an object of mass 6.4 kg that has momentum of 128 kg m s^{-1}.

2 A train of mass 24 000 kg moving at a velocity of 15.0 m s^{-1} is brought to rest by a braking force of 6000 N. Calculate:

  a the initial momentum of the train,

  b the time taken for the brakes to stop the train.

3 An aircraft of total mass 45 000 kg accelerates on a runway from rest to a velocity of 120 m s^{-1} when it takes off. During this time, its engines provide a constant driving force of 120 kN.

  Calculate:

  a the gain of momentum of the aircraft,

  b the 'take off' time.

4 The velocity of a vehicle of mass 600 kg was reduced from 15 m s^{-1} by a constant force of 400 N which acted for 20 s then by a constant force of 20 N for a further 20 s.

  a Sketch the force v. time graph for this situation.

  b (i) Calculate the initial momentum of the vehicle,
   (ii) Use the force v. time graph to determine the total change of momentum.
   (iii) Hence calculate the final velocity of the vehicle.

Fig 2.4 *A golf ball impact*

A sports person knows that the harder a ball is hit, the further it travels. The impact changes the momentum of the ball in a very short time when the object exerting the impact force is in contact with the ball.

- If the ball is initially stationary and the impact causes it to accelerate to speed v in time t, the gain of momentum of the ball due to the impact = mv, where m is the mass of the ball.

  Therefore, the force of the impact $F = \dfrac{\text{change of momentum}}{\text{contact time } t} = \dfrac{mv}{t}$

- If the ball is moving with an initial velocity, u, and the impact changes its velocity to v in time t, the change of momentum of the ball = $mv - mu$.

  Therefore, the force of impact $F = \dfrac{\text{change of momentum}}{\text{contact time } t} = \dfrac{mv - mu}{t}$

Worked example

A ball of mass 0.63 kg initially at rest was struck by a bat which gave it a velocity of 35 m s^{-1}. The contact time between the bat and ball was 25 ms. Calculate:

a the momentum gained by the ball,

b the average force of impact on the ball.

Solution

a Momentum gained = 0.63 kg $\times$ 35 m s^{-1} = 22 kg m s^{-1},

b Impact force = $\dfrac{\text{gain of momentum}}{\text{contact time}} = \dfrac{22 \text{ kg m s}^{-1}}{0.025 \text{ s}} = 880$ N

2.2.1 Vehicle safety reminders

The AS specification looks at the physics of vehicle safety features such as crumple zones, seatbelts, collapsible steering wheels, and airbags. These and other features such as side-impact bars are all designed to lessen the effect of an impact on people in the vehicle. As explained at AS level, the essential idea is to increase the time taken by an impact so the acceleration or deceleration is less and therefore the impact force is less. The result is the same using the idea of momentum; for a given change of momentum, the force is reduced if the impact time is increased. However, as explained in 2.3, the ideas can be developed much further by using the concept of momentum.

2.2.2 Force v. time graphs for impacts

The variation of an impact force with time on a ball can be recorded using a force sensor connected via suitably long wires or a radio link to a computer. The force sensor is attached to the object (e.g. a bat) that causes the impact. Because equal and opposite forces act on the ball, the force on the ball due to the bat varies in exactly the same way as the force on the bat due to the ball. The variation of force with time is displayed on the computer screen.

Figure 2.6 shows a typical force v. time graph for an impact. The graph shows that the impact force increases then decreases during the impact. As explained on p. 17, the area under the graph is equal to the change of momentum. The average force of impact can be worked out from the change of momentum divided by the contact time.

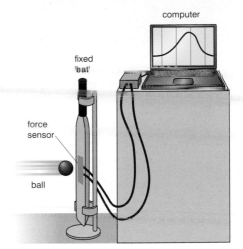

Fig 2.5 Investigating an impact force on a ball

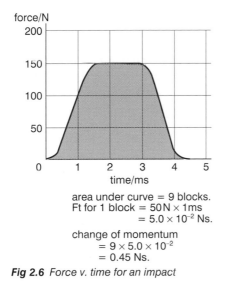

area under curve = 9 blocks.
Ft for 1 block = 50 N × 1ms
= 5.0×10^{-2} Ns.

change of momentum
= $9 \times 5.0 \times 10^{-2}$
= 0.45 Ns.

Fig 2.6 Force v. time for an impact

2.2.3 Rebound impacts

When a ball hits a wall and rebounds, its momentum changes direction due to the impact. If the ball hits the wall normally, it rebounds normally so the direction of its momentum is reversed. The velocity and, therefore, the momentum after the impact are in the opposite direction to the velocity before the impact and therefore have the opposite sign. Figure 2.7 shows the idea.

Suppose the ball hits the wall normally with an initial speed u and it rebounds at speed v in the opposite direction. Since its direction of motion reverses on impact, a sign convention is necessary to represent the two directions. Using + for 'towards the wall' and − for 'away from the wall', its initial momentum = $+mu$, and its final momentum = $-mv$.

Therefore, its change of momentum = final momentum − initial momentum
$$= (-mv) - (mu)$$

The impact force $F = \dfrac{\text{change of momentum}}{\text{contact time, } t} = \dfrac{(-mv) - (mu)}{t}$

Note If there is no loss of speed on impact, then $v = u$

so the impact force $\quad F = \dfrac{(-mu) - (mu)}{t} = -\dfrac{2mu}{t}$

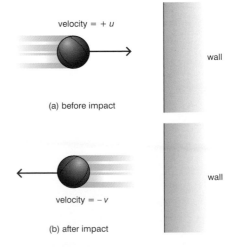

velocity = $+u$

wall

(a) before impact

velocity = $-v$

wall

(b) after impact

Fig 2.7 A rebound

Worked example
A tennis ball of mass 0.20 kg moving at a speed of 18 m s^{-1} was hit by a bat, causing the ball to go back in the direction it came from at a speed of 15 m s^{-1}. The contact time was 0.12 s. Calculate:

a the change of momentum of the ball,

b the impact force on the ball.

Solution

a Mass of ball $m = 0.20$ kg, initial velocity $u = +18 \text{ m s}^{-1}$, final velocity $= -15 \text{ m s}^{-1}$,

Change of momentum $= mv - mu = (0.20 \times -15) - (0.20 \times 18)$
$= -3.0 - 3.6 = -6.6 \text{ kg m s}^{-1}$

b Impact force $= \dfrac{\text{change of momentum}}{\text{time taken}} = \dfrac{-6.6 \text{ kg m s}^{-1}}{0.12 \text{ s}} = -55 \text{ N}$

The minus sign indicates the force on the ball is in the same direction as velocity after the impact.

QUESTIONS

1 A 2000 kg lorry reversing at a speed of 0.8 m s^{-1} backs accidentally into a steel fence. The fence stops the lorry 0.5 s after the lorry first makes contact with the fence. Calculate:

  a the initial momentum of the lorry,

  b the force of the impact.

2 A car of mass 600 kg travelling at a speed of 3.0 m s^{-1} is struck from behind by another vehicle. The impact lasts for 0.4 s and causes the speed of the car to increase to 8.0 m s^{-1}. Calculate:

  a the change of momentum of the car due to the impact,

  b the impact force.

3 A molecule of mass 5.0×10^{-26} kg moving at a speed of 420 m s^{-1} hits a surface at right angles to the surface and rebounds at the same speed in the opposite direction in an impact lasting 0.22 ns. Calculate:

  a the change of momentum,

  b the force on the molecule.

4 Repeat the calculation in question **3** for a molecule of the same mass at the same speed which hits the surface at 60° to the normal and rebounds without loss of speed at 60° to the normal, as shown in Figure 2.8. You will need to work out the component of the molecule's velocity parallel to the normal before and after the impact. Assume the contact time is the same.

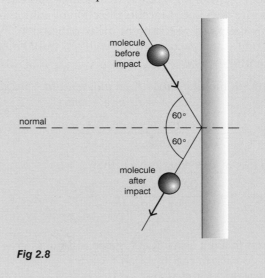

molecule before impact

60°

normal

60°

molecule after impact

Fig 2.8

Conservation of momentum

2.3.1 Newton's 3rd law of motion

> **When two objects interact, they exert equal and opposite forces on each other.**

In other words, if object A exerts a force on object B, there must be an equal and opposite force acting on object A due to object B.

For example,

- an object resting on a table exerts a force on the table which exerts an equal and opposite force on the object;
- a person leaning against a wall exerts a force on the wall which exerts an equal and opposite force on the person;
- a hammer hitting a nail exerts a force on the nail which exerts an equal and opposite force on the hammer;
- the Earth exerts a force due to gravity on an object which exerts an equal and opposite force on the Earth;
- a jet engine exerts a force on hot gas in the engine to expel the gas; the gas being expelled exerts an equal and opposite force on the engine.

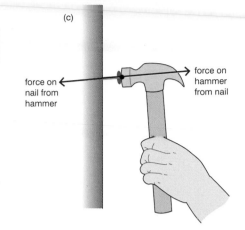

Fig 2.9 Newton's 3rd Law

2.3.2 The Principle of Conservation of Momentum

When an object is acted on by a resultant force, its momentum changes. If there is no change of its momentum, there can be no resultant force on the object. Now consider several objects which interact with each other. If no external resultant force acts on the objects, the total momentum does not change. However, interactions between the objects can transfer momentum between them. But the total momentum does not change.

> **The Principle of Conservation of Momentum states that for a system of interacting objects, the total momentum remains constant, provided no external resultant force acts on the system.**

Consider two objects that collide with each other then separate. As a result, the momentum of each object changes. They exert equal and opposite forces on each other when they are in contact. So the change of momentum of one object is equal and opposite to the change of momentum of the other object. In other words, if one object gains momentum, the other object loses an equal amount of momentum. So the total amount of momentum is unchanged.

Let's look in detail at the example of two snooker balls A and B in collision, as shown in Figure 2.10.

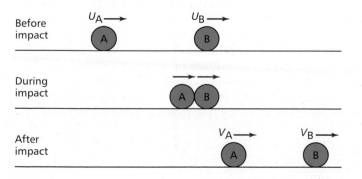

Fig 2.10 Conservation of momentum

- The impact force F_1 on ball A changes the velocity of A from u_A to v_A in time t

Therefore, $\quad F_1 = \dfrac{m_A v_A - m_A u_A}{t}$,

where t = the time of contact between A and B,

and m_A = the mass of ball A.

- The impact force F_2 on ball B changes the velocity of B from u_B to v_B in time t

Therefore, $\quad F_2 = \dfrac{m_B v_B - m_B u_B}{t}$,

where t = the time of contact between A and B,

and m_B = the mass of ball B.

Because the two forces are equal and opposite to each other, $F_2 = -F_1$

Therefore

$$\frac{m_B v_B - m_B u_B}{t} = -\frac{(m_A v_A - m_A u_A)}{t}$$

Cancelling t on both sides gives

$$m_B v_B - m_B u_B = -m_A v_A + m_A u_A$$

Rearranging this equation gives

$$m_B v_B + m_A v_A = m_A u_A + m_B u_B$$

Therefore,

the total final momentum = the total initial momentum

In other words, the total momentum is unchanged by this collision.

Note If the colliding objects stick together as a result of the collision, they have the same final velocity. The above equation may therefore be written

$$(m_B + m_A)\, V = m_A u_A + m_B u_B$$

2.3.3 Testing conservation of momentum

Figure 2.11 shows an arrangement that can be used to test conservation of momentum using a motion sensor linked to a computer. The mass of each trolley is measured before the test. With trolley B at rest, trolley A is given a push so it moves towards trolley B at constant velocity. The two trolleys stick together on impact. The computer records and displays the velocity of trolley A throughout this time. The computer display shows that the velocity of trolley A dropped suddenly when the impact took place. The velocity of trolley A immediately before the collision, u_A, and after the collision (V) can be measured. The measurements should show that the total momentum of both trolleys after the collision is equal to the momentum of trolley A before the collision. In other words,

$$(m_B + m_A)\, V = m_A u_A$$

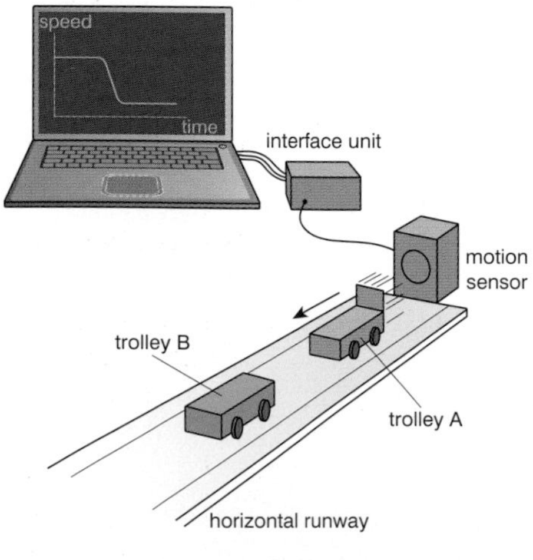

Fig 2.11 Testing conservation of momentum

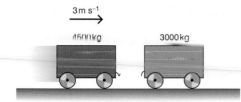

Fig 2.12 *Representing a vector*

Worked example

A rail wagon of mass 4500 kg moving along a level track at a speed of 3.0 m s^{-1} collides with and couples to a second rail wagon of mass 3000 kg which is initially stationary. Calculate the speed of the two wagons immediately after the collision.

Solution

Total initial momentum

$$= \text{initial momentum of A} + \text{initial momentum of B}$$
$$= (4500 \times 3.0) + (3000 \times 0) = 13\,500 \text{ kg m s}^{-1}$$

Total final momentum

$$= \text{total mass of A and B} \times \text{velocity } V \text{ after the collision}$$
$$= (4500 + 3000)\, V = 7500\, V$$

Using the Principle of Conservation of Momentum,

$$7500\, V = 13\,500$$
$$V = \frac{13\,500}{7500} = 1.8 \text{ m s}^{-1}$$

2.3.4 Head-on collisions

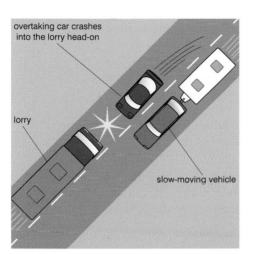

Fig 2.13 *A crash calculation*

Consider two objects moving in opposite directions that collide with each other. Depending on the masses and initial velocities of the two objects, the collision could cause them both to stop. The momentum of the two objects after the collision would then be zero. This could only happen if the initial momentum of one object was exactly equal and opposite to that of the other object. In general, if two objects move in opposite directions before a collision, then the vector nature of momentum needs to be taken into account by assigning numerical values of velocity + or − according to the direction.

For example, if a car of mass 600 kg travelling at a velocity of 25 m s^{-1} collides head-on with a lorry of mass 2400 kg travelling at a velocity of 10 m s^{-1} in the opposite direction, the total momentum before the collision is 9000 kg m s^{-1} in the direction the lorry was moving in. As momentum is conserved in a collision, the total momentum after the collision is the same as the total momentum before the collision. Prove for yourself that if the two vehicles stick together after the collision, they must have had a velocity of 3.0 m s^{-1} (= 9000 kg m s^{-1}/3000 kg) in the direction the lorry was moving in immediately after the impact.

QUESTIONS

1 A rail wagon of mass 3000 kg moving at a velocity of 1.2 m s^{-1} collides with a stationary wagon of mass 2000 kg. After the collision, the two wagons couple together. Calculate their speed immediately after the collision.

2 A rail wagon of mass 5000 kg moving at a velocity of 1.6 m s^{-1} collides with a stationary wagon of mass 3000 kg. After the collision, the 3000 kg wagon moves away at a velocity of 1.5 m s^{-1}. Calculate the speed and direction of the 5000 kg wagon after the collision.

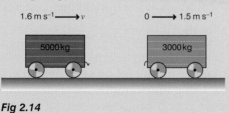

Fig 2.14

3 In a laboratory experiment, a trolley of mass 0.50 kg moving at a speed of 0.25 m s^{-1} collided with a trolley of mass 1.0 kg moving in the opposite direction at a speed of 0.20 m s^{-1}. The two trolleys coupled together on collision. Calculate their speed and direction immediately after the collision.

4 A ball of mass 0.80 kg moving at a speed of 2.5 m s^{-1} along a straight line collided with a ball of mass 2.5 kg which was initially stationary. As a result of the collision, the 2.5 kg ball was given a velocity of 1.0 m s^{-1} along the same line. Calculate the speed and direction of the 0.80 kg ball immediately after the collision.

Elastic and inelastic collisions

Drop a bouncy rubber ball from a measured height onto a hard floor. The ball should bounce back almost to the same height. Try the same with a cricket ball and there will be very little bounce! A **perfectly elastic** ball would be one that bounces back to exactly the same height. Its kinetic energy just after impact must equal its kinetic energy just before impact. Otherwise, it cannot regain its initial height. There is no loss of kinetic energy in a perfectly elastic collision.

> **A perfectly elastic collision is one where there is no loss of kinetic energy.**

- A squash ball hitting a hard surface bounces off the surface with little or no loss of speed. If the ball is perfectly elastic, there is no loss of speed on impact and no loss of kinetic energy.
- A very low speed impact between two cars is almost perfectly elastic, provided no damage is done. Some of the initial kinetic energy of the two vehicles may be converted to sound. However, if the collision causes damage to the vehicles, the kinetic energy after the collision is less than before so the collision is not elastic.

> **A totally inelastic collision is one where the colliding objects stick together.**

- A railway wagon that collides with and couples to another wagon is an example of a totally inelastic collision. Some of the initial kinetic energy is converted to other forms of energy.
- A vehicle crash in which the colliding vehicles lock together is another example of a totally inelastic collision. The total kinetic energy after the collision is less than the total kinetic energy before the collision.

A partially inelastic collision is where the colliding objects:

1 move apart, and

2 have less kinetic energy after the collision than before.

To work out if a collision is elastic or inelastic, the kinetic energy of each object before and after the collision must be worked out.

Examples

1 For a ball of mass m falling in air from a measured height H and rebounding to a height h:

(i) the kinetic energy immediately before impact = loss of potential energy through height $H = mgH$,

(ii) the kinetic energy immediately after impact = gain of potential energy through height $h = mgh$.

So the height ratio $\dfrac{h}{H}$ gives the fraction of the initial kinetic energy that is recovered as kinetic energy after the collision.

2 For a collision between two objects, the kinetic energy of each object can be worked out using the kinetic energy formula $E_K = \frac{1}{2}mv^2$, where m is the mass of the object and v is its speed. Using this formula, the total initial kinetic energy and the total final kinetic energy can be worked out if the mass, initial speed and speed after collision of each object is known.

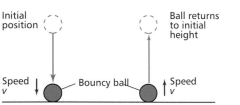

Fig 2.15 *An elastic impact*

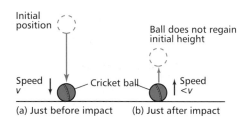

Fig 2.16 *A partially elastic impact*

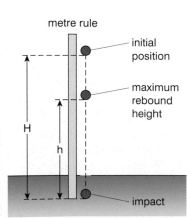

Fig 2.17 *Testing an impact*

Worked example

A railway wagon of mass 8000 kg moving at 3.0 m s^{-1} collides with an initially stationary wagon of mass 5000 kg. The two wagons separate after the collision. The 8000 kg wagon moves at a speed of 1.0 m s^{-1} without change of direction after the collision. Calculate:

a the speed and direction of the 5000 kg wagon after the collision,

b the loss of kinetic energy due to the collision.

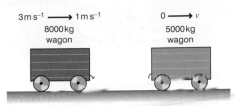

Fig 2.18

Solution

a The total initial momentum = 8000 × 3.0 = 24 000 kg m s^{-1}

The total final momentum = (8000 × 1.0) + 5000 V, where V is the speed of the 5000 kg wagon after the collision.

Using the Principle of Conservation of Momentum

$$8000 + 5000\,V = 24\,000$$

$$5000\,V = 24\,000 - 8000 = 16\,000$$

$$V = \frac{16\,000}{5000} = 3.2 \text{ m s}^{-1}$$

b kinetic energy of the 8000 kg wagon before the collision

$$= \tfrac{1}{2} \times 8000 \times 3.0^2 = 36\,000 \text{ J}$$

kinetic energy of the 8000 kg wagon after the collision

$$= \tfrac{1}{2} \times 8000 \times 1.0^2 = 4000 \text{ J}$$

kinetic energy of the 5000 kg wagon after the collision

$$= \tfrac{1}{2} \times 5000 \times 3.2^2 = 25\,600 \text{ J}$$

∴ loss of kinetic energy due to the collision

$$= 36\,000 - (4000 + 25\,600) = 6400 \text{ J}$$

Fig 2.19 *This dramatic collision was used to demonstrate that special casks used to transport radioactive materials by rail could withstand high speed impacts. In this collision, a remotely controlled diesel locomotive was driven into a stationary cask. Even though the locomotive was destroyed, the cask itself was intact afterwards.*

QUESTIONS

1 a A squash ball is released from rest above a flat surface. Describe how its energy changes if:
 (i) it rebounds to the same height,
 (ii) it rebounds to a lesser height.

b In **a** (ii), the ball is released from a height of 1.2 m above the surface and it rebounds to a height of 0.9 m above the surface. Show that 25% of its kinetic energy is lost in the impact.

2 A vehicle of mass 800 kg moving at a speed of 15.0 m s^{-1} collided with a vehicle of mass 1200 kg moving in the same direction at a speed of 5.0 m s^{-1}. The two vehicles locked together on impact. Calculate:

a the velocity of the two vehicles immediately after impact,

b the loss of kinetic energy due to the impact.

3 An ice puck of mass 1.5 kg moving at a speed of 4.2 m s^{-1} collides head on with a second ice puck of mass 1.0 kg moving in the opposite direction at a speed of 4.0 m s^{-1}. After the impact, the 1.5 kg ice puck continues in the same direction at a speed of 0.8 m s^{-1}. Calculate:

a the speed and direction of the 1.0 kg ice puck after the collision,

b the loss of kinetic energy due to the collision.

4 The bumper cars at a fairground are designed to withstand low-speed impacts without damage. A bumper car of mass 250 kg moving at a velocity of 0.9 m s^{-1} collides elastically with a stationary car of mass 200 kg. Immediately after the impact, the 250 kg car has a velocity of 0.1 m s^{-1} in the same direction as it was initially moving in.

a (i) Calculate the velocity of the 200 kg car immediately after the impact.

 (ii) Show that the collision was an elastic collision.

b Without further calculations, discuss the effect of the impact on the driver of each car.

Explosions

Fig 2.20 *The gun barrel recoils when the shell is fired. Large springs fitted to the barrel absorb the recoil energy of the barrel*

When two objects fly apart after being initially at rest, they recoil from each other with equal and opposite amounts of momentum. Consider Figure 2.21 where a trolley of mass m_A and a trolley of mass m_B, initially at rest, move away at speeds v_A and v_B respectively.

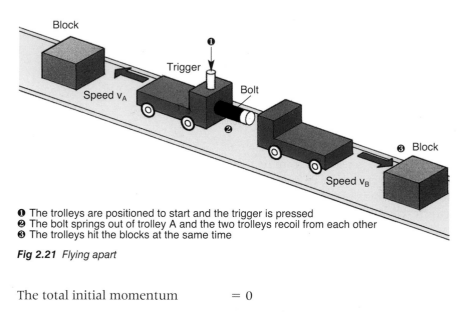

❶ The trolleys are positioned to start and the trigger is pressed
❷ The bolt springs out of trolley A and the two trolleys recoil from each other
❸ The trolleys hit the blocks at the same time

Fig 2.21 *Flying apart*

The total initial momentum $= 0$

The total momentum
immediately after the explosion $=$ momentum of A $+$ momentum of B
$$= m_A v_A + m_B v_B$$

Using the Principle of Conservation of Momentum, $m_A v_A + m_B v_B = 0$

$$\therefore m_B v_B = -m_A v_A$$

The minus sign means that the two masses move away from each other in opposite directions. For example, if $m_A = 1.0$ kg, $v_A = 2$ m s^{-1} and $m_B = 0.5$ kg, then $v_B = -m_A v_A / m_B = -4.0$ m s^{-1}. So A and B move away at speeds of 2 m s^{-1} and 4 m s^{-1} in opposite directions.

Testing a model explosion

In Figure 2.21, when the spring is released from one of the trolleys, the two trolleys, A and B, push each other apart. The bricks are positioned so that the trolleys hit the bricks at the same moment. The distance travelled by each trolley to the point of impact with the brick is equal to its speed multiplied by the time taken to travel that distance. Because the time taken is the same for the two trolleys, the distance ratio is the same as the speed ratio. Because the trolleys have equal (and opposite) amounts of momentum, the ratio of their speeds is the inverse of the mass ratio. The distance ratio should therefore be equal to the inverse of the mass ratio. In other words, if trolley A travels twice as far as trolley B, then the mass of A must be half the mass of B (so they carry away equal amounts of momentum).

QUESTIONS

1 A shell of mass 2.0 kg is fired at a speed of $140 \, \text{m s}^{-1}$ from an artillery gun of mass 800 kg. Calculate the recoil velocity of the shell.

2 In a laboratory experiment to measure the mass of an object X, two identical trolleys A and B, each of mass 0.50 kg, were initially stationary on a track. Object X was fixed to trolley A. When a trigger was pressed, the two trolleys moved apart in opposite directions at speeds of $0.30 \, \text{m s}^{-1}$ and $0.25 \, \text{m s}^{-1}$.

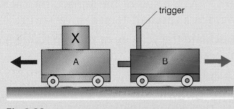

Fig 2.22

a Which of the two speeds given above was the speed of trolley A? Give a reason for your answer.

b Show that the mass of X must have been 0.10 kg.

3 Two trolleys, X of mass 1.2 kg and Y of mass 0.8 kg, are initially stationary on a level track.

a When a trigger is pressed on one of the trolleys, a spring pushes the two trolleys apart. Trolley Y moves away at a velocity of $0.15 \, \text{m s}^{-1}$.
  (i) Calculate the velocity of X.
  (ii) Calculate the total kinetic energy of the two trolleys immediately after the impact.

b In Question **2**, if the test had been carried out with trolley X held firmly, calculate the speed at which Y would have recoiled, assuming the energy stored in the spring before release is equal to the total kinetic energy calculated in **a** (ii).

4 A person in a stationary boat of total mass 150 kg throws a rock of mass 2.0 kg out of the boat. As a result, the boat recoils at a speed of $0.12 \, \text{m s}^{-1}$. Calculate:

a the speed at which the rock was thrown from the boat,

b the kinetic energy gained by:
  (i) the boat,   (ii) the rock.

CHAPTER SUMMARY

• Momentum = mass × velocity

• Force = $\dfrac{\text{change of momentum}}{\text{time taken}}$

• The Principle of Conservation of Momentum states that when two or more bodies interact, the total momentum is unchanged, provided no external forces act on the bodies.

• An elastic collision is one in which the total kinetic energy after the collision is the same as before the collision.

• A totally inelastic collision is one in which the colliding objects stick together.

• In an explosion where two objects fly apart, the two objects carry away equal and opposite momentum.

1 An object of mass 7.0 kg, initially at rest, is acted on by a force of 14 N for 10 s. Calculate:

   a the gain of momentum of the object,

   b the velocity of the object after 10 s.

2 A vehicle of mass 600 kg travelling at a velocity of 15 m s^{-1} is acted on by a braking force of 150 N. Calculate:

   a the momentum of the object at 15 m s^{-1},

   b the time taken to stop the object.

3 An object of mass 5.0 kg, initially at rest, was acted on by a force of 8.0 N in 12 s then brought to rest by a different force in 20 s.

   a Show that the change of momentum of the object is 96 N s.

   b Calculate the speed of the object after 12 s.

   c Calculate the force needed to bring the object to rest in 20s.

4 A stream of identical atoms of mass 1.0×10^{-25} kg hit a vertical surface normally at a speed of 750 m s^{-1} at a rate of 2000 atoms per second. The atoms stick to the surface on impact.

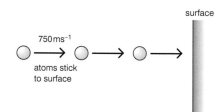

surface

750 ms^{-1}

atoms stick to surface

Calculate:

   a the loss of momentum of a single atom,

   b the average force of the atoms on the surface.

5 A molecule of mass 2.5×10^{-26} kg moving at a speed of 520 m s^{-1} collides normally with a wall and rebounds normally without loss of speed.

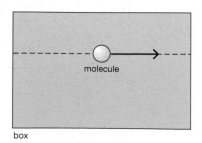

molecule

box

   a Calculate the change of momentum of the molecule.

   b The molecule is in a rectangular box and collides repeatedly with the same side of the box every 2.0 ms. Calculate the average force of impact of the molecule on the box.

6 A railway wagon of mass 2500 kg moving at a speed of 2.4 m s^{-1} collides with a stationary wagon of mass 1500 kg on a level track. The two wagons couple together and move away at the same velocity after the impact.

   a Calculate their velocity after the impact.

   b (i) Calculate the loss of kinetic energy due to the impact.
   (ii) Discuss the energy changes that take place as a result of the impact.

7 In a road accident, a van of mass 1500 kg moving at a speed of 28 m s^{-1} ran into the back of a car of mass 900 kg moving in the same direction at a speed of 11 m s^{-1}. As a result of the impact, the car was pushed forward at a speed of 18 m s^{-1}.

   a Calculate the velocity of the van immediately after the impact.

   b Calculate:
   (i) the loss of kinetic energy of the van,
   (ii) the gain of kinetic energy of the car,
   (iii) the total change of kinetic energy of the two vehicles.

   c Discuss the effect of the impact on a person in the car.

8 In a radioactive decay, a nucleus of mass 4.0×10^{-25} kg initially at rest emitted a particle of mass 6.7×10^{-27} kg with a velocity of 1.5×10^{7} m s^{-1}.

   a Calculate the velocity of recoil of the nucleus.

   b Calculate the kinetic energy of:
   (i) the recoil nucleus,
   (ii) the α-particle.

Motion in a circle

Uniform circular motion

In a cycle race, the cyclists pedal furiously at top speed. The speed of the perimeter of each wheel is the same as the cyclist's speed, provided the wheels do not slip on the ground. If the cyclist's speed is constant, the wheels must turn at a steady rate. An object rotating at a steady rate is said to be in **uniform circular motion**.

Consider a point on the perimeter of a wheel of radius r rotating at a steady speed.

- The circumference of the wheel $= 2\pi r$

- The frequency of rotation $f = \dfrac{1}{T}$, where T is the time for one rotation.

The speed of a point on the perimeter $= \dfrac{\text{circumference}}{\text{time for 1 rotation}} = \dfrac{2\pi r}{T} = 2\pi r f$

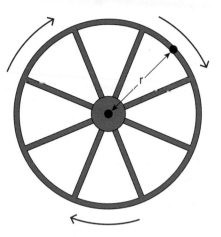

Fig 3.1 In uniform circular motion

Worked example

A cyclist is travelling at a speed of 13 m s^{-1} on a bicycle which has wheels of radius 390 mm. Calculate:

a the time for one rotation of the wheel

b (i) the frequency of rotation of the wheel.
   (ii) the number of rotations of the wheel in 1 minute.

Solution

a Rearranging speed $v = \dfrac{2\pi r}{T}$ gives the time for 1 rotation, $T = \dfrac{2\pi r}{v}$

Therefore, $T = \dfrac{2\pi \times 0.39 \text{ m}}{13 \text{ m s}^{-1}} = 0.19 \text{ s}$

b (i) Frequency $f = \dfrac{1}{T} = \dfrac{1}{0.19 \text{ s}} = 5.3 \text{ Hz}$

(ii) Number of rotations in 1 minute $= 60 \times 5.3 = 318$

3.1.1 Angular displacement

The London Eye is a very popular tourist attraction. The wheel has a diameter of 130 m and takes passengers high above the surrounding buildings, giving a glorious view on a clear day. Each full rotation of the wheel takes 30 minutes. Each capsule therefore takes its passengers through an angle of $0.2°$ each second $\left(= \dfrac{0.2\pi}{180} \text{ radians each second as } 360° = 2\pi \text{ radians} \right)$. Therefore, each capsule turns through an angle of:

- $2°$ in 10 seconds,

- $20° \left(= \dfrac{\pi}{9} \text{ radians} \right)$ in 100 seconds,

- $90° \left(= \dfrac{\pi}{2} \text{ radians} \right)$ in 450 seconds.

Fig 3.2 The London Eye

For any object in uniform circular motion, the object turns through an angle of $\dfrac{2\pi}{T}$ radians each second, where T is the time taken for 1 complete rotation.

In other words, the angular displacement of the object each second is $\frac{2\pi}{T}$.

Therefore, the **angular displacement** of the object in time t is given by

$$\theta \text{ (in radians)} = \frac{2\pi t}{T} = 2\pi ft$$

where T is the time for one rotation and $f\left(=\frac{1}{T}\right)$ is the frequency of rotation.

Notes

1 In time t, an object in uniform circular motion at speed v moves along the arc of the circle through a distance $s = vt = \frac{2\pi rt}{T} = \theta r$.

2 Angular speed, $\omega = \dfrac{\text{angular displacement, } \theta}{\text{time taken, } t} = \dfrac{2\pi}{T}$

3 The unit of ω is the radian per second (rad s^{-1})

Worked example

A cyclist travels at a speed of 12 m s^{-1} on a bicycle which has wheels of radius 0.40 m. Calculate:

a the frequency of rotation of each wheel,

b the angular speed of each wheel,

c the angle the wheel turns through in 0.10 s:
   (i) in radians,
   (ii) in degrees.

Solution

a Circumference of wheel $= 2\pi r = 2\pi \times 0.4 = 2.5$ m

Time for 1 wheel rotation, $T = \dfrac{\text{circumference}}{\text{speed}} = \dfrac{2.5}{12} = 0.21$ s

Frequency $= \dfrac{1}{T} = \dfrac{1}{0.21} = 4.8$ Hz

b Angular speed $= \dfrac{2\pi}{T} = 30$ rad s^{-1}

c (i) Angle the wheel turns through in 0.10 s, $\theta, = \dfrac{2\pi t}{T} = \dfrac{2\pi \times 0.10}{0.21}$
      $= 3.0$ radians

   (ii) $\theta = 3.0 \times \dfrac{360}{2\pi} = 172°$

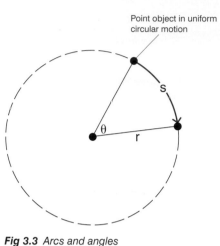

Point object in uniform circular motion

Fig 3.3 *Arcs and angles*

QUESTIONS

1 Calculate the angular displacement in radians of the tip of the minute hand of a clock in:

   a 1 second,

   b 1 minute,

   c 1 hour.

2 An electric motor turns at a frequency of 50 Hz. Calculate:

   a its time period,

   b the angle it turns through in radians in:
      (i) 1 ms,
      (ii) 1 second.

3 The Earth takes exactly 24 hours for 1 full rotation. Calculate:

   a the speed of rotation of a point on the equator,

   b the angle the Earth turns through in 1 second in:
      (i) degrees,   (ii) radians.

   The radius of the Earth = 6400 km.

4 A satellite in a circular orbit of radius 8000 km takes 120 minutes per orbit. Calculate:

   a its speed,

   b its angular displacement in 1.0 s in:
      (i) degrees,   (ii) radians.

Centripetal acceleration

The **velocity** of an object moving round a circle at constant speed continually changes direction. Because its velocity changes, the object therefore accelerates. If this seems odd because the speed is constant, remember that acceleration is change of velocity per second. Passengers on the London Eye might not notice they are being accelerated but if the wheel was made to rotate much faster, they undoubtedly would notice.

The velocity of an object in uniform circular motion at any point is along the tangent to the circle at that point. The direction of the velocity changes continuously as the object moves round on its circular path. The change in the direction of the velocity is towards the centre of the circle. So its acceleration is towards the centre of the circle and is referred to as **centripetal acceleration**. Centripetal means 'towards the centre of the circle'.

For an object moving at constant speed v in a circle of radius r, it can be shown that

$$\text{its centripetal acceleration, } a = \frac{v^2}{r}$$

Proof of this equation is not required for the A2 specification. However, a proof is given to provide a better understanding of the idea of centripetal acceleration.

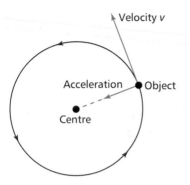

Fig 3.4 Centripetal acceleration

Proof of $a = \frac{v^2}{r}$

- Consider an object in uniform circular motion at speed v moving in a short time interval δt from position A to position B along its path. Therefore the distance AB along the circle, $\delta s = v\,\delta t$. Figure 3.5 shows the idea.
- The line from the object to the centre of the circle at C turns through angle θ when the object moves from A to B. The velocity direction of the object turns through the same angle θ, as shown in Figure 3.5.
- The change of velocity, δv = velocity at B – velocity at A, is shown in the velocity vector triangle in Figure 3.5.
- The triangles ABC and the velocity vector triangle have the same shape because they both have two sides of equal length with the same angle θ between the two sides.

Provided θ is small, then $\qquad \dfrac{\delta v}{v} = \dfrac{\delta s}{r}$

Because $\delta s = v\,\delta t$, then $\qquad \dfrac{\delta v}{v} = \dfrac{v\,\delta t}{r}$

Therefore, acceleration, $\qquad a = \dfrac{\text{change of velocity } \delta v}{\text{time taken } \delta t}$

$\qquad\qquad\qquad\qquad\qquad = \dfrac{v^2}{r} \text{ towards the centre.}$

Note Since $v = \omega r$, then $a = \dfrac{v^2}{r} = \dfrac{(\omega r)^2}{r} = \omega^2 r$

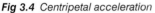

Fig 3.5 Proving $a = \frac{v^2}{r}$

3.2.1 Centripetal force

To make an object move round on a circular path, it must be acted on by a resultant force which changes its direction of motion. Figure 3.6 shows a 'hammer' being whirled round in a circle. The tension in the cable pulls on the ball and changes its direction continuously. When the cable is released, the ball flies off at a tangent.

The resultant force on an object moving round a circle at constant speed is referred to as the **centripetal force** because it acts towards the centre of the circle.

- For an object whirling round on the end of a string, the tension in the string is the centripetal force.
- For a satellite moving round the Earth, the force of gravity between the satellite and the Earth is the centripetal force.
- For a planet moving round the Sun, the force of gravity between the planet and the Sun is the centripetal force.
- For a capsule on the London Eye, the centripetal force is the resultant of the support force on the capsule and the force of gravity on it.
- In Chapter 8, you will meet the use of a magnetic field to bend a beam of charged particles (e.g. electrons) in a circular path. The magnetic force on the moving charged particles is the centripetal force.

Any object that moves in circular motion is acted on by a resultant force which always acts towards the centre of the circle. The resultant force is the centripetal force and therefore causes a centripetal acceleration.

Notes

1 If the object is acted on by a single force only (e.g. a satellite in orbit round the Earth), that force is the centripetal force and causes the centripetal acceleration.

2 The centripetal force is at right angles to the direction of the object's velocity. Therefore, no work is done by the centripetal force on the object because there is no displacement in the direction of the force. The kinetic energy of the object is therefore constant so its speed is unchanged.

Equation for centripetal force

For an object moving at constant speed v along a circular path of radius r, its centripetal acceleration $a = \dfrac{v^2}{r}$.

Therefore, applying Newton's second law for constant mass in the form '$F = ma$' gives

$$\textbf{centripetal force } F = \frac{mv^2}{r}$$

Fig 3.6 *Centripetal force in action*

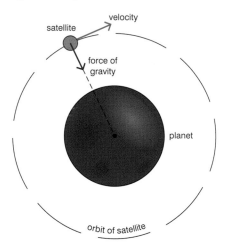

Fig 3.7 *A satellite in uniform circular motion*

QUESTIONS

1 The wheel of the London Eye has a diameter of 130 m and takes 30 minutes for a full rotation. Calculate:
   a the speed of a capsule,
   b (i) the centripetal acceleration of a capsule,
      (ii) the centripetal force on a person of mass 65 kg in a capsule.

2 An object of mass 0.15 kg moves round a circular path of radius 0.42 m at a steady rate once every 5.0 seconds. Calculate:
   a the speed and acceleration of the object,
   b the centripetal force on the object.

3 a The Earth moves round the Sun on a circular orbit of radius 1.5×10^{11} m, taking $365\frac{1}{4}$ days for each complete orbit. Calculate:
      (i) the speed,
      (ii) the centripetal acceleration of the Earth on its orbit round the Sun.

   b A satellite is in orbit just above the surface of a spherical planet which has the same radius as the Earth and the same acceleration of free fall at its surface. Calculate:
      (i) the speed,
      (ii) the time for 1 complete orbit of this satellite.

The radius of the Earth = 6400 km

Acceleration of free fall = 9.8 m s^{-2}

4 A hammer thrower whirls a 2.0 kg hammer on the end of a rope in a circle of radius 0.8 m. The hammer took 0.6 s to make one full rotation just before it was released. Calculate:
   a the speed of the hammer just before it was released,
   b its centripetal acceleration,
   c the centripetal force on the hammer just before it was released.

On the road

Even on a very short journey, the effects of circular motion can be important. For example, a vehicle that turns a corner too fast could skid or topple over. A vehicle that goes over a curved bridge too fast might even lose contact briefly with the road surface. To make any object move on a circular path, the object must be acted on by a resultant force which is always towards the centre of curvature of its path.

Examples

1 Over the top of a hill

Consider a vehicle of mass m moving at speed v along a road that passes over the top of a hill or over the top of a curved bridge.

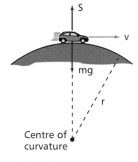

Fig 3.8 *Over the top*

At the top of the hill, the support force S from the road on the vehicle is directly upwards in the opposite direction to its weight, mg. The resultant force on the vehicle is the difference between the weight and the support force. This difference acts towards the centre of curvature of the hill as the centripetal force. In other words,

$$mg - S = \frac{mv^2}{r}, \text{ where } r \text{ is the radius of curvature of the hill}$$

The vehicle would lose contact with the road if its speed is equal to or greater than a certain speed, v_0. If this happens, then $S = 0$ so $mg = \frac{mv_0^2}{r}$

Therefore, the vehicle speed should not exceed v_0, where $v_0^2 = gr$, otherwise the vehicle will lose contact with the road surface at the top of the hill. Prove for yourself that a vehicle that travels over a curved bridge of radius of curvature 5 m would lose contact with the road surface if its speed exceeded 7 m s^{-1}.

2 On a roundabout

Consider a vehicle of mass m moving at speed v in a circle of radius r as it moves round a roundabout on a level road. The centripetal force is provided by the force of friction between the vehicle's tyres and the road surface. In other words,

$$\text{force of friction } F = \frac{mv^2}{r}$$

For no skidding or slipping, the force of friction between the tyres and the road surface must be less than a limiting value F_0 which is proportional to the vehicle's weight.

Therefore, for no slipping, the speed of the vehicle must be less than a certain value v_0 which is given by the equation,

$$\text{limiting force of friction } F_0 = \frac{mv_0^2}{r}$$

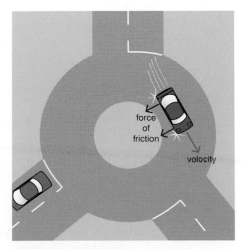

Fig 3.9 *On a roundabout*

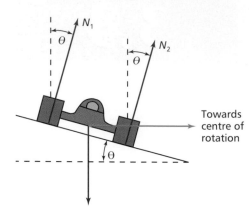

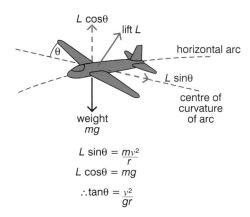

Fig 3.10 A racing car taking a bend

$L \cos\theta$

lift L

horizontal arc

θ

$L \sin\theta$

centre of
curvature
of arc

weight
mg

$L \sin\theta = \frac{mv^2}{r}$

$L \cos\theta = mg$

$\therefore \tan\theta = \frac{v^2}{gr}$

Fig 3.11 An aircraft circling

3 On a banked track

A race track is often banked where it curves. Motorway slip roads in cities often bend in a tight curve. Such a road is usually banked to enable vehicles to drive round without any sideways friction on the tyres. Rail tracks on curves are usually banked to enable trains to move round the curve without slowing down too much.

- Without any banking, the centripetal force is provided only by sideways friction between the vehicle wheels and the road surface. As explained in the previous example, the vehicle on a bend slips outwards if its speed is too high.
- On a banked track, the speed can be higher. To understand why, consider Figure 3.10 which represents the front-view of a racing car of mass m on a banked track, where $\theta =$ the angle of the track to the horizontal. For there to be no sideways friction on the tyres due to the road, the horizontal component of the support forces N_1 and N_2 must act as the centripetal force.

Resolving these forces into horizontal components ($= (N_1 + N_2) \sin \theta$) and vertical components ($= (N_1 + N_2) \cos \theta$),

- because $(N_1 + N_2) \sin \theta$ acts as the centripetal force, then $(N_1 + N_2) \sin \theta = \frac{mv^2}{r}$
- because $(N_1 + N_2) \cos \theta$ balances the weight (mg), then $(N_1 + N_2) \cos \theta = mg$.

Therefore $\qquad \tan \theta = \frac{(N_1 + N_2) \sin \theta}{(N_1 + N_2) \cos \theta} = \frac{mv^2}{mgr}$

Simplifying this equation gives the condition for no sideways friction; $\tan \theta = \frac{v^2}{gr}$

In other words, there is no sideways friction if the speed v is such that $v^2 = gr \tan \theta$.

Note An aircraft banks when it turns in a circle. The horizontal component of the lift force acts as the centripetal force. Figure 3.11 shows the idea. The radius of the circle, r, depends on the speed and the angle of banking in accordance with the equation $v^2 = gr \tan \theta$.

QUESTIONS

$g = 9.8 \,\text{m s}^{-2}$

1 A vehicle of mass 1200 kg passes over a bridge of radius of curvature 15 m at a speed of $10 \,\text{m s}^{-1}$. Calculate:

  a the centripetal acceleration of the vehicle on the bridge,

  b the support force on the vehicle when it is at the top.

2 The maximum speed for no skidding of a vehicle of mass 750 kg on a roundabout of radius 20 m is $9.0 \,\text{m s}^{-1}$. Calculate, for this speed:

  a the centripetal acceleration,

  b the centripetal force on the vehicle.

3 Explain why a circular athletics track that is banked is suitable for sprinters but not for marathon runners.

4 At a racing car circuit, the track is banked at an angle of 25° to the horizontal on a bend which has a radius of curvature of 350 m.

  a Calculate the speed of a vehicle on the bend if there is to be no sideways friction on its tyres.

  b Discuss and explain what could happen to a vehicle that took the bend too fast.

At the fairground

Many of the rides at a fairground take people round in circles. Some examples are analysed below. It is worth remembering that centripetal acceleration values of more than 2–3 g can be dangerous to the average person.

Examples

1 The Big Dipper

A ride that takes you at high speed through a big dip pushes you into your seat as you pass through the dip. The difference between the support force on you (acting upwards) and your weight acts as the centripetal force.

At the bottom of the dip, the support force S on you is vertically upwards, as shown in Figure 3.12.

Therefore, for a speed v at the bottom of a dip of radius of curvature r,

$$S - mg = \frac{mv^2}{r}$$

So the support force $S = mg + \frac{mv^2}{r}$

The extra force you experience due to your motion is therefore $\frac{mv^2}{r}$.

2 The very long swing

Consider a person of mass m on a very long swing of length L, released from height h above the equilibrium position. The maximum speed is when the swing passes through the lowest point. This can be worked out by equating the loss of potential energy to the gain of kinetic energy.

$$\tfrac{1}{2}mv^2 = mgh$$

where v is its speed as it passes through the lowest point.

$$\text{Therefore } v^2 = 2gh$$

The person on the swing is on a circular path of radius L. At the lowest point, the support force S on the person due to the rope is in the opposite direction to the person's weight, mg. The difference, $S - mg$, acts towards the centre of the circular path and provides the centripetal force. Therefore

$$S - mg = \frac{mv^2}{L}$$

Because $v^2 = 2gh$, $S - mg = \frac{2mgh}{L}$

In other words, $\frac{2mgh}{L}$ represents the extra support force the person experiences due to circular motion. Prove for yourself that for $h = L$ (i.e. a 90° swing), the extra support force is equal to twice the person's weight.

3 The Big Wheel

This ride takes its passengers round in a vertical circle on the inside of the circumference of a very large wheel. The wheel turns fast enough to stop the passengers falling out as they pass through the highest position.

At maximum height, the reaction R from the wheel on each person acts downwards. Therefore, the resultant force at this position = $mg + R$. This reaction force and the weight provide the centripetal force. Therefore, at the highest position when the wheel speed is v,

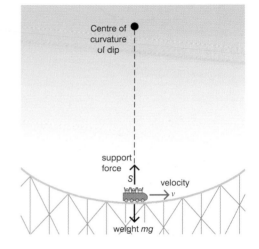

Fig 3.12 In a dip

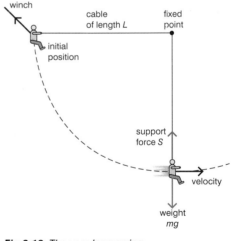

Fig 3.13 The very long swing

> ### NOTE
> A person in a Big Wheel with capsules (e.g. the London Eye) would be unsupported at speed v_0. Such a wheel must turn slower otherwise passengers would lose contact with the capsule floor.

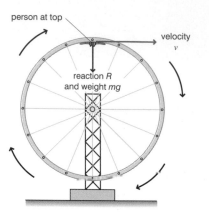

Fig 3.14 *The Big Wheel*

$$mg + R = \frac{mv^2}{r} \qquad \text{where } r \text{ is the radius of the wheel}$$

$$\therefore \quad R = \frac{mv^2}{r} - mg$$

At a certain speed v_0 such that $v_0^2 = gr$, then $R = 0$ so there would be no force on the person due to the wheel.

QUESTIONS

$g = 9.8 \text{ m s}^{-2}$

1 A train on a fairground ride is initially stationary before it descends through a height of 45 m into a dip which has a radius of curvature of 78 m, as shown in Figure 3.15.

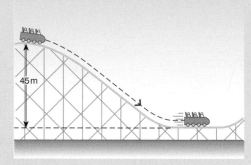

Fig 3.15

a Calculate the speed of the train at the bottom of the dip, assuming air resistance and friction are negligible.

b Calculate:
   (i) the centripetal acceleration of the train at the bottom of the dip,
   (ii) the extra support force on a person of weight 600 N in the train.

2 A very long swing at a fairground is 32 m in length. A person of mass 69 kg on the swing descends from a position when the swing is horizontal. Calculate:

a the speed of the person at the lowest point,

b the centripetal acceleration at the lowest point,

c the support force on the person at the lowest point.

3 The Big Wheel at a fairground has a radius of 12.0 m and rotates in a vertical plane once every 6.0 seconds. Calculate:

a the speed of rotation of the perimeter of the wheel,

b the centripetal acceleration of a person on the perimeter,

c the support force on a person of mass 72 kg at the highest point.

4 The wheel of the London Eye has a diameter of 130 m and takes 30 minutes to complete one revolution. Calculate the change, due to rotation of the wheel, of the support force on a person of weight 500 N in a capsule at the top of the wheel.

CHAPTER SUMMARY

1 For an object of mass m in uniform circular motion on a circle of radius r:

- its **speed** $v = \dfrac{2\pi r}{T}$, where T is the time for one rotation,

- its **frequency of rotation** $f = \dfrac{1}{T}$,

- its **angular displacement**, in radians, in time $t = 2\pi f t = \dfrac{2\pi t}{T}$,

- its **centripetal acceleration**, $a = \dfrac{v^2}{r}$ towards the centre of the circle,

- the **centripetal force** on the object $= \dfrac{mv^2}{r}$

2 Examples

- Car of mass m going over the top of a hill; support force $S = mg - \dfrac{mv^2}{r}$

- Object of mass m going through the bottom of a dip; support force $S = mg + \dfrac{mv^2}{r}$

- Person on the inside of a vertical fairground wheel at the top; reaction force $R = \dfrac{mv^2}{r} - mg$

- Banked track at angle θ to horizontal; $v^2 = gr \tan \theta$ for no sideways friction

$g = 9.8 \text{ m s}^{-2}$

1 An object moves on a circular path at constant speed. Explain:

   a why the object's velocity continually changes even though its speed is constant,

   b the object accelerates even though its speed is constant.

2 The Moon moves round the Earth once every $27\frac{1}{3}$ days on a circular orbit of radius 380 000 km. Calculate:

   a the speed of the Moon,

   b its centripetal acceleration.

3 A pulley wheel of diameter 24 mm fitted to an electric motor in a machine rotates at a frequency of 30 Hz when the machine is in normal operation. A belt fitted to the wheel is used to drive a drum in the machine, as shown below.

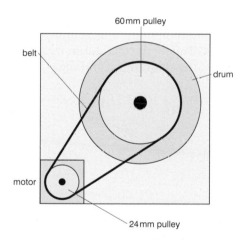

   a Calculate:
   (i) the speed of the belt on the wheel,
   (ii) the centripetal acceleration of the belt attached to the wheel as it moves round the pulley wheel.

   b The belt drives the drum via a second pulley wheel of diameter 60 mm attached to the drum axle. Calculate:
   (i) the frequency of rotation of the second pulley wheel,
   (ii) the centripetal acceleration of the belt as it passes round the second pulley wheel.

4 A cyclist travels at a speed of 15 m s⁻¹ on a bicycle fitted with wheels of diameter 850 mm.

   a Calculate:
   (i) the frequency of rotation of each wheel,
   (ii) the centripetal acceleration of the tyre on each wheel.

   b The rear wheel of the bicycle is driven by a chain which passes round a gear wheel of diameter 55 mm attached to the axle of the rear wheel.

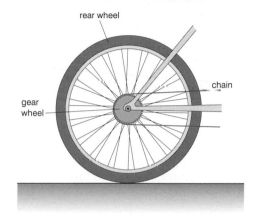

   (i) Calculate the centripetal acceleration of the chain as it passes round the gear wheel.
   (ii) Explain why the chain will come off the gear wheel if its speed is too great.

5 a Explain why a car on a roundabout will slide to the outside of the roundabout if it travels too fast on the roundabout.

   b (i) Calculate the centripetal acceleration of a vehicle travelling round a roundabout of diameter 40 m when the speed of the vehicle is 8 m s⁻¹.
   (ii) For no slippage on the roundabout, the frictional force on the vehicle tyres must be less than 0.6 × the vehicle weight. Calculate the maximum speed of the vehicle on the roundabout for no slippage.

6 On a fairground ride, a train of mass 1500 kg moving at a speed of 1.5 m s⁻¹ descends from the highest point of the track through a height of 42 m to the bottom of a dip and then passes over a 'hill' which is 15 m higher than the bottom of the dip.

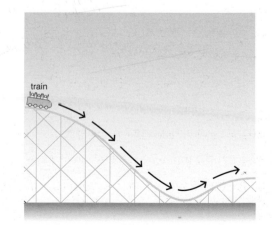

a (i) Calculate the speed of the train at the bottom of the dip.

    (ii) Show that the speed of the train as it passes over the top of the hill is 23 m s^{-1}. (Assume air resistance and friction are negligible.)

b (i) The dip has a radius of curvature of 65 m. Show that a person of mass 80 kg in the train experiences an extra support force of 1020 N on passing through the bottom of the dip.

    (ii) The passengers in the train momentarily leave their seats when the train passes over the hill. Show that the radius of curvature of the hill is 54 m.

7 a Explain why a train can travel round a horizontal curve at a higher speed if the track is banked rather than flat.

  b Discuss why the train would leave the track if it travelled round the curve too fast.

8 The figure below shows a cross-section of an automatic brake fitted to a rotating shaft. The brake pads are held on the shaft by springs.

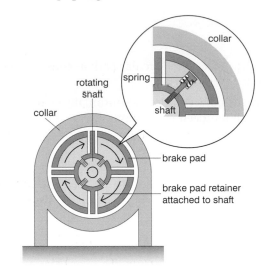

a Explain why the brake pads press against the inner surface of the stationary collar if the shaft rotates too fast.

b Each brake pad and its retainer has a mass of 0.30 kg and its centre of mass is 60 mm from the centre of the shaft. The tension in the spring attached to each pad is 250 N. Calculate the maximum frequency of rotation of the shaft for no braking.

Oscillations

Measuring oscillations

4

4.1

There are many examples of oscillations in everyday life. A car that travels over a bump bounces up and down for a short time afterwards. Every microcomputer has an electronic oscillator to drive its internal clock. A child on a swing moves forwards then backwards repeatedly. In this simple example, one full cycle of motion is from maximum height at one side to maximum height on the other side then back again. The lowest point is referred to as the **equilibrium** position as it is where the child eventually comes to a standstill. The child in motion is said to **oscillate** about equilibrium.

Further examples of oscillating motion include:

- an object on a spring moving up and down repeatedly,

- a pendulum moving to-and-fro repeatedly,

- a ball bearing rolling from side-to-side,

- a small boat rocking from side to side.

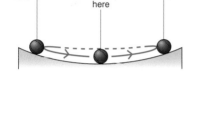

4.1.1 Displacement v. time for an oscillating object

An oscillating object moves repeatedly one way then in the opposite direction through its equilibrium position. The **displacement** of the object (i.e. distance and direction) from equilibrium continually changes during the motion. In one full cycle after passing through equilibrium, the displacement of the object:

- increases as it moves away from equilibrium, then

- decreases as it returns to equilibrium, then

- reverses and increases as it moves away from equilibrium in the opposite direction, then

- decreases as it returns to equilibrium.

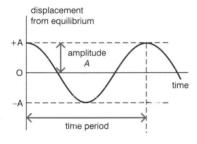

Fig 4.1 Oscillating motion

The **amplitude** of the oscillations is the maximum displacement of the oscillating object from equilibrium. If the amplitude is constant and no frictional forces are present, the oscillations are described as **free** oscillations. See p. 47.

The **time period** of the oscillating motion is the time for one complete cycle of oscillations. One full cycle after passing through any position, the object passes through that same position in the same direction.

The **frequency** of oscillations is the number of cycles per second made by an oscillating object.

The unit of frequency is the hertz (Hz) which is 1 cycle per second.

For oscillations of frequency f, the time period $T_P = \dfrac{1}{f}$

Note The angular frequency ω of the oscillating motion is defined as $\dfrac{2\pi}{T_P} (= 2\pi f)$.

The unit of ω is the radian per second (rad s^{-1}). Although angular frequency is not part of the A2 physics specification, you may meet it if you are studying A level mathematics.

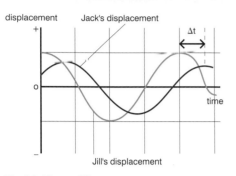

displacement

Jack's displacement

Jill's displacement

Fig 4.2 *Phase difference*

4.1.2 Phase difference

Imagine two children on adjacent identical swings. The time period, T_P of the oscillating motion is the same, as the swings are identical. If one child reaches maximum displacement on one side a certain time, Δt, later than the other child, they oscillate out of phase. Their **phase difference** stays the same as they oscillate, always corresponding to a fraction of a cycle equal to $\frac{\Delta t}{T_P}$. For example, if the time period is 2.0 s and one child reaches maximum displacement on one side 0.5 seconds later than the other child, the later child will always be a quarter of a cycle $\left(= \frac{0.5 \text{ s}}{2.0 \text{ s}} \right)$ behind the other child. Their phase difference, in radians, is therefore $0.5\,\pi \left(= 2\pi \frac{\Delta t}{T_P} \right)$.

In general, for two objects oscillating at the same frequency,

$$\text{their phase difference, in radians, } = 2\pi \frac{\Delta t}{T_P}$$

where Δt is the time between successive instants when the two objects are at maximum displacement in the same direction.

Notes

1. 2π radians = 360° so the phase difference in degrees is $360 \frac{\Delta t}{T_P}$.

2. The two objects oscillate in phase if $\Delta t = T_P$. The phase difference of 2π is therefore equivalent to zero.

3. Table of phase differences

Δt	0	0.25 T_P	0.50 T_P	0.75 T_P	T_P
Phase difference in radians	0	$\frac{\pi}{2}$	π	$\frac{3\pi}{2}$	2π
in degrees	0	90	180	270	360

QUESTIONS

1 Describe how the velocity of a bungee jumper changes from the moment he jumps off the starting platform to the moment he next returns to the platform.

2 a What is meant by free oscillations?

  b A metre rule is clamped to a table so that part of its length projects at right angles from the edge of the table, as shown in Figure 4.3. A 100 g mass is attached to the free end of the rule. When the free end of the rule is depressed downwards then released, the mass oscillates. Describe how you would find out if the oscillations of the mass are free oscillations.

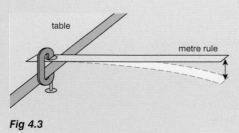

Fig 4.3

3 An object suspended from the lower end of a vertical spring is displaced downwards from equilibrium by a distance of 20 mm then released. It takes 9.6 s to undergo 20 complete cycles of oscillation. Calculate:

  a its time period,

  b its frequency of oscillation.

4 Two identical pendulums X and Y each consist of a small metal sphere attached to a thread of a certain length. Each pendulum makes 20 complete cycles of oscillation in 16 s. State the phase difference, in radians, between the motion of X and that of Y if:

  a X passes through equilibrium 0.2 s after Y passes through equilibrium in the same direction,

  b X reaches maximum displacement at the same time as Y reaches maximum displacement in the opposite direction.

An oscillating object speeds up as it returns to equilibrium and it slows down as it moves away from equilibrium. Figure 4.4 shows one way to record the displacement of an oscillating pendulum.

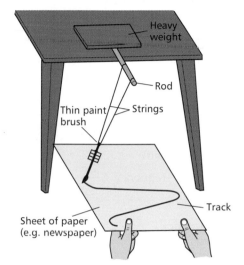

Fig 4.4 *Investigating oscillations*

The variation of displacement with time is shown in Figure 4.5 (i). Provided friction is negligible, the amplitude of the oscillations is constant.

The variation of velocity with time is given by the gradient of the displacement v. time graph, as shown by Figure 4.5 (ii).

- The velocity is greatest where the gradient of the displacement v. time graph is greatest (i.e. at zero displacement when the object passes through equilibrium).
- The velocity is zero where the gradient of the displacement v. time graph is zero (i.e. at maximum displacement).

The variation of acceleration with time is given by the gradient of the velocity v. time graph, as shown by Figure 4.5 (iii).

- The acceleration is greatest where the gradient of the velocity v. time graph is greatest. This is when the velocity is zero and occurs at maximum displacement.
- The acceleration is zero where the gradient of the velocity v. time graph is zero. This is when the displacement is zero.

By comparing Figure 4.5 (i) and (iii) directly, it can be seen that

> **the acceleration is always in the opposite direction to the displacement.**

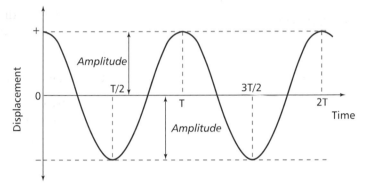

Fig 4.5 *(i) Displacement v. time*

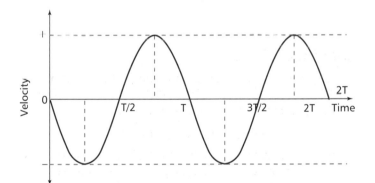

Fig 4.5 *(ii) Velocity v. time*

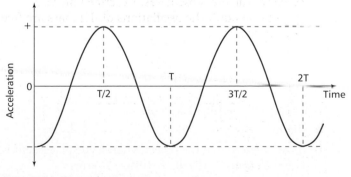

Fig 4.5 *(iii) Acceleration v. time*

In other words, if one direction is referred to as the positive direction and the other as the negative direction, the acceleration direction is always the opposite sign to the displacement direction.

Simple harmonic motion is defined as oscillating motion in which the acceleration is

1 proportional to the displacement,

2 always in the opposite direction to the displacement.

$$\text{Acceleration, } a = -\text{ constant} \times \text{displacement } x$$

The constant depends on the time period T_P of the oscillations. The shorter the time period, the faster the oscillations which means the larger the acceleration at any given displacement. So the constant is greater the shorter the time period. As shown in 4.3, the constant in this equation is ω^2, where ω, the angular frequency, $= \dfrac{2\pi}{T_P} (= 2\pi f)$.

Therefore the defining equation for simple harmonic motion is

acceleration, $\quad a = -\omega^2 x, \quad$ where $x = $ displacement

$$\omega = \text{angular frequency} = \frac{2\pi}{T_P}$$

This equation may be written as

acceleration, $\quad a = -(2\pi f)^2 x, \quad$ where $f = $ frequency

NOTES

1 The time period is independent of the amplitude of the oscillations.

2 Maximum displacement $x_{MAX} = \pm A$, where A is the amplitude of the oscillations. Therefore,

• when $x_{MAX} = +A$, the acceleration $a = -(2\pi f)^2 A$, and

• when $x_{MAX} = -A$, the acceleration $a = +(2\pi f)^2 A$.

QUESTIONS

1 A small object attached to the end of a vertical spring (Fig. 4.6) oscillates with an amplitude of 25 mm and a time period of 2.0 s. The object passes through equilibrium moving upwards at time $t = 0$. What is the displacement and direction of motion of the object:

a $\frac{1}{4}$ cycle later,   b $\frac{1}{2}$ cycle later,

c $\frac{3}{4}$ cycle later,   d 1 cycle later?

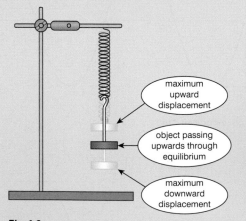

Fig 4.6

2 For the oscillations in 1, calculate:

a the frequency,

b the acceleration of the object when its displacement is:
(i) +25 mm,   (ii) 0,   (iii) −25 mm.

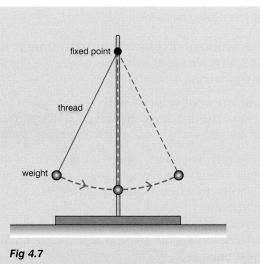

Fig 4.7

3 A simple pendulum consists of a small weight on the end of a thread. The weight is displaced from equilibrium and released. It oscillates with an amplitude of 32 mm, taking 20 s to execute 10 oscillations. Calculate:

a its frequency,

b its initial acceleration.

4 For the oscillations in 3, the object is released at time $t = 0$. State the displacement and calculate the acceleration when:

a $t = 10$ s,

b time $= 15$ s.

More about sine waves

4.3.1 Circles and waves

Consider a small object P in uniform circular motion, as shown in Figure 4.8. Measured from the centre of the circle at O, the coordinates of P are therefore $x = r \cos \theta$ and $y = r \sin \theta$, where θ is the angle between the x-axis and the radial line OP. Figure 4.9 shows how the x-coordinate changes as angle θ changes. The curve is a cosine wave. It has the same shape as the simple harmonic motion curves in Figure 4.5.

4.3.2 Oscillating shadows

To see the link between simple harmonic motion and sine curves, consider the motion of the ball and the pendulum bob in Figure 4.9. A projector is used to cast a shadow of the ball (P) in uniform circular motion on to a screen alongside the shadow of the bob (Q) of a simple pendulum oscillating above the circle. The two shadows keep up with each other exactly when their time periods are matched. In other words, P and Q at any instant have the same horizontal position and have the same horizontal motion. The acceleration of Q is therefore the same as the acceleration of P.

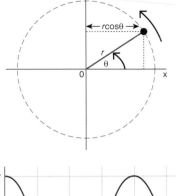

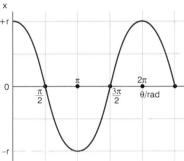

Fig 4.8 Circles and waves

- Because the ball is in uniform circular motion, its acceleration $a = -\dfrac{v^2}{r}$ where the minus sign indicates its direction towards O. Since speed $v = 2\pi rf$ (see p. 29), then $a = -(2\pi f)^2 r$.

- The component of acceleration of the ball parallel to the screen, $a_x = a \cos \theta$, $\therefore$ the acceleration of P, $a_x = -(2\pi f)^2 r \cos \theta = -(2\pi f)^2 x$

Because the bob's motion is the same as the motion of the ball's shadow,

$$\text{the acceleration of the bob, } a_x = -(2\pi f)^2 x$$

This is the defining equation for simple harmonic motion and it shows why the constant of proportionality is $(2\pi f)^2$.

Notes

1. The bob oscillates along the x-axis between $x = -r$ and $x = +r$. Its amplitude of oscillation, $A = r$.

2. The displacement of the bob from equilibrium is therefore given by $x = A \cos \theta$, where θ is the angle the ball moves through from its position when $x = A$. At time t after the ball passes through this position,

$$\theta \text{ (in radians)} = \frac{2\pi t}{T_P} = 2\pi ft.$$

Therefore $x = A \cos (2\pi ft)$.

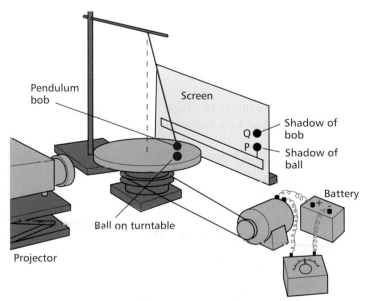

4.3.3 Sine wave solutions

For any object oscillating at frequency f in simple harmonic motion, its acceleration a at displacement x is given by

$$a = -(2\pi f)^2 x$$

The variation of displacement with time depends on the initial displacement and the initial velocity (i.e. the displacement and velocity at time $t = 0$). For example:

Fig 4.9 Comparing simple harmonic motion with circular motion

Where the damping is strong enough, an object displaced from equilibrium and released returns to equilibrium without oscillating. The greater the damping, the longer it takes for the object to return to equilibrium. For example, a mass on a spring in thick oil would return to equilibrium after being displaced and released much more slowly than if it was in thin oil.

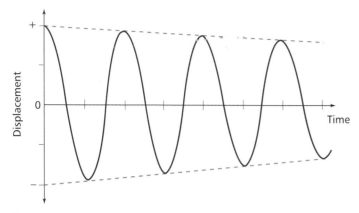

Fig 4.16 *Light damping*

Practical examples

1 **The suspension system of a car** consists of a coiled spring near each wheel between the wheel axle and the car chassis. When the wheel is jolted, for example on a bumpy road, the spring smoothes out the force of the jolts. An oil damper fitted with each spring prevents the chassis from bouncing up and down too much.

Without oil dampers, the occupants of the car would continue to be thrown up and down until the oscillations died away. The flow of oil through valves in the piston of each damper provides a frictional force which damps the oscillating motion of the chassis. The dampers are designed to ensure the chassis returns to its 'equilibrium' position in the shortest possible time after each jolt with little or no oscillations. Such damping is referred to as **critical damping**.

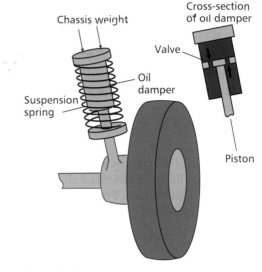

Fig 4.17 *Car suspension*

2 **Swing doors** need to be damped to prevent them swinging back on people. Imagine walking through a swing door without dampers; if you walk too slowly through it, it might bounce back and hit you as you are walking away from it. A damper fitted to the door slows its motion and stops it from swinging back. The damper needs to provide heavier than critical damping so the door closes slowly.

QUESTIONS

1 a Describe the energy changes of a simple pendulum oscillating in air during one cycle of oscillation after it passes through equilibrium.

  b Sketch graphs on the same axes to show how the potential energy and the kinetic energy of a freely oscillating object varies with its displacement from equilibrium.

2 A glider of mass 0.45 kg on a frictionless air track is attached to two stretched springs at either end, as shown in Figure 4.18. A force of 3.0 N is needed to displace the glider from equilibrium and hold it at a displacement of 50 mm. The glider is then released and it oscillates freely on the air track. Calculate:

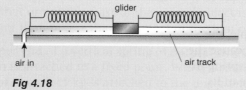

Fig 4.18

  a the spring constant k for the system,

  b (i) the initial potential energy of the system when the glider is held at a displacement of 50 mm,
      (ii) the maximum kinetic energy of the glider.

3 a In each of the following examples, describe the energy changes after the instant of release:
      (i) A child on a swing displaced from equilibrium then released.
      (ii) Water in a U-shaped tube displaced from equilibrium then released.

  b Discuss how effective a car suspension damper would be if the oil in the damper was replaced by oil that was much more viscous.

4 The amplitude of an oscillating mass on a spring decreases by 4% each cycle from an initial amplitude of 100 mm. Calculate the amplitude after:

  a 5 cycles of oscillation,

  b 20 cycles of oscillation.

Forced oscillations and resonance

4.6

Imagine pushing someone on a swing at regular intervals. If each push is timed suitably, the swing goes higher and higher. The pushes are a simple example of a **periodic force** which is a force applied at regular intervals.

- When the system oscillates without a periodic force being applied to it, its frequency is referred to as its **natural frequency**.
- When a periodic force is applied to an oscillating system, the response depends on the frequency of the periodic force. The system undergoes **forced oscillations** when a periodic force is applied to it.

4.6.1 Investigating forced oscillations

Figure 4.19 shows how a periodic force can be applied to an oscillating system consisting of a mass attached to two stretched springs.

The bottom end of the lower spring is attached to a mechanical oscillator which is connected to a signal generator. The top end of the upper spring is fixed. The mechanical oscillator pulls repeatedly on the lower spring at a frequency that can be adjusted by adjusting the signal generator. The frequency of the oscillator is referred to as the **applied frequency**. The response of the system is measured from the amplitude of oscillations of the mass.

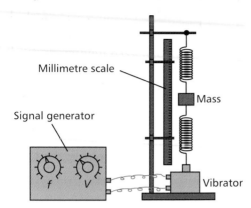

Fig 4.19 Forced oscillations

The variation of the response with the applied frequency is shown in Figure 4.20.

Consider the effect of increasing the applied frequency:

- When the applied frequency is less than the natural frequency of the mass–spring system, the amplitude of oscillations increases then decreases repeatedly as the periodic force from the oscillator moves in and out of phase with the oscillations of the system.
- If the applied frequency is adjusted closer to the natural frequency, the amplitude of oscillations still increases then decreases repeatedly but it reaches a larger maximum value and takes longer for each cycle.
- The amplitude of oscillations is greatest when the applied frequency is equal to the natural frequency, provided the damping is light. The periodic force is then exactly in phase with the oscillations. The system is said to be in **resonance** when the applied frequency is equal to the natural frequency.

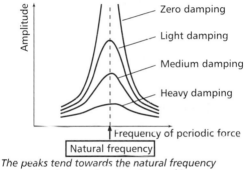

The peaks tend towards the natural frequency as the damping becomes less and less

Fig 4.20 Resonance curves

> **For an oscillating system with little or no damping, at resonance, the applied frequency of the periodic force = the natural frequency of the system**

1 At resonance, the periodic force acts on the system at the same point in each cycle, causing the amplitude to increase to a maximum value limited only by damping. At maximum amplitude, energy supplied by the periodic force is lost at the same rate because of the effects of damping. So the system oscillates with a constant amplitude at resonance.

2 The applied frequency at resonance, the resonant frequency, is equal to the natural frequency only when there is little or no damping. Resonance occurs at a lower frequency than the natural frequency if the damping is not light. The lighter the damping, the closer the resonant frequency is to the natural frequency.

3 If the applied frequency is increased beyond the natural frequency, the amplitude of oscillations once again increases then decreases repeatedly with a maximum amplitude that reduces as the applied frequency increases. Once again, the periodic force acts in and out of phase with the oscillations, causing the amplitude to increase and decrease repeatedly.

6 Electric fields

6.1 Field patterns

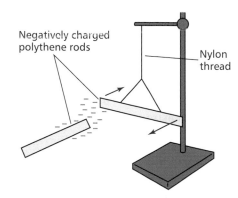

Fig 6.1 Electrostatic forces

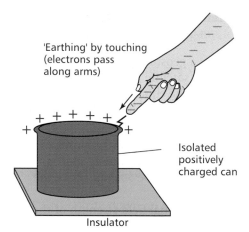

Fig 6.2 Discharge to Earth

6.1.1 Static electricity

Most plastic materials can be charged quite easily by rubbing with a dry cloth. When charged, they can usually pick up small bits of paper. The bits of paper are attracted to the charged piece of plastic. Do charged pieces of plastic material attract one another? Figure 6.1 shows an arrangement to test for attraction. A charged perspex ruler will attract a charged polythene comb, but two charged rods of the same material always repel one another.

Like charges repel; Unlike charges attract

Electrons are responsible for charging in most situations. An uncharged atom contains equal numbers of protons and electrons. Add one or more electrons to an uncharged atom and it becomes negatively charged. Remove one or more electrons from an uncharged atom and it becomes positively charged. An uncharged solid contains equal numbers of electrons and protons. To make it negatively charged, electrons must be added to it. To make it positively charged, electrons must be removed from it. When an uncharged perspex rod is rubbed with an uncharged dry cloth, electrons transfer from the rod to the cloth so the rod becomes positively charged and the cloth becomes negatively charged.

- Electrical conductors such as metals contain lots of free electrons. These are electrons which move about inside the metal and are not attached to any one atom. To charge a metal up, it must first be isolated from the Earth. Otherwise, any charge given to it is neutralised by electrons transferring between the conductor and the Earth. Then the isolated conductor can be charged by direct contact with any charged object. If an isolated conductor is charged positively then 'earthed', electrons transfer from the Earth to the conductor to neutralise or discharge it.
- Insulating materials do not contain free electrons. All the electrons in an insulator are attached to individual atoms. Some insulators, such as perspex or polythene, are easy to charge because their surface atoms easily gain or lose electrons.

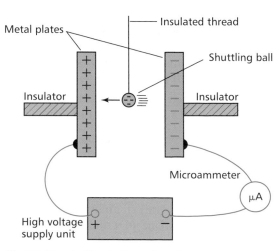

Fig 6.3 The shuttling ball experiment

The shuttling ball experiment shows that an electric current is a flow of charge. A conducting ball is suspended by an insulating thread between two vertical plates, as in Figure 6.3. When a high voltage is applied across the two plates, the ball bounces back and forth between them. Each time it touches the negative plate, the ball gains some electrons and becomes negatively charged. It is then repelled by the negative plate and pulled across to the positive plate. When contact is made, electrons on the ball transfer to the positive plate so the ball now becomes positively charged and is repelled back to the negative plate to repeat the cycle. Therefore, the electrons from the high voltage supply pass along the wire to the negative plate. There, they are ferried across to the other plate by the ball. Then they pass along the wire back to the supply. A microammeter in series with the plates shows that the shuttling ball causes a current round the circuit. If the plates are brought closer together, the ball shuttles back and forth even more rapidly. As a result, the microammeter reading increases because charge is ferried across at a faster rate.

Suppose the ball shuttles back and forth at frequency f. The time taken for each cycle is therefore $\frac{1}{f}$. The amount and type of charge on the ball depends on the voltage of the plate it last made contact with. Therefore, if the charge ferried across the gap each cycle is Q, the average current round the

$$\text{circuit} = Qf\left(= \frac{\text{charge } Q}{\text{time for 1 cycle}}\right).$$

Note

The simplest atom is the hydrogen atom ^1_1H which consists of a proton as its nucleus with an electron in orbit round the nucleus. Every other type of atom has a nucleus composed of protons and neutrons with electrons in orbit round the nucleus. The proton and the electron have equal and opposite charges. The magnitude of the charge of an electron or a proton, $e = 1.6 \times 10^{-19}$ C. See pp. 136–137.

Worked example

$e = 1.6 \times 10^{-19}$ C

In a shuttling ball experiment, the microammeter reading was 20 nA when the frequency of the shuttling ball was 4.0 Hz. Calculate

a the charge carried by the ball,

b the number of electrons needed for the charge calculated in **a**.

Solution

a $Q = \dfrac{I}{f} = \dfrac{20 \times 10^{-9}\,\text{A}}{4.0\,\text{Hz}} = 5.0 \times 10^{-9}$ C

b number of electrons $= \dfrac{Q}{e} = \dfrac{5.0 \times 10^{-9}}{1.6 \times 10^{-19}} = 3.1 \times 10^{10}$

The gold leaf electroscope is used to detect charge. If a charged object is in contact with the metal cap of the electroscope, some of the charge on the object transfers to the electroscope. As a result, the gold leaf and the metal stem which is attached to the cap gain the same type of charge and the leaf rises because it is repelled by the stem.

If another object with the same type of charge is brought near the electroscope, the leaf rises further because the object forces some charge on the cap to transfer to the leaf and stem.

Fig 6.4 *The electroscope*

6.1.2 Chips and charge

A tiny amount of charge on the pins of an electronic chip can be enough to destroy circuits inside the chip. This can happen if the pins are touched in the presence of a charged body. This is because the pins are earthed when they are touched. As a result, electrons transfer between the pins and earth. If the connection to earth is removed, the pins remain charged when the charged body is removed. People handling microchips wear antistatic clothing and they work in rooms fitted with antistatic floors. Microchips are stored in antistatic packets and handled with special tools. Antistatic materials allow charge to flow across the surface.

6.1.3 Field lines and patterns

Any two charged objects exert equal and opposite forces on each other without being directly in contact. An electric field is said to surround each charge. Suppose a small positive charge is placed as a test charge near a body with a much bigger charge which is also positive. If the test charge is free to move, it will follow a path away from the body with the bigger charge. The path a free test charge follows is called a **line of force** or a **field line**.

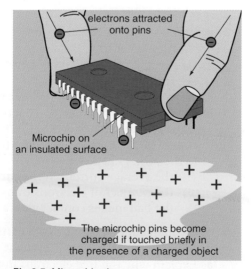

Fig 6.5 *Microchip damage*

The field lines of an electric field are the lines which positive test charges follow. The direction of an electric field line is the direction a positive test charge would move along. Figure 6.6 shows the patterns of fields around different charged objects. Each pattern is produced by semolina grains sprinkled on oil. An electric field is set up across the surface of the oil by connecting two metal conductors in the oil to the output terminals of a high voltage supply unit. The grains line up along the field lines, like plotting compasses in a magnetic field.

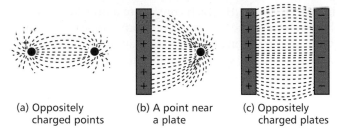

(a) Oppositely charged points   (b) A point near a plate   (c) Oppositely charged plates

Fig 6.6 *Electric field patterns*

- Oppositely charged point objects create a field as shown in Figure 6.6 (a). The field lines become concentrated at the points. A positive test charge released from an off-centre position would follow a curved path to the negative point charge.
- A point object near an oppositely charged flat plate produces a field as shown in Figure 6.6 (b). The field lines are concentrated at the point object but they are at right angles to the plate where they meet.
- Two oppositely charged plates create a field as shown in Figure 6.6 (c). The field lines run parallel from one plate to the other, meeting the plates at right angles. The field is **uniform** between the plates as the field lines are parallel to each other.

QUESTIONS

$e = 1.6 \times 10^{-19}$ C

1 Explain each of the following observations in terms of transfer of electrons:
   a An insulated metal can is given a positive charge by touching it with a positively charged rod.
   b A negatively charged metal sphere suspended on a thread is discharged by connecting it to the ground using a wire.

2 a In the shuttling ball experiment, explain why the ball shuttles faster if:
   (i) the potential difference between the plates is increased,
   (ii) the plates are brought closer together.
   b A ball shuttles between two oppositely charged metal plates at a frequency of 2.5 Hz. The ball carries a charge of 30 nC each time it shuttles from one plate to the other. Calculate:
   (i) the average current in the circuit,
   (ii) the number of electrons transferred each time the ball makes contact with a metal plate.

3 An insulated metal conductor is earthed before a negatively charged object is brought near to it.
   a Explain why the free electrons in the conductor move as far away from the charged object as they can.

b The conductor is then briefly earthed. The charged object is then removed from the vicinity of the conductor. Explain why the conductor is left with an overall positive charge.

4 a A positively charged point object is placed near an earthed metal plate, as shown in Figure 6.7.

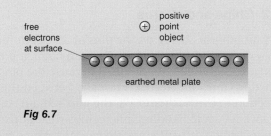

free electrons at surface   positive point object

earthed metal plate

Fig 6.7

   (i) Explain why electrons gather at the surface of the metal plate near the object.
   (ii) Explain why there is a force of attraction between the object and the metal plate.
   b Sketch the pattern of the field lines of the electric field:
   (i) between two oppositely charged parallel plates,
   (ii) between a positively charged point object and an earthed metal plate.

6.2.1 Inside an electric field

A charged object in an electric field experiences a force due to the field. Provided the object's size and charge are both sufficiently small, the object may be used as a 'test' charge to measure the strength of the field at any position in the field.

> **The electric field strength, E, at a point in the field is defined as the force per unit charge on a positive test charge placed at that point.**

The unit of E is the newton per coulomb ($N\,C^{-1}$).

If a positive test charge Q at a certain point in an electric field is acted on by force F due to the electric field, the electric field strength, E, at that point is given by the equation

$$E = \frac{F}{Q}$$

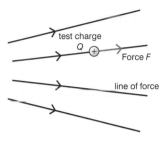

Electric field strength, $E = \dfrac{F}{Q}$
(at Q)

Fig 6.8 Electric field strength

Notes

1 Rearranging this equation gives $\boldsymbol{F = QE}$ for the force F on a test charge Q at a point in the electric field where the electric field strength is E.

2 Electric field strength is a vector which is in the same direction as the force on a positive test charge. In other words, the direction of a field line at any point is the direction of the electric field strength at that point. The force on a small charge in an electric field is

   • in the same direction as the electric field if the charge is positive,
   • in the opposite direction to the electric field if the charge is negative.

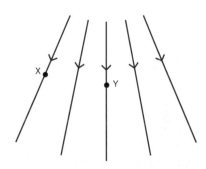

Worked example

$e = 1.6 \times 10^{-19}$ C

Figure 6.9 shows the field lines of an electric field.

a Calculate the magnitude of electric field strength at X if a $+3.5$ μC 'test' charge at X experiences a force of 70 mN.

b At a second position Y in the field, the electric field strength is 15 000 N C^{-1} in a direction downwards. Calculate the force on an electron at Y and state the direction of the force.

Fig 6.9 Representing a vector

Solution

a $E = \dfrac{F}{Q} = \dfrac{70 \times 10^{-3}\,\text{N}}{3.5 \times 10^{-6}\,\text{C}} = 2.0 \times 10^{4}\,\text{N C}^{-1}$

b $F = QE = 1.6 \times 10^{-19}\,\text{C} \times 15\,000\,\text{N C}^{-1} = 2.4 \times 10^{-15}\,\text{N}$

The direction of the force on an electron at Y is directly upwards because the field line at Y is directly downwards and the charge on an electron is negative.

The lightning conductor

Air is an insulator provided it is not subjected to an electric field that is too strong. Such a field ionises the air molecules by pulling electrons out of the molecules. In a thunderstorm, a lightning strike to the ground occurs when a cloud becomes more and more charged and the electric field in the air becomes stronger and stronger. The insulating property of air suddenly breaks down and a massive discharge of electric charge occurs between the cloud and the ground.

Fig 6.10 Lightning

A lightning conductor is a metal rod at the top of a tall building. The rod is connected to the ground by means of a thick metal conductor. When a charged cloud is overhead, it creates a very strong electric field near the tip of the conductor. Air molecules near the tip are ionised by this very strong field. The ions discharge the thundercloud so no lightning strike occurs.

6.2.2 The electric field between two parallel plates

Figure 6.6 (c) shows that the field lines between two oppositely charged flat conductors are parallel to each other and at right angles to the plates. The field pattern for two oppositely charged flat plates is similar, as shown in Figure 6.11. The field lines are:

- parallel to each other,
- at right angles to the plates,
- from the positive plate to the negative plate.

The field between the plates is **uniform**. This is because the electric field strength has the same magnitude and direction everywhere between the plates. The electric field strength E can be calculated from the potential difference V between the plates and their separation d using the equation

$$E = \frac{V}{d}$$

To prove this equation, consider a small charge Q between the plates, as in Figure 6.11.

1 The force F on a small charge Q in the field is given by $F = QE$, where E is the electric field strength between the plates.

2 If the charge is moved from the positive to the negative plate, the work done W by the field on Q is given by $W = $ force $F \times$ distance moved, $d = QEd$

3 By definition, the potential difference between the plates, V is the work done per unit charge when a small charge is moved through potential difference V.

Therefore, $V = \dfrac{W}{Q} = \dfrac{QEd}{Q} = Ed$ so rearranging $V = Ed$ gives $E = \dfrac{V}{d}$

Worked example
A pair of parallel plates at a separation of 80 mm are connected to a high voltage supply unit which maintains a constant p.d. of 6000 V between the plates. Calculate:

a the electric field strength between the plates,

b the magnitude and direction of the force on a positive ion of charge 4.8×10^{-19} C when it is between the plates.

Solution

a $E = \dfrac{V}{d} = \dfrac{6000 \text{ V}}{80 \times 10^{-3} \text{ m}} = 7.5 \times 10^4 \text{ V m}^{-1}$

b $F = QE = 4.8 \times 10^{-19} \text{ C} \times 7.5 \times 10^4 \text{ V m}^{-1} = 3.6 \times 10^{-14} \text{ N}$

The force on the ion is directly towards the negative plate.

6.2.3 Field factors

An electric field exists near any charged body. The greater the charge on the body, the stronger the electric field is. For a charged metal conductor, the charge on it is spread across its surface. The more concentrated the charge is on the surface, the greater the strength of the electric field is above the surface.

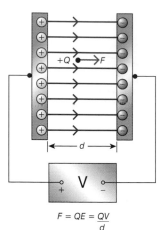

$F = QE = \dfrac{QV}{d}$

Fig 6.11 *The electric field strength between two parallel plates*

NOTE

The unit of E may be written as the newton per coulomb (N C^{-1}) or the volt per metre (V m^{-1}).

The link between the two can be seen because $F = QE = \dfrac{QV}{d}$.

Rearranging this equation gives $\dfrac{F}{Q} = \dfrac{V}{d} \; (= E)$. Therefore, the newton per coulomb and the volt per metre are both acceptable as the unit of E.

- Figure 6.12 shows the electric field pattern between a V-shaped conductor opposite a flat plate when a constant p.d. is applied between the plate and the conductor. The field lines are concentrated at the tip of the V because that is where charge on the V-shaped conductor is most concentrated.

- The electric field between two oppositely charged parallel plates depends on the concentration of charge on the surface of the plates. The charge on the plates distributes itself evenly across the facing surfaces. Measurements show that the electric field strength between the plates is proportional to the charge per unit area on the facing surfaces. Therefore, for charge Q on a plate of surface area A, the electric field strength E between the plates is proportional to $\frac{Q}{A}$. Introducing a constant of proportionality, ε_0 (referred to as 'epsilon nought'), into this equation gives $\frac{Q}{A} = \varepsilon_0 E$. The value of ε_0 is 8.85×10^{-12} farads per metre (F m^{-1}), where the farad (the unit of capacitance; see p. 76) is 1 coulomb per volt.

ε_0 is referred to as the absolute permittivity of free space. It represents that charge per unit area on a surface in a vacuum that produces an electric field of strength 1 volt per metre above the surface. The formula $\frac{Q}{A} = \varepsilon_0 E$ is not required for the A2 specification but we will meet ε_0 in the next section.

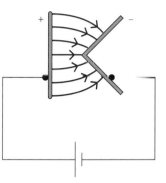

Fig 6.12 The electric field near a metal tip

QUESTIONS

$e = 1.6 \times 10^{-19}$ C

1 A +40 nC point charge Q_1 is placed in an electric field.

  a Calculate the magnitude of the force on Q_1 if the electric field strength where Q_1 is placed is 3.5×10^4 V m^{-1}.

  b Q_1 is moved to a different position in the electric field. The force on Q_1 at this position is 1.6×10^{-3} N. Calculate the magnitude of the electric field strength at this position.

2 Figure 6.13 shows the path of a charged dust particle in an electric field.

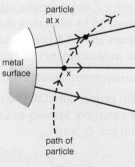

Fig 6.13

  a The electric field strength at X is 65 kV m^{-1}. The force due to the field on the particle when it is at X is 8.2×10^{-3} N towards the metal surface.
  (i) What type of charge does X carry?
  (ii) Calculate the charge carried by the particle.

  b (i) Calculate the magnitude of the force on the particle when it is at Y where the electric field strength is 58 kV m^{-1}.
  (ii) State the direction of the force on the particle when it is at Y.

3 A high voltage supply unit is connected across a pair of parallel plates which are at a separation of 50 mm.

  a The voltage is adjusted to 4.5 kV. Calculate:

  (i) the electric field strength between the plates,
  (ii) the electric force on a droplet in the field that carries a charge of 8.0×10^{-19} C.

  b The separation between the plates is altered without changing the p.d. between the plates. The droplet in **a** is now acted on by a force of 4.5×10^{-14} N. Calculate the new separation between the plates.

4 A certain gas in a tube is subjected to an electric field of increasing strength. The gas becomes conducting when the electric field reaches a strength of 35 kV m^{-1}.

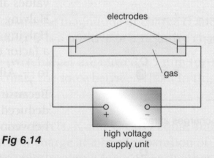

Fig 6.14

  a The electrodes in the tube are at a spacing of 84 mm. Assuming the field between the electrodes is uniform before the gas conducts, calculate the potential difference between the electrodes that is necessary to produce an electric field of strength 35 kV m^{-1} in the tube.

  b (i) Calculate the force on an electron in the tube when the electric field strength is 35 kV m^{-1}.
  (ii) Explain why the gas becomes conducting only when the electric field strength in the tube reaches a certain value.

Point charges

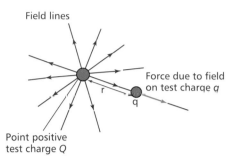

Fig 6.18 Force near a point charge Q

A point charge is a convenient expression for a charged object in a situation where distances under consideration are much greater than the size of the object. The same idea applies to a distant star which is considered as a point object because its diameter is much smaller than the distance to it from the Earth. A 'test' charge in an electric field is a point charge that does not alter the electric field in which it is placed. This would happen if an object with a sufficiently large charge is placed in an electric field and it causes a change in the distribution of charge that creates the field.

Consider the electric field due to a point charge $+Q$, as shown in Figure 6.18. The field lines radiate from the point charge because a test charge $+q$ in the field would experience a force directly away from Q wherever it was placed. Coulomb's Law gives the force F on the test charge q as

$$F = \frac{1}{4\pi\varepsilon_0}\frac{Qq}{r^2}$$

Therefore, as electric field strength $E = \frac{F}{q}$ by definition, the electric field strength at distance r from Q is given by

$$E = \frac{Q}{4\pi\varepsilon_0 r^2}$$

Note that if Q is negative, the above formula gives a negative value of E corresponding to the field lines pointing inwards towards Q.

Worked example

$$\frac{1}{4\pi\varepsilon_0} = 9.0 \times 10^9 \text{ m F}^{-1}, e = 1.6 \times 10^{-19} \text{ C}$$

Calculate the electric field strength due to a nucleus of charge $+82\,e$ at a distance of 0.35 nm.

Solution

$$E = \frac{Q}{4\pi\varepsilon_0 r^2} = \frac{9.0 \times 10^9 \times (+82 \times 1.6 \times 10^{-19})}{(0.35 \times 10^{-9})^2} = 9.6 \times 10^{11} \text{ V m}^{-1}$$

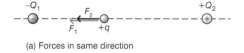

(a) Forces in same direction

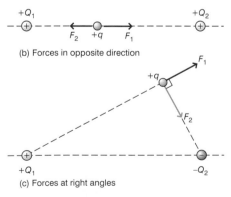

(b) Forces in opposite direction

(c) Forces at right angles

Fig 6.19 Combined electric fields

6.4.1 Electric field strength as a vector

If a test charge is in an electric field due to several point charges, each charge exerts a force on the test charge. The resultant force F on the test charge gives the resultant electric field strength at the position of the test charge. Consider the following situations:

- **Forces in the same direction**: Figure 6.19 (a) shows a test charge $+q$ on the line between a negative point charge Q_1 and a positive point charge Q_2. The test charge experiences a force $F_1 = q\,E_1$ where E_1 is the electric field strength due to Q_1 and a force $F_2 = q\,E_2$ where E_2 is the electric field strength due to Q_2. The two forces act in the same direction because Q_1 attracts q and Q_2 repels q. So the resultant force $F = F_1 + F_2 = q\,E_1 + q\,E_2$. Therefore, the resultant electric field strength $E = \frac{F}{q} = \frac{(qE_1 + qE_2)}{q} = E_1 + E_2$

- **Forces in opposite directions**: Figure 6.19 (b) shows a test charge $+q$ on the line between two positive point charges Q_1 and Q_2. The test charge experiences a force $F_1 = q\,E_1$ where E_1 is the electric field strength due to Q_1

and a force $F_2 = q E_2$ where E_2 is the electric field strength due to Q_2. The two forces act in opposite directions because Q_1 repels q and Q_2 repels q. Assuming F_1 is greater than F_2, the resultant force $F = F_1 - F_2 = q E_1 - q E_2$.

Therefore, the resultant electric field strength $E = \dfrac{F}{q} = \dfrac{(qE_1 - qE_2)}{q} = E_1 - E_2$

- **Forces at right angles to each other**: Figure 6.19 (c) shows a test charge $+q$ on perpendicular lines from two positive point charges Q_1 and Q_2. The test charge experiences a force $F_1 = q E_1$ where E_1 is the electric field strength due to Q_1 and a force $F_2 = q E_2$ where E_2 is the electric field strength due to Q_2. The two forces are perpendicular to each other, F_1 along the line between q and Q_1 and F_2 along the line between q and Q_2. The magnitude of the resultant force F is given by Pythagoras' formula $F^2 = F_1^2 + F_2^2$. Therefore, as the resultant electric field strength $E = F/q$, then $E^2 = E_1^2 + E_2^2$ can be used to calculate the resultant electric field strength.

In general, the resultant electric field strength is the vector sum of the individual electric field strengths.

Worked example

$\dfrac{1}{4\pi\varepsilon_0} = 9.0 \times 10^9$ m F^{-1}

A $+65$ μC point charge Q_1 is at a distance of 50 mm from a $+38$ μC charge Q_2. A $+12$ pC charge q is placed at M, midway between Q_1 and Q_2.

Calculate:

a the resultant electric field strength at M,

b the magnitude and direction of the force on q.

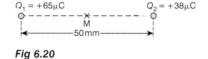

Fig 6.20

Solution

a The electric field strength due to Q_1 at M, $E_1 = \dfrac{Q_1}{4\pi\varepsilon_0 r_1^2}$ where $r_1 = 25$ mm

Therefore, $E_1 = 9.0 \times 10^9 \times \dfrac{65 \times 10^{-6}}{(25 \times 10^{-3})^2} = 9.4 \times 10^8$ V m^{-1} away from Q_1

The electric field strength due to Q_2 at M, $E_2 = \dfrac{Q_2}{4\pi\varepsilon_0 r_2^2}$, where $r_2 = 25$ mm

Therefore, $E_2 = 9.0 \times 10^9 \times \dfrac{38 \times 10^{-6}}{(25 \times 10^{-3})^2} = 5.5 \times 10^8$ V m^{-1} away from Q_2

As E_1 and E_2 are in opposite directions, the resultant electric field strength $E = E_1 - E_2 = 9.4 \times 10^8 - 5.5 \times 10^8 = 3.9 \times 10^8$ V m^{-1} away from Q_1 towards Q_2

b The resultant force on $q = qE = +12 \times 10^{-12} \times 3.9 \times 10^8 = 4.7 \times 10^{-3}$ N

6.4.2 More about radial fields

The electric field surrounding a charged metal sphere is radial, like the field due to a point charge. The charge on the metal surface is evenly distributed on its surface. The field has the same strength as if all the charge was concentrated at the centre of the sphere.

For a sphere of radius R with a charge Q,

- At distance r from the centre of the sphere, the electric field strength

$E = \dfrac{Q}{4\pi\varepsilon_0 r^2}$

- At the surface of the sphere, the electric field strength $E = \dfrac{Q}{4\pi\varepsilon_0 R^2}$

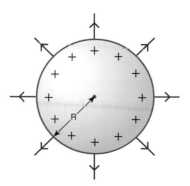

Fig 6.21 The electric field near a charged hollow metal sphere

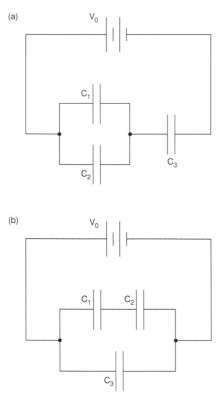

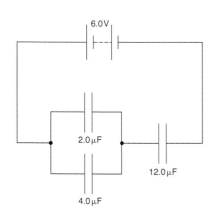

Fig 7.8

Fig 7.9

7.2.3 **Combinations with capacitors in series and parallel**

Figure 7.8 shows two arrangements where 3 capacitors are connected to a battery.

- In (a), two capacitors C_1 and C_2 in parallel are connected in series to a third capacitor C_3 and the battery.
- In (b), the two capacitors C_1 and C_2 in series are connected in parallel with the third capacitor C_3 and the battery.

The steps below show how to work out the charge and p.d. of each capacitor, given the capacitance values and the battery p.d. V_0.

1 Calculate the total capacitance C by using the appropriate combination rule to find the combined capacitance C' of C_1 and C_2 then use the other combination rule to work out the combined capacitance of C_3 and C'.

2 Work out the total charge stored Q using $Q = CV$.

3 For (a), charge Q is stored by C_3 and the same amount of charge is shared between C_1 and C_2 in proportion to their capacitances. After working out the charge stored by each capacitor, use $V = \dfrac{Q}{C}$ to work out the p.d. across each capacitor.

For (b), the battery p.d. V_0 is across C_3 and is shared between C_1 and C_2 in inverse proportion to their capacitances. After working out the p.d. across each capacitor, use $Q = CV$ to work out the charge stored by each capacitor.

Worked example 1

A 2.0 μF capacitor and a 4.0 μF capacitor are in parallel with each other. The parallel combination is in series with a 12.0 μF capacitor and a 6.0 V battery, as shown in Figure 7.9. Calculate:

a the total capacitance of the combination,

b the charge stored by the combination,

c the charge and p.d. for each capacitor.

Solution

a $C' = 2.0 + 4.0 = 6.0\ \mu$F

$\therefore$ the total capacitance C is given by $\dfrac{1}{C} = \dfrac{1}{6.0} + \dfrac{1}{12.0} = 0.167 + 0.083 = 0.25\ \mu\text{F}^{-1}$

$\therefore C = \dfrac{1}{0.25} = 4.0\ \mu$F

b The charge stored $Q = CV = 4.0 \times 6.0 = 24\ \mu$C

c C_3; charge stored $= Q = 24\ \mu$C. $\therefore$ p.d. across $C_3 = \dfrac{Q}{C_3} = \dfrac{24\ \mu\text{C}}{12\ \mu\text{F}} = 2.0$ V

C_1 and C_2; $\dfrac{C_1}{C_2} = \dfrac{2\ \mu\text{F}}{4\mu\text{F}} = 0.5$, then $\dfrac{Q_1}{Q_2} = \dfrac{C_1}{C_2} = 0.5$

As $Q = Q_1 + Q_2 = 24\ \mu$C, then $Q_1 = 8\ \mu$C and $Q_2 = 16\ \mu$C

$\therefore V_1 = \dfrac{Q_1}{C_1} = \dfrac{8\ \mu\text{C}}{2\ \mu\text{F}} = 4$ V.

$V_2 = \dfrac{Q_2}{C_2} = \dfrac{16\ \mu\text{C}}{4\ \mu\text{F}} = 4$ V.

Note $V_1 = V_2 = 6.0\ \text{V} - V_3$

Worked example 2

A 3.0 μF capacitor and a 6.0 μF capacitor are in series with each other. The series combination is in parallel with a 4.0 μF capacitor and a 12.0 V battery, as shown in Figure 7.10. Calculate:

a (i) the total capacitance of the combination,
   (ii) the charge stored by the combination,

b the charge and p.d. for each capacitor.

Solution

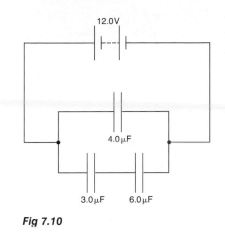

Fig 7.10

a (i) $\dfrac{1}{C'} = \dfrac{1}{3.0} + \dfrac{1}{6.0} = 0.333 + 0.167 = 0.5 \ \mu F^{-1}, \ \therefore C' = \dfrac{1}{0.5} = 2.0 \ \mu F$

   $\therefore$ the total capacitance $C = C' + C_3 = 2.0 + 4.0 = 6.0 \ \mu F$

   (ii) The charge stored $Q = CV = 6.0 \times 12.0 = 72 \ \mu C$

b C_3; p.d. $V_3 =$ battery p.d. $= 12$ V

   charge stored $Q_3 = C_3 V_3 = 4.0 \ \mu F \times 12.0 \ V = 48 \ \mu C.$

   C_1 and C_2; charge stored by the combination $= Q - Q_3 = 72 - 48 = 24 \ \mu C$

   They store the same amount of charge as they are in series with each other.

   $\therefore \ Q_1 = Q_2 = 24 \ \mu C$

   $\therefore \ V_1 = \dfrac{Q_1}{C_1} = \dfrac{24 \ \mu C}{3.0 \ \mu F} = 8.0 \ V.$

   $V_2 = \dfrac{Q_2}{C_2} = \dfrac{24 \ \mu C}{6.0 \ \mu F} = 4.0 \ V.$

   Note $V_1 + V_2 = V_3 = 12 \ V$

QUESTIONS

1 A 3.0 V battery is connected to a 2.0 μF capacitor in parallel with a 3.0 μF capacitor. Sketch the circuit diagram and calculate:

   a the combined capacitance of the two capacitors,

   b the charge stored and the p.d. across each capacitor.

2 a A 4.5 V battery is connected to a 6.0 μF capacitor in series with a 4.0 μF capacitor. Calculate:
      (i) the combined capacitance of the two capacitors,
      (ii) the charge stored and the p.d. across each capacitor.

   b A 10 μF capacitor is connected in parallel with the 6.0 μF capacitor.
      (i) Sketch the new circuit diagram and calculate the total capacitance of the three capacitors.
      (ii) Calculate the charge and p.d. across each capacitor.

3 A student is given 3 capacitors of values 10 μF, 22 μF and 47 μF. Sketch the 6 different possible combinations using all three capacitors and calculate the capacitance of each combination.

4 A 4.0 μF capacitor in series with a 10.0 μF capacitor are connected to a 6.0 V battery. A 2.0 μF capacitor is then connected to the battery in parallel with the two capacitors in series.

   a Sketch the circuit diagram for this arrangement and calculate its total capacitance.

   b Calculate the charge and p.d. for each capacitor in the arrangement.

Energy stored in a charged capacitor

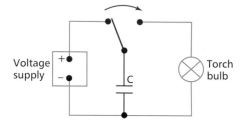

Fig 7.11 *Releasing stored energy*

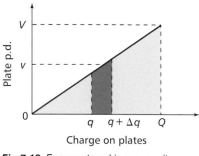

Fig 7.12 *Energy stored in a capacitor*

When a capacitor is charged, energy is stored in it. A charged capacitor discharged across a torch bulb will release its energy in a brief flash of light from the bulb, as long as the capacitor has been charged initially to the operating p.d. of the bulb. Charge flow is rapid enough to give a large enough current to light the bulb, but only for a brief time. The bulb could be replaced by a miniature electric motor which would spin briefly when the capacitor is discharged through it.

How much energy is stored in a charged capacitor? The charge is forced onto the plates by the battery. In the charging process, the p.d. across the plates increases in proportion to the charge stored, as shown in Figure 7.12.

Consider one step in the process of charging a capacitor of capacitance C when the charge on the plates increases by a small amount Δq from q to $q + \Delta q$. The work done ΔW to force the extra charge Δq on to the plates is given by $\Delta W = v\Delta q$, where v is the average p.d. during this step. $v\Delta q$ is represented in Figure 7.12 by the area of the vertical strip of width Δq and height v under the line. Therefore, the area of this strip represents the work done ΔW in this small step.

Now consider all the small steps from zero p.d. to the final p.d. V. The total work done W is obtained by adding up the work done for each small step. In other words, W is represented by the total area under the line from zero p.d. to p.d. V. As this area is a triangle of height V and base length Q ($= CV$), the total work done W = triangle area $= \frac{1}{2} \times$ height $\times$ base $= \frac{1}{2}VQ$

Because the energy stored in the capacitor is equal to the work done on it to charge it, the energy stored $= \frac{1}{2}VQ$.

$$\text{Energy stored by the capacitor, } W = \tfrac{1}{2}QV$$

Note Using $Q = CV$, the above equation may be written as $W = \frac{1}{2}CV^2$

7.3.1 Measuring the energy stored in a charged capacitor

A joulemeter is used to measure the energy transfer from a charged capacitor to a light bulb when the capacitor discharges. The capacitor p.d. V is measured and the joulemeter reading recorded before the discharge starts. When the capacitor has discharged, the joulemeter reading is recorded again. The difference of the two joulemeter readings is the energy transferred from the capacitor during the discharge process. This is the total energy stored in the capacitor before it discharged. This can be compared with the calculation of the energy stored using $W = \frac{1}{2}CV^2$.

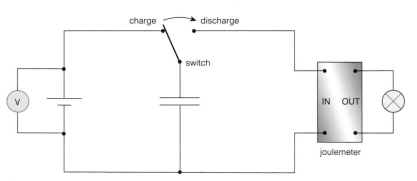

Fig 7.13 *Measuring energy stored*

7.3.2 The energy stored in a thundercloud

Imagine a thundercloud and the Earth below like a pair of charged parallel plates. Because the thundercloud is charged, a strong electric field exists between the thundercloud and the ground. The potential difference between the thundercloud and the ground, $V = Ed$, where E is the electric field strength and d is the height of the thundercloud above the ground.

- For a thundercloud carrying a constant charge Q, the energy stored $W = \frac{1}{2}QV = \frac{1}{2}QEd$.

- If the thundercloud is forced by winds to rise to a new height d', the energy stored $W' = \frac{1}{2}QEd'$.

- As the electric field strength is unchanged (since it depends on the charge per unit area; see p. 67), therefore, the increase in the energy stored $= W' - W = \frac{1}{2}QEd' - \frac{1}{2}QEd = \frac{1}{2}QE\,\Delta d$, where $\Delta d = d' - d$.

This increase in the energy stored is because work is done by the force of the wind to overcome the electrical attraction between the thundercloud and the ground and make the charged thundercloud move away from ground.

The insulating property of air breaks down if it is subjected to an electric field of strength more than about 300 kV m^{-1}. Prove for yourself that, for every metre rise of the thundercloud carrying a maximum charge of 20 C, the energy stored would increase by 3 MJ. At a height of 500 m, the energy stored would be 1500 MJ.

QUESTIONS

1 Calculate the charge and energy stored in a 10 μF capacitor charged to a p.d. of:

   a 3.0 V,

   b 6.0 V.

2 A 50 000 μF capacitor is charged from a 9 V battery then discharged through a light bulb in a flash of light lasting 0.2 s. Calculate:

   a the charge and energy stored in the capacitor before discharge,

   b the average power supplied to the light bulb.

3 A 2.2 μF capacitor is connected in series with a 10 μF capacitor and a 3.0 V battery. Calculate the charge and energy stored in each capacitor.

4 In Figure 7.14, a 4.7 μF capacitor is charged from a 12.0 V battery by connecting the switch to X. The switch is then reconnected to Y to charge a 2.2 μF capacitor from the first capacitor.

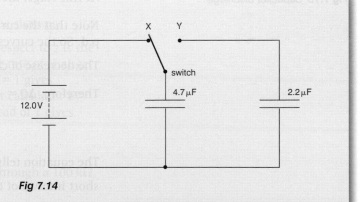

Fig 7.14

Calculate:

   a the initial charge and energy stored in the 4.7 μF capacitor,

   b the combined capacitance of the two capacitors,

   c the final p.d. across the two capacitors,

   d the final energy stored in each capacitor.

   Account for the loss of energy stored.

7.4.2 Investigating capacitor discharge

Figure 7.16 shows how to measure the p.d. across a capacitor as it discharges through a fixed resistor. An oscilloscope is used as it has a very high resistance so the discharge current from the capacitor passes only through the fixed resistor. The oscilloscope is used to measure the capacitor p.d. at regular intervals. A data logger or a digital voltmeter could be used instead of the oscilloscope.

The measurements may be used to plot a graph of voltage against time. The time taken for the voltage to decrease to 37% (= 1/e) of the initial value can be measured from the graph and compared with the calculated value of RC.

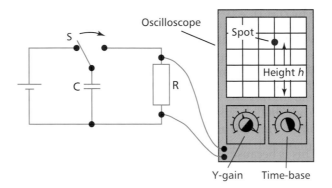

Fig 7.16 *Measuring capacitor discharge*

7.4.3 The significance of the time constant

The time constant RC is the time taken, in seconds, for the capacitor to discharge to 37% of its initial charge. Given values of R and C, the time constant can be quickly calculated and used as an approximate measure of how quickly the capacitor discharges. In the worked example on p. 85, the time constant of 220 s gives a 'rule of thumb' estimate of the time taken to discharge significantly but not completely. Also, $5RC$ gives a 'rule of thumb' estimate for the time taken to discharge by over 99%. Prove for yourself that $t = 5RC$ gives a value which is less than 1% of the initial value.

7.4.4 Applications of capacitor discharge

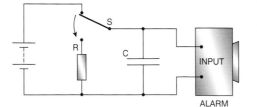

Fig 7.17 *A time-delayed alarm circuit*

1 **Any electronic timing circuit or time-delay circuit** makes use of capacitor discharge through a fixed resistor. Figure 7.17 shows an alarm circuit where the alarm rings if the input voltage to the electronic circuit drops below a certain value after the switch is reset. The time delay between resetting the switch and the alarm ringing can be increased by increasing the resistance R or the capacitance C. Such a change to the circuit would make the discharge of C through R slower so increasing the time for the capacitor voltage to decrease sufficiently to make the alarm ring.

2 **Capacitor smoothing** is used in applications where sudden voltage variations or 'glitches' can have undesirable effects. For example, mains appliances being switched on or off in a building could affect computers connected to the mains supply in the building. A large capacitor in a computer supplies current if the mains supply is interrupted so the computer circuits continue to function normally.

QUESTIONS

1 A 50 μF capacitor is charged by connecting it to a 6.0 V battery then discharged through a 100 kΩ resistor.

 a Calculate:
   (i) the charge stored in the capacitor immediately after it has been charged,
   (ii) the time constant of the circuit.

 b (i) Estimate how long the capacitor would take to discharge to about 2 V.
   (ii) Estimate the resistance of the resistor that you would use in place of the 100 kΩ resistor if the discharge is to be 99% completed within about 5 s.

2 A 68 μF capacitor is charged to a p.d. of 9.0 V then discharged through a 20 kΩ resistor.

 a Calculate:
   (i) the charge stored by the capacitor at a p.d. of 9.0 V,
   (ii) the initial discharge current.

 b Calculate the p.d. and the discharge current 5.0 s after the discharge started.

3 A 2.2 μF capacitor is charged to a p.d. of 6.0 V and then discharged through a 100 kΩ resistor. Calculate:

 a the charge and energy stored in this capacitor at 6.0 V,
 b the p.d. across the capacitor 0.5 s after the discharge started,
 c the energy stored at this time.

4 A 4.7 μF capacitor is charged to a p.d. of 12.0 V and then discharged through a 220 kΩ resistor. Calculate:

 a the energy stored in this capacitor at 12.0 V,
 b the time taken for the p.d. to fall from 12.0 V to 3.0 V,
 c the energy lost by the capacitor in this time.

CHAPTER SUMMARY

The **capacitance** of a capacitor is defined as the charge stored per unit p.d.

The **unit of capacitance** is the farad (F), equal to 1 coulomb per volt. Note that $1 \mu F = 10^{-6}$ F.

Capacitor equation $C = \dfrac{Q}{V}$

Capacitor combination rules

1 Capacitors in parallel; combined capacitance $C = C_1 + C_2 + C_3 + \ldots$

2 Capacitors in series; combined capacitance $\dfrac{1}{C} = \dfrac{1}{C_1} + \dfrac{1}{C_2} + \dfrac{1}{C_3} + \ldots$

Energy stored by the capacitor, $W = \frac{1}{2}QV = \frac{1}{2}CV^2$

Capacitor discharge

1 **Time constant**, $\tau = RC$

2 **Exponential decrease equation** for current or charge or p.d.; $x = x_0\, e^{-t/RC}$

8.2.3 Force on a moving charge in a magnetic field

A beam of charged particles crossing a vacuum tube is an electric current across the tube. Suppose each charged particle has a charge Q and moves at speed v. In a time interval t, each particle travels a distance vt. Its passage is equivalent to current $I = \dfrac{Q}{t}$ along a wire of length $\ell = vt$.

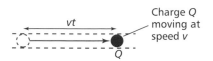

Fig 8.12 *Force on a moving charge*

If the particles pass through a uniform magnetic field in a direction at right angles to the field lines, each particle experiences a force F due to the field. If the particles were confined to a wire, the force would be given by $F = BI\ell$. For moving charges, the same equation applies where $I = \dfrac{Q}{t}$ and $\ell = vt$. Therefore, for a charged particle moving across a uniform magnetic field in a direction at right angles to the field, $F = BI\ell = B \times \dfrac{Q}{t} \times vt = BQv$.

More generally, if the direction of motion of a charged particle in a magnetic field is at angle θ to the lines of the field, then $B \sin \theta$ is used in the equation for F. This is because $B \sin \theta$ is the component of the magnetic field perpendicular to the direction of motion of the charged particle.

For a particle of charge Q moving through a uniform magnetic field at speed v in a direction at angle θ to the field, the force on the particle is given by

$$F = BQv \sin \theta$$

Notes

1   If the velocity of the charged particle is at right angles to the direction of the magnetic field, $\theta = 90°$ so the equation becomes $F = BQv$ because $\sin 90° = 1$.

2   If the velocity of the charged particle is parallel to the direction of the magnetic field, $\theta = 0$ so $F = 0$ because $\sin 0 = 0$.

8.2.4 The Hall probe

Hall probes are used to measure magnetic field strength. Knowledge of the Hall Effect is not required for the A2 specification. It is included here as a practical use of '$F = BQv$' and to provide information about the Hall probe as a magnetic field sensor.

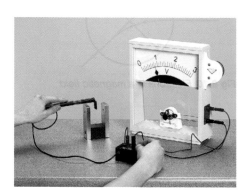

A Hall probe contains a slice of semiconducting material. Figure 8.13 shows the slice in a magnetic field with the field lines perpendicular to the flat side of the slice. A constant current passes through the slice as shown. The charge carriers (which are electrons in an n-type semiconductor) are deflected by the field. As a result, a potential difference is created between the top and bottom edges of the slice. This effect is known as the **Hall Effect** after its discoverer.

The p.d., referred to as the Hall voltage, is proportional to the magnetic flux density, provided the current is constant. This is because each charge carrier passing through the slice is subjected to a magnetic force $F_{mag} = BQv$, where v is the speed of the charge carrier. Once the Hall voltage has been created, the magnetic deflection of a charge carrier entering the slice is opposed by the force on it due to the electric field created by the Hall voltage. The electric field force

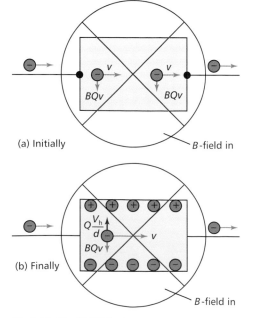

(a) Initially

(b) Finally

Fig 8.13 *The Hall Effect*

$F_{elec} = \dfrac{QV_H}{d}$, where V_H represents the Hall voltage and d is the distance between the top and bottom edges of the slice. Therefore, $\dfrac{QV_H}{d} = BQv$ gives $V_H = Bvd$.

For constant current, v is constant so V_H is proportional to B.

QUESTIONS

$e = 1.6 \times 10^{-19}$ C

1 **a** In Figure 8.10, how would the force on the electrons in the magnetic field differ if:
   (i) the magnetic field was reversed in direction,
   (ii) the magnetic field was reduced in strength,
   (iii) the speed of the electrons was increased?

   b Calculate the force on an electron that enters a uniform magnetic field of flux density 150 mT at a velocity of 8.0×10^6 m s^{-1} at an angle of:
   (i) 90°,
   (ii) 30° to the field

2 Electrons in a vertical wire move upwards at a speed of 2.5×10^{-3} m s^{-1} into a uniform horizontal magnetic field of magnetic flux density 95 mT. The field is directed along a line from South to North as shown in Figure 8.14. Calculate the force on each electron and determine its direction.

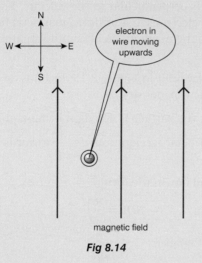

magnetic field

Fig 8.14

3 A beam of protons moving at constant speed is directed into a uniform magnetic field in the same direction as the field.

   a Explain why the beam is not deflected by the field.

   b Describe and explain how the path of the beam in the field would have differed if the beam had been directed into the field at a slight angle to the field lines.

4 In a Hall probe, electrons passing through the semiconductor slice experience a force due to a magnetic field.

   a Explain why a potential difference is created across the slice as a result of the application of the magnetic field.

   b When the magnetic flux density is 90 mT, each electron moving through the slice experiences a force of 6.4×10^{-20} N due to the magnetic field. Calculate:
   (i) the mean speed of the electrons passing through the slice,
   (ii) the force on each electron if the magnetic flux density is increased to 120 mT.

Charged particles in circular orbits

Magnetic fields are used to control beams of charged particles in many devices, from television tubes to high energy accelerators. The force of the magnetic field on a moving charged particle is at right angles to the direction of motion of the particle.

- No work is done by the magnetic field on the particle as the force acts at right angles to the velocity of the particle. Its direction of motion is changed by the force but not its speed. The kinetic energy of the particle is unchanged by the magnetic field.
- In accordance with Fleming's left hand rule, the magnetic force is perpendicular to the velocity at any point along the path. The force therefore acts towards the centre of curvature of the circular path.
- The particle moves on a circular path. The force causes a centripetal acceleration because it is perpendicular to the velocity. Figure 8.15 shows the deflection of a beam of electrons in a uniform magnetic field. The path is a complete circle because the magnetic field is uniform and the particle remains in the field.

The radius, r, of the circular orbit in Figure 8.15 depends on the speed v of the particles and the magnetic flux density B.

At any point on the orbit, the particle is acted on by a magnetic force $F = BQv$ and it experiences a centripetal acceleration, $a = \dfrac{v^2}{r}$ towards the centre of the circle.

Applying Newton's second law in the form $F = ma$ gives

$$BQv = \frac{mv^2}{r}$$

Rearranging this equation gives

$$r = \frac{mv}{BQ}$$

The equation for r shows that

1 r decreases if B is increased,

2 r increases if v is increased,

3 particles in a beam with different values of specific charge, Q/m, are separated by a magnetic field.

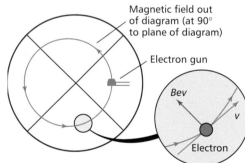

8.15 *A circular orbit in a magnetic field*

Labels on figure: Magnetic field out of diagram (at 90° to plane of diagram); Electron gun; Bev; v; Electron

8.3.1 Applications

The following applications make use of the essential principle that charged particles move on circular paths when in a magnetic field and moving at right angles to the field lines.

1 Measurement of the specific charge, $\dfrac{e}{m}$, of the electron

The fine beam tube shown in Figure 8.16 contains hydrogen gas at low pressure. When a beam of electrons from the electron gun in the tube passes through the gas, the atoms along the beam path emit light due to collisions with electrons. So the path of the beam is seen as a fine trace of light in the tube. A pair of coils, placed either side of the tube, is supplied with a direct current to produce a uniform magnetic field through the tube.

Provided the initial direction of the beam is at right angles to the magnetic field lines, the beam curves round in a circle. The stronger the field, the smaller the circle. With the anode voltage V_A constant, the coil current is adjusted in steps so

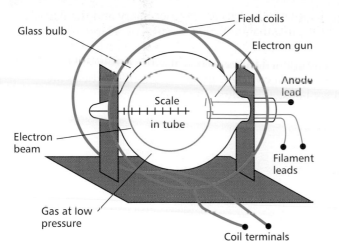

Fig 8.16 Using a fine beam tube

the beam diameter can be measured directly from the scale inside the tube. In this way, the magnetic flux density B is measured for several different values of the beam radius, r.

As explained below, the speed of the electrons depends on the anode voltage, V_A, in accordance with the equation $\frac{1}{2}m v^2 = eV_A$. Combining this with the equation $r = \frac{mv}{Be}$ gives $r = \frac{k}{B}$ where the constant $k = \left(\frac{2mV_A}{e}\right)^{\frac{1}{2}}$.

Using the measurements of r and B to plot a graph of r against $\frac{1}{B}$ gives a straight line through the origin with a gradient equal to k.

Therefore, $\frac{e}{m}$ can be determined if the value of k is measured from the graph and used in the equation $\frac{e}{m} = \frac{2V_A}{k^2}$.

Notes

1 B can be measured using a Hall probe without the tube present.

2 V_A is measured directly using a suitable voltmeter connected across the high voltage supply unit.

3 The speed v depends on V_A according to the equation $\frac{1}{2}mv^2 = eV_A$. The equation is because the kinetic energy gained by each electron, $\frac{1}{2}mv^2$, on being accelerated from the filament to the anode is due to the work done, eV_A, on the electron by the anode.

4 The specific charge of the electron $= 1.76 \times 10^{11}$ C kg^{-1}. The value was first determined by J.J. Thomson in 1895. Before Thomson made this measurement, the hydrogen ion was known to have the largest specific charge of any charged particle. Thomson showed that the electron's specific charge is 1860 times larger than that of the hydrogen ion. However, Thomson could not conclude that the electron has a much smaller mass than the hydrogen ion as the charge of the electron was not known at that time. The charge of the electron was measured by R. Millikan in 1915.

2 The cyclotron

The cyclotron was invented in 1930 by E.O. Lawrence. It consists of 2 hollow D-shaped electrodes (referred to as 'dees') in a vacuum chamber. A high-frequency alternating voltage is applied between the dees. A beam of charged particles is directed into one of the dees near the centre of the cyclotron. A uniform magnetic field is applied perpendicular to the plane of the dees.

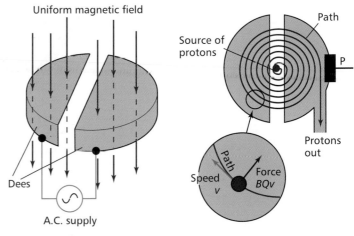

Fig 8.17 The cyclotron

The charged particles are forced on a circular path by the magnetic field, causing the particles to emerge from the dee they were directed into. The particles emerging from the dee when the alternating voltage reverses are accelerated into the other dee where they are forced on a circular path by the magnetic field. When they emerge from this dee, the alternating voltage reverses again and accelerates the particles into the first dee where the process is repeated. This occurs because the time taken, T, by a particle to move round its semi-circular path in the dee $= \frac{\pi r}{v}$, where r is the radius of the path and v is the particle speed. As explained previously, $r = \frac{mv}{BQ}$ so $T = \frac{m\pi}{BQ}$. For an alternating voltage of frequency f, the time for one half cycle $= \frac{1}{2f}$. Therefore, $\frac{1}{2f} = \frac{m\pi}{BQ}$ so $f = \frac{BQ}{2\pi m}$. The equation shows that the frequency is independent of the radius and the speed so the charged particles cross between the dees each time the voltage reverses.

The particles gain speed each time they are accelerated from one dee to the other. The radius of the circular path, therefore, is larger each time a particle travels into and out of a dee. The particles emerge from the cyclotron when the radius of orbit is equal to the dee radius R. As $v = \frac{BQr}{m}$, the speed of the particles on exit from the cyclotron $= \frac{BQR}{m}$.

The **synchrotron** accelerates charged particles to much higher energies than a cyclotron. The magnetic field is increased to keep the particles in an orbit of constant radius as they are boosted to higher and higher speeds. As the radius of orbit is constant, semi-circular dees are not necessary and the particles move round a ring-shaped tube in a magnetic field created by a large number of electromagnets positioned round the ring. A high-frequency alternating voltage, applied between electrodes positioned in the ring, is used to accelerate the charged particles in the ring to high energies. In operation, the particles are injected into the ring and are boosted in 'bursts' to high energies each time the magnetic field is increased.

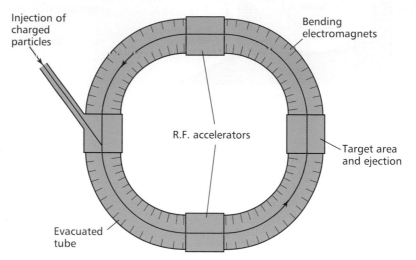

Fig 8.18 *The synchrotron*

3 The mass spectrometer

The mass spectrometer is used to analyse the type of atoms present in a sample. The atoms of the sample are ionised and directed in a narrow beam at constant velocity into a uniform magnetic field. Each ion is deflected in a semi-circle by the magnetic field onto a detector, as shown in Figure 8.19. The radius of curvature of the path of each ion depends on the specific charge $\frac{Q}{m}$ of the ion in accordance with the equation $r = \frac{mv}{BQ}$. Each type of ion is deflected by a different amount onto the detector. The detector is linked to a computer which is programmed to show the relative abundance of each type of ion in the sample.

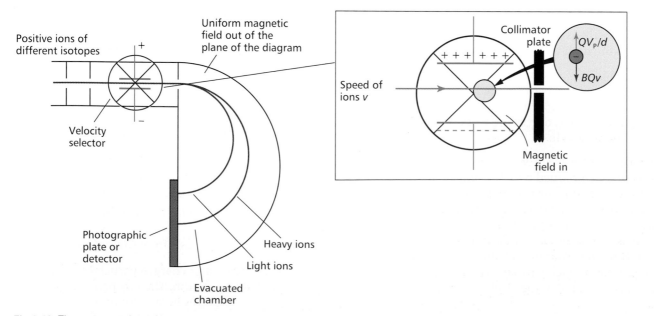

Fig 8.19 *The mass spectrometer*

The ions in the beam enter the magnetic field at the same speed. When they are produced from the sample, they have a continuous range of speeds. Before they enter the magnetic field, they are formed into a beam and directed through a velocity selector, as shown in Figure 8.19. The velocity selector consists of a magnet and a pair of parallel plates at spacing d and voltage V_P due to a high voltage supply. The magnet and the plates are aligned so each ion passing through the velocity selector is acted on by an electric field force, $F_{elec} = \dfrac{QV_P}{d}$, in the opposite direction to

the magnetic field force $F_{mag} = B_S Q v$ where B_S is the magnetic flux density of the magnet in the velocity selector.

Ions moving at a certain speed such that $B_S Q v = \dfrac{QV_P}{d}$ experience equal and opposite forces and so pass through undeflected. All other ions are deflected and do not pass through the collimator slit. So the beam emerging from the collimator consists of different types of ions, all with the same speed $v = \dfrac{V_P}{B_S d}$.

QUESTIONS

$e = 1.6 \times 10^{-19}$ C, e/m for the electron $= 1.76 \times 10^{11}$ C kg^{-1}

1 A beam of electrons at a speed of 3.2×10^7 m s^{-1} are directed into a uniform magnetic field of flux density 8.5 mT in a direction perpendicular to the field lines. The electrons move on a circular orbit in the field.

a (i) Explain why the electrons move on a circular orbit.
   (ii) Calculate the radius of the orbit.

b The flux density is adjusted until the radius of orbit is 65 mm. Calculate the flux density for this new radius.

2 In a fine beam tube, electrons were accelerated from rest through a certain p.d. before being directed at a speed of 2.9×10^7 m s^{-1} in a narrow beam into a uniform magnetic field.

a The beam followed a circular path of radius 35 mm in the magnetic field. Calculate the flux density of the magnetic field.

b The speed of the electrons in the beam was halved as a result of reducing the anode voltage. Calculate the new radius of curvature of the beam in the field.

3 The first cyclotron, used to accelerate protons, was 0.28 m in diameter and was in a magnetic field of flux density 1.1 T.

a Show that protons emerged from this cyclotron at a maximum speed of 1.5×10^7 m s^{-1}.

b Calculate the maximum kinetic energy, in MeV, of a proton from this accelerator.

The mass of a proton $= 1.67 \times 10^{-27}$ kg.

1 MeV $= 1.6 \times 10^{-13}$ J

4 In a mass spectrometer, a beam of different ions moving at a speed of 7.6×10^4 m s^{-1} was directed into a uniform magnetic field of flux density 680 mT, as shown in Figure 8.18.

a An ion was deflected through 180° to a position on the detector which was 28 mm from the detector. Calculate the specific charge of the ion.

b A different type of ion was deflected onto the same detector when the magnetic flux density was changed to 400 mT. Calculate the specific charge of this ion.

CHAPTER SUMMARY

1 a $F = BI\ell \sin \theta$ gives the force F on a current-carrying wire of length ℓ in a uniform magnetic field B at angle θ to the field lines, where I is the current.

   b The direction of the force is given by Fleming's left hand rule where the field direction is the direction of the field component perpendicular to the wire.

2 a $F = BQv \sin \theta$ gives the force F on a particle of charge Q moving through a uniform magnetic field B at speed v in a direction at angle θ to the field .

   b If the velocity of the charged particle is perpendicular to the field, $F = BQv$.

   c The direction of the force is given by Fleming's left hand rule, provided the current is in the direction that positive charge would flow in.

3 $BQv = \dfrac{mv^2}{r}$ gives the radius of the orbit of a charge moving in a direction at right angles to the lines of a magnetic field.

Fig 9.4 *Michael Faraday*

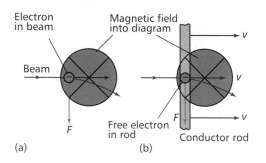

Fig 9.5 *Deflection of electrons in a magnetic field*

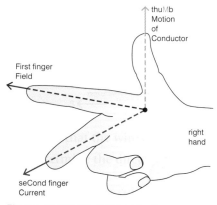

Fig 9.6 *Fleming's right hand rule*

So the induced e.m.f. × the current = energy transferred per unit charge from the source × the charge flow per second = energy transferred per second from the source.

Michael Faraday 1791–1861

Electromagnetic induction was discovered by Michael Faraday in 1831 at the Royal Institution, London. Faraday knew that a current passing along a wire produced a magnetic field near the wire and he wanted to know if a magnet could be used to produce a current. Using a magnetic compass near a loop of wire as a detector of current, he showed that the compass deflected whenever the magnet was moved in or out of the wire. He used the term 'electromotive force' (e.m.f.) to describe the voltage induced in a wire. When he demonstrated his discoveries to an invited audience at the Royal Institution, he was asked the question 'What use is electricity, Mr Faraday?'. He replied with another question 'What use is a new baby?'. No one can tell what can grow from a new discovery.

9.1.2 Understanding electromagnetic induction

When a beam of electrons is directed across a magnetic field, each electron experiences a force at right angles to its direction of motion and to the field direction. A metal rod is like a tube containing lots of free electrons. If the rod is moved across a magnetic field, as shown in Figure 9.5, the magnetic field forces the free electrons in the rod to one end away from the other end. So, one end of the rod becomes negative and the other end positive. In this way, an e.m.f. is induced in the rod. The same effect happens if the magnetic field is moved and the rod is stationary. As long as there is relative motion between the rod and the magnetic field, an e.m.f. is induced in the rod. If the relative motion ceases, the induced e.m.f. becomes zero because the magnetic field no longer exerts a force on the electrons in the rod. Note that when the rod is part of a complete circuit, the electrons are forced round the circuit. In other words, the induced e.m.f. drives a current round the circuit.

9.1.3 The dynamo rule

In Figure 9.5, the magnetic field is into the plane of the diagram and the motion of the conductor is towards the right. The electrons in the rod are forced downwards. The direction of the induced current can also be worked out using Fleming's right hand rule, also referred to as the dynamo rule, as shown in Figure 9.6. The direction of the induced current is, in accordance with the current convention, opposite to the direction of the flow of electrons in the conductor.

QUESTIONS

1 A coil of wire is connected to a sensitive meter.

  a Explain why the meter shows a brief reading when a magnet is pushed into the coil.

  b State two ways in which the meter reading could be made larger.

2 An electric motor consists of a coil of wire between the poles of a magnet. The motor is connected to a lamp. A thread wrapped round the motor spindle is used to support a weight, as shown in Figure 9.2.

  a Explain why the lamp lights when the weight descends.

  b What difference would have been made if the magnet had been much stronger?

3 **a** Explain why a lamp connected to a dynamo lights when the dynamo turns.

  b Why is the dynamo easier to turn when the lamp is disconnected?

4 A horizontal rod aligned along a line from east to west is dropped through a horizontal magnetic field which is directed from south to north.

  a (i) What is the direction of the velocity of the rod?

    (ii) Determine which end of the rod is positive. Explain your answer.

  b Explain why no e.m.f. is induced in the rod if it is aligned from north to south then dropped in the field.

9.2.1 Coils, currents and fields

A magnetic field is produced in and around a coil when the electromagnet is connected to a battery and a current is passed through it. A magnetic compass near the electromagnet is deflected when current passes through the coil. For a long coil or solenoid, the pattern of the magnetic field lines is like the pattern for a bar magnet – except the magnetic field lines near a bar magnet loop round from the north pole to the south pole of the magnet. Figure 9.7 shows the magnetic field pattern of a current-carrying solenoid. The field lines pass through the solenoid and loop round outside the solenoid from one end (the north pole) to the other end (the south pole). If each end in turn is viewed from outside the solenoid:

- current passes a**N**ticlockwise (or cou**N**terclockwise) round the '**N**orth pole' end,
- current passes clockwise round the 'south pole' end.

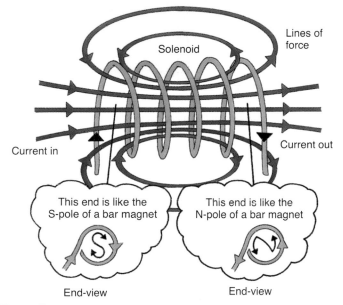

Fig 9.7 *The magnetic field near a solenoid*

Lenz's Law

When a bar magnet is pushed into a coil connected to a meter, the meter deflects. If the bar magnet is pulled out of the coil, the meter deflects in the opposite direction. What determines the direction of the induced current? Consider the North pole of a bar magnet approaching end X of a coil, as shown in Figure 9.8.

The induced current passing round the circuit creates a magnetic field due to the coil. The coil field must act against the incoming North pole, otherwise it would pull the N-pole in faster, making the induced current bigger, pulling the N-pole in even faster still, etc. Clearly, conservation of energy forbids this creation of kinetic and electrical energy from nowhere. So, the induced current creates a magnetic field in the coil which opposes the incoming N-pole. The induced polarity of end X must therefore be a N-pole so as to repel the incoming N-pole. Therefore, the current must go round end X of the coil in an anticlockwise direction, as shown.

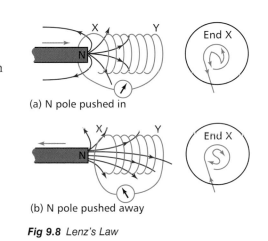

Fig 9.8 Lenz's Law

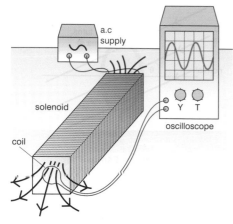

solenoid

coil

Fig 9.13 *A changing magnetic field*

3 A fixed coil in a changing magnetic field

Figure 9.13 shows a small coil on the axis of a current-carrying solenoid. The magnetic field of the solenoid passes through the small coil. If the current in the solenoid changes, an e.m.f. is induced in the small coil. This is because the magnetic field through the coil changes so the flux linkage through it changes, causing an induced e.m.f. Because the induced e.m.f. is proportional to the rate of change of flux linkage through the coil and the flux linkage is proportional to the current I in the solenoid, the magnitude of the induced e.m.f is, therefore, proportional to the rate of change of current in the solenoid.

QUESTIONS

1 A uniform magnetic field of flux density 72 mT is confined to a region of width 60 mm, as shown in Figure 9.14. A rectangular coil of length 50 mm and width 20 mm has 15 turns. The coil is moved into the magnetic field at a speed of 10 mm s^{-1} with its longer edge parallel to the edge of the magnetic field.

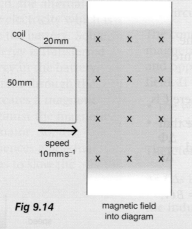

coil

20 mm

50 mm

speed
10 mm s^{-1}

Fig 9.14   magnetic field
into diagram

a Calculate:
  (i) the flux linkage through the coil when it is completely in the field,
  (ii) the time taken for the flux linkage to increase from zero to its maximum value,
  (iii) the induced e.m.f. in the coil as it enters the field.

b (i) Sketch a graph to show how the flux linkage through the coil changes with time from the instant the coil enters the field to when it leaves the field completely.
  (ii) Sketch a graph to show how the induced e.m.f. in the coil varies with time.

2 A rectangular coil of length 40 mm and width 25 mm has 20 turns. The coil is in a uniform magnetic field of flux density 68 mT.

a Calculate the flux linkage through the coil when the coil is at right angles to the field lines.

b The coil is removed from the field in 60 ms. Calculate the mean value of the induced e.m.f.

3 A circular coil of diameter 24 mm has 40 turns. The coil is placed in a uniform magnetic field of flux density 85 mT with its plane perpendicular to the field lines.

a Calculate:
  (i) the area of the coil in m^2,
  (ii) the flux linkage through the coil.

b The coil was reversed in a time of 95 ms. Calculate:
  (i) the change of flux linkage through the coil,
  (ii) the magnitude of the induced e.m.f.

4 A small circular coil of diameter 15 mm and 25 turns is placed in a fixed position on the axis of a solenoid, as shown in Figure 9.13. The magnetic flux density of the solenoid at this position varies with current according to the equation $B = kI$, where $k = 1.2 \times 10^{-3}$ T A^{-1}.

a Calculate the flux linkage through the coil when the current in the solenoid is 1.5 A.

b The current in the solenoid was reduced from 1.5 A to zero in 0.20 s. Calculate the magnitude of the induced e.m.f. in the small coil.

The alternating current generator

Alternating current generators are used in power stations and in mobile and emergency generators. In this section, the simple a.c. generator is considered as an application of electromagnetic induction. Detailed knowledge of the a.c. generator is not required in the A2 specification.

9.3.1 The simple a.c. generator

The simple a.c. generator consists of a rectangular coil that spins in a uniform magnetic field, as shown in Figure 9.15. When the coil spins at a steady rate, the flux linkage changes continuously. At an instant when the normal to the plane of the coil is at angle θ to the field lines, the flux linkage through the coil, $N\Phi = BAN \cos \theta$, where B is the magnetic flux density, A is the coil area and N is the number of turns on the coil.

For a coil spinning at a steady frequency, f, $\theta = 2\pi ft$ at time t after $\theta = 0$. So the flux linkage $N\Phi$ ($= BAN \cos 2\pi ft$) changes with time as shown in Figure 9.16.

- The gradient of the graph is the change of flux linkage per second, $N\dfrac{\Delta\Phi}{\Delta t}$, so it represents the induced e.m.f. It can be shown mathematically that the induced e.m.f. alternates in accordance with the equation $\varepsilon = \varepsilon_0 \sin 2\pi ft$, where f is the frequency of rotation of the coil and ε_0 is the peak e.m.f.

- The induced e.m.f is zero when the sides of the coil move parallel to the field lines. At this position, the rate of change of flux is zero and the sides of the coil do not cut the field lines.

- The induced e.m.f. is a maximum when the sides of the coil cut at right angles across the field lines. At this position, the e.m.f. induced in each wire of each side $= B\ell v$, where v is the speed of each wire and ℓ is its length. So, for N turns and two sides, the induced e.m.f. at this position $\varepsilon_0 = 2 NB\ell v$. The equation shows that the peak e.m.f. can be increased by increasing the speed (i.e. the frequency of rotation) or using a stronger magnet or a bigger coil or a coil with more turns.

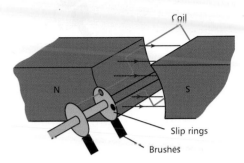

Fig 9.15 *The a.c. generator*

(a)

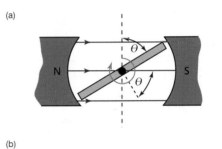

(b)

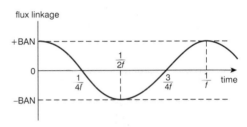

Fig 9.16 *Flux linkage in a spinning coil*

An a.c. generator in a power station has 3 coils at 120° to each other. Each coil produces an alternating voltage 120° out of phase with the voltage from the other coils.

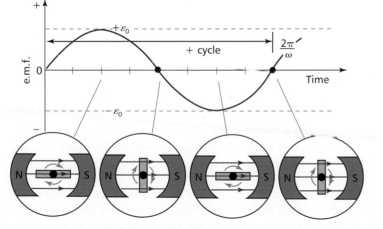

Fig 9.17 *E.m.f. v. time for an a.c. generator*

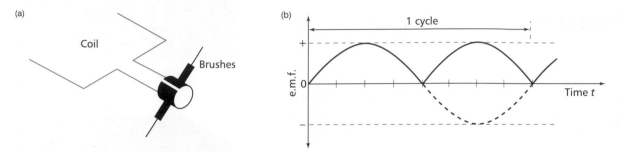

Fig 9.18 *The d.c. generator   (a) The split ring commutator, (b) e.m.f. v. time*

QUESTIONS

1 a An a.c. generator produces an alternating e.m.f. with a peak value of 8.0 V and a frequency of 20 Hz. Sketch a graph to show how the e.m.f. varies with time.

b The frequency of rotation of the a.c. generator in **a** is increased to 30 Hz. On the same axes, sketch a graph to show how the e.m.f. varies with time at 30 Hz.

2 A rectangular coil of N turns and area A spins at a constant frequency f in a uniform magnetic field of flux density B. Complete the table to show how the flux linkage and induced e.m.f. relate to the orientation of the coil during one cycle of rotation.

Time	Orientation of coil	Flux linkage	Induced e.m.f.
0	Parallel to field	?	$+\varepsilon_0$
0.25/f	Perpendicular to field	$+BAN$	?
0.50/f	Parallel to field	?	?
0.75/f	Perpendicular to field	?	?

3 The coil of an a.c. generator has 80 turns, a length of 65 mm and a width of 38 mm. It spins in a uniform magnetic field of flux density 130 mT at a constant frequency of 50 Hz.

a Calculate the maximum flux linkage through the coil.

b (i) Show each side of the coil moves at a speed of 6.0 m s^{-1}.
   (ii) Show that the peak voltage is 8.1 V.

4 An electric motor is to be used to move a variable load. The motor is connected in series with a battery and an ammeter.

a Explain why the motor current is very small when the load is zero.

b Explain why the motor current increases when the load is increased.

Note A d.c. generator can be made by replacing the two slip rings of the a.c. generator with a split-ring, as shown in Figure 9.18. The e.m.f. does not reverse its polarity because the connections between the split-ring and the brushes reverse every half-cycle.

9.3.2 Back e.m.f.

An e.m.f. is induced in the spinning coil of an electric motor because the flux linkage through the coil changes. The induced e.m.f. ε is referred to as a **back e.m.f.** because it acts against the p.d. V applied to the motor in accordance with Lenz's Law. At any instant, $V - \varepsilon = IR$, where I is the current through the motor coil and R is the circuit resistance.

Because the induced e.m.f. is proportional to the speed of rotation of the motor, the current changes as the motor speed changes.

- At low speed, the current is high because the induced e.m.f. is small.
- At high speed, the current is low because the induced e.m.f. is high.

Note that multiplying the equation $V - \varepsilon = IR$ by I throughout gives $IV - I\varepsilon = I^2R$.

Rearranging this equation gives

electrical power supplied by the source	=	electrical power transferred to mechanical power	+	electrical power wasted due to the circuit resistance
IV		$I\varepsilon$		I^2R

The above power equation shows that electrical power supplied to the motor that is not used as mechanical power is wasted due to the resistance heating effect of the current.

- When the motor spins without driving a load, it spins at high speed so the current is very small. Its speed is limited by friction in the bearings and air resistance. It uses little or no power.
- When the motor is used to drive a load, its speed is less than when it is 'off-load' so the current is much larger. The power it uses from the voltage source that is not transferred as mechanical power to the load is wasted due to the resistance heating effect of the current.

The transformer

A transformer changes an alternating p.d. to a different peak value. Any transformer consists of two coils: the primary coil and the secondary coil. The two coils have the same iron core. When the primary coil is connected to a source of alternating p.d., an alternating magnetic field is produced in the core. The field passes through the secondary coil. So, an alternating e.m.f. is induced in the secondary coil by the changing magnetic field. The symbol for the transformer is shown in Figure 9.19.

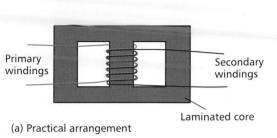

(a) Practical arrangement

(b) Transformer symbol

Fig 9.19 *The transformer*

9.4.1 The transformer rule

A transformer is designed so that all the magnetic flux produced by the primary coil passes through the secondary coil.

Let Φ = the flux in the core passing through each turn at an instant when an alternating p.d. V_P is applied to the primary coil.

- The flux linkage in the secondary coil = $N_S \Phi$, where N_S is the number of turns on the secondary coil. From Faraday's Law, the induced e.m.f. in the secondary coil, $V_S = N_S \dfrac{\Delta \Phi}{\Delta t}$

- The flux linkage in the primary coil = $N_P \Phi$, where N_P is the number of turns on the primary coil. From Faraday's Law, the induced e.m.f. in the primary coil = $N_P \dfrac{\Delta \Phi}{\Delta t}$. The induced e.m.f. in the primary coil opposes the p.d. applied to the primary coil, V_P.

Assuming the resistance of the primary coil is negligible, the applied p.d.
$$V_P = N_P \frac{\Delta \Phi}{\Delta t}$$

Dividing the equation for V_S by the equation for V_P gives $\dfrac{V_S}{V_P} = N_S \dfrac{\Delta \Phi}{\Delta t} \Big/ N_P \dfrac{\Delta \Phi}{\Delta t}$

Cancelling $\dfrac{\Delta \Phi}{\Delta t}$ from this equation gives the **transformer rule**

$$\frac{V_S}{V_P} = \frac{N_S}{N_P}$$

- **A step-up transformer** has more turns on the secondary coil than on the primary coil. So the secondary voltage is stepped up compared with the primary voltage (i.e. $N_S > N_P$ so $V_S > V_P$)

- **A step-down transformer** has fewer turns on the secondary coil than on the primary coil. So the secondary voltage is stepped down compared with the primary voltage (i.e. $N_S < N_P$ so $V_S < V_P$).

9.4.2 Transformer efficiency

The efficiency of a transformer $= \dfrac{\text{power delivered by the secondary coil}}{\text{power supplied to the primary coil}} = \dfrac{I_S V_S}{I_P V_P} (\times 100\%)$

When a device (e.g. a lamp) is connected to the secondary coil, because the efficiency of a transformer is almost equal to 100%,

the electrical power supplied = the electrical power supplied
to the primary coil   by the secondary

Therefore, the current ratio $\dfrac{I_S}{I_P} = \dfrac{V_P}{V_S} = \dfrac{N_P}{N_S}$

- In a step-up transformer, the voltage is stepped up and the current is stepped down.
- In a step-down transformer, the voltage is stepped down and the current is stepped up.

9.4.3 The grid system

Electricity from power stations in the United Kingdom is fed into the National Grid system which supplies electricity to most parts of the country. The National Grid is a network of cables, underground and on pylons, which covers all regions of the UK. Each power station generates alternating current in 3 phases (see p. 107) at a precise frequency of 50 Hz at about 25 kV.

Step-up transformers at the power station increase the alternating voltage to 400 kV or more for long-distance transmission via the grid system. Step-down transformers operate in stages, as shown in Figure 9.20. Factories are supplied with all three phases at either 33 kV or 11 kV. Homes are supplied via a local transformer sub-station with single-phase a.c. at 230 V.

Transmission of electrical power over long distances is much more efficient at high voltage than at low voltage. The reason is that the current needed to deliver a certain amount of power is reduced if the voltage is increased. So power wasted due to the heating effect of the current through the cables is reduced. To deliver power P at voltage V, the current required $I = \dfrac{P}{V}$.

If the resistance of the cables is R, the power wasted through heating the cables is $I^2R = \dfrac{P^2R}{V^2}$. Therefore, the higher the voltage, the smaller the ratio of the wasted power to the power transmitted.

For example, for transmission of 1 MW of power through cables of resistance 500 Ω at 25 kV, the current necessary would be 40 A (= 1 MW/25 kV) so the power wasted would be 0.8 MW (= I^2R = $40^2 \times 500$ W). Prove for yourself that at 400 kV, the power wasted would be about 3 kW.

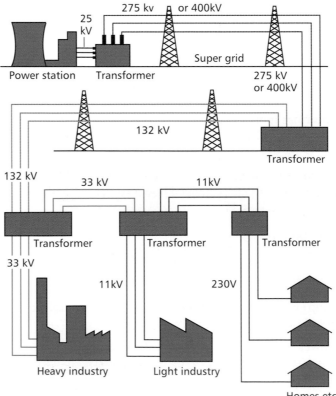

Fig 9.20 *The grid system*

QUESTIONS

1 a Explain why an alternating e.m.f. is induced in the secondary coil of a transformer when the primary coil is connected to an alternating voltage supply.

b In terms of electrical power, explain why the current through the primary coil of a transformer increases when a device is connected to the secondary coil.

2 a Explain why a transformer is designed so that as much of the magnetic flux produced by the primary coil of a transformer as possible passes through the secondary coil.

b Explain why a transformer works using alternating current but not using direct current.

3 A transformer has a primary coil with 120 turns and a secondary coil with 2400 turns.

a Calculate the primary voltage needed for a secondary voltage of 230 V.

b A 230 V, 60 W lamp is connected to its secondary coil. Calculate the current through:
  (i) the secondary coil,
  (ii) the primary coil. State any assumptions made in this calculation.

4 a Explain why transmission of electrical power over a long distance is more efficient at high voltage than at low voltage.

b A power cable of resistance 200 Ω is to be used to deliver 2.0 MW of electrical power at 120 kV from a power station to an industrial estate. Calculate:
  (i) the current through the cable,
  (ii) the power wasted in the cable.

CHAPTER SUMMARY

Magnetic flux, $\Phi = BA$

Flux linkage through a coil of N turns $= N\Phi = NBA$ where B is the magnetic flux density perpendicular to area A.

Lenz's Law states that the direction of the induced current is always such as to oppose the change that causes the current.

Faraday's law of electromagnetic induction states that the induced e.m.f. in a circuit is equal to the rate of change of flux linkage through the circuit.

Equation for Faraday's Law; induced e.m.f.

$\varepsilon = -N \dfrac{\Delta\Phi}{\Delta t}$, where $N \dfrac{\Delta\Phi}{\Delta t}$ is the change in flux linkage per second.

For a moving conductor in a uniform magnetic field, the induced e.m.f. $= B\ell v$

For a changing magnetic field in a fixed coil, induced e.m.f. $= NA \dfrac{\Delta B}{\Delta t}$

Units

The unit of magnetic flux density B is the **tesla** (T).

The unit of magnetic flux and of flux linkage is the **weber** (Wb), equal to $1\,\text{T m}^2$ or $1\,\text{V s}$.

The unit of rate of change of flux (or rate of change of flux linkage) is the weber per second (Wb s^{-1}), equal to 1 V.

Examination-style questions

1 In a ribbon microphone, a metal ribbon vibrates between the poles of a magnet when sound waves reach the microphone.

    a Explain why an e.m.f. is induced across the ends of the ribbon when it vibrates.

    b How would the e.m.f. be affected if:
       (i) a stronger magnet was used,
       (ii) a ribbon of greater mass was used?

2 **a** A bar magnet was positioned near a coil connected to a centre-reading meter. When the bar magnet was pushed into the coil, the meter pointer deflected briefly to the right.
      (i) Explain why the pointer deflected briefly.
      (ii) State and explain what is observed when the magnet is withdrawn from the coil.

    b In **a**, the flux density of the magnet was 25 mT and the area of the 30 turn coil was 4.0×10^{-4} m^2. The magnet was pushed into the coil in 0.20 s. Calculate:
      (i) the flux linkage through the coil,
      (ii) the mean induced e.m.f.

3 A U-shaped magnet was placed at the centre of a horizontal stretched steel wire such that the magnetic field was vertical. When the wire was plucked at its centre, an alternating e.m.f. was induced between the ends of the wire.

    a Explain why an alternating e.m.f. was induced between the ends of the wire.

    b The length of wire between the poles was 28 mm and the magnetic flux density of the magnet was 78 mT. The peak voltage produced was 3.4 mV. Calculate the maximum speed of the wire between the poles.

4 **a** A straight conducting rod PQ of length 0.10 m moves through a uniform magnetic field at a speed of 20 mm s^{-1}. The induced e.m.f. was 0.60 mV when the conductor was moving perpendicular to the field. Calculate:
      (i) the flux swept out in 5.0 s,
      (ii) the magnetic flux density.

    b In **a**, the field was vertically downwards and the rod was horizontal, as shown in the diagram opposite.
      (i) State the polarity of each end of the rod.
      (ii) If the rod was part of a complete circuit, state and explain the direction in which the induced current would pass through it.

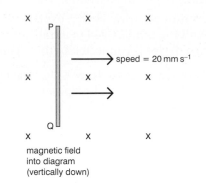

magnetic field into diagram (vertically down)

5 A rectangular coil of length 50 mm and width 20 mm has 25 turns. The diagram below shows the coil just before it was moved at a constant speed of 5 mm s^{-1} into a uniform magnetic field of flux density 86 mT. The field lines are perpendicular to the plane of the coil.

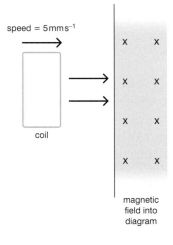

    a Show that the coil takes 4.0 s to enter the field and calculate the flux linkage through the coil when it is completely in the field.

    b Sketch a graph to show how:
      (i) the flux linkage through the coil changes with time,
      (ii) the induced e.m.f. varies with time t from $t = 0$ when the coil enters the field to $t = 5.0$ s.

6 An a.c. generator is used to provide electricity for a lighting circuit.

    a Explain why the generator is easier to turn when the lamps are switched off.

    b The generator coil has 120 turns on a rectangular coil of length 40 mm and width 30 mm. The coil spins in a magnetic field of flux density 220 mT.

(i) When the generator spins at a frequency of 20 Hz, show that the peak voltage is 4.0 V.

(ii) Calculate the peak voltage when the frequency is 23 Hz.

7 A bar magnet was held vertically in a horizontal coil connected to a data recorder, as shown in the diagram below. When the magnet was released, the data recorder was used to measure the voltage induced in the coil every 5 ms. The diagram shows how the voltage changed with time.

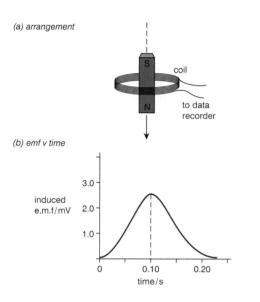

(a) arrangement

coil

to data recorder

(b) emf v time

induced e.m.f/mV

a (i) Without calculations, sketch a graph to show how the flux linkage through the coil changed with time.

(ii) Use your graph to explain the shape of the voltage v. time graph.

b Sketch the voltage v. time graph that would have been produced if the bar magnet had been released from a position above the coil so that it dropped through the coil.

8 A transformer is used to step down an alternating voltage of 230 V to 12 V. The transformer has a primary coil with 1000 turns.

a Calculate the number of turns on the secondary coil.

b The transformer is used to supply power to a 12V, 60 W lamp. Calculate the current in:
(i) the secondary coil,
(ii) the primary coil when the lamp is on.

c The lamp is connected to the transformer by means of a cable of resistance 0.4 Ω.
(i) Estimate the power wasted due to the heating effect of the current in the cable.
(ii) Discuss whether or not it would be better to replace the lamp and transformer with a 230 V, 60 W lamp connected to the mains using the same cable.

Fig 10.1 *Heat transfer in winter*

When you are outdoors in winter, you need to wrap up well otherwise heat transfer from your body to the surroundings takes place and you lose energy. In summer, if you are in a very hot room, you gain energy from the room due to heat transfer.

Energy transfer between two objects takes place if:

- One object exerts a force on the other one and makes it move. In other words, one object does work on the other (see p. 8 for more about work).
- One object is hotter than the other so heat transfer takes place by means of conduction, convection or radiation. In other words, heat transfer is energy transfer due to a temperature difference.

10.1.1 Internal energy

The brake pads of a moving vehicle become hot if the brakes are applied for long enough. The work done by the frictional force between the brake pads and the wheel heats the brake pads. The brake pads gain energy from the kinetic energy of the vehicle. The temperature of the brake pads increases as a result and the internal energy of each brake pad increases.

As explained below, the internal energy of an object is the energy of its molecules due to their individual movements. The internal energy of an object due to its temperature is sometimes referred to as **thermal energy**. However, some of the internal energy of an object might be due to other causes. For example, an iron bar that is magnetised has more internal energy than if it is unmagnetised because of the magnetic interaction between its atoms.

The internal energy of an object changes as a result of:

- heat transfer or energy transfer by radiation to or from the object, or
- work done on or by the object, including work done by electricity.

If the internal energy of an object is constant, either:

- there is no heat transfer or energy transfer due to radiation and no work is done, or
- heat transfer, energy transfer due to radiation and work done 'balance' each other out.

For example, the internal energy of a lamp filament increases when the lamp is switched on because work is done by the electricity supply pushing electrons through the filament. The filament becomes hot as a result. When it reaches its operating temperature, heat transfer to the surroundings takes place and it radiates light. Work done by the electricity supply pushing electrons through the filament is balanced by heat transfer and light radiated from the filament.

10.1.2 About molecules

A molecule is the smallest particle of a pure substance that is characteristic of the substance. For example, a water molecule consists of two hydrogen atoms joined to an oxygen atom.

An atom is the smallest particle of an element that is characteristic of the element. For example, a hydrogen atom consists of a proton and an electron.

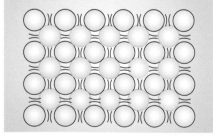

A solid is made up of particles arranged in a regular 3-dimensional structure. There are strong forces of attraction between the particles. Although the particles can vibrate, they cannot move out of their positions in the structure.

When a solid is heated, the particles gain energy and vibrate more and more vigorously. Eventually they may break away from the solid structure and become free to move around. When this happens, the solid has turned into liquid: it has melted.

- In a solid, the atoms and molecules are held to each other by forces due to the electrical charges of the protons and electrons in the atoms. The molecules in a solid vibrate randomly about fixed positions. The higher the temperature of the solid, the more the molecules vibrate. The energy supplied to raise the temperature of a solid increases the kinetic energy of the molecules. If the temperature is raised sufficiently, the solid melts. This happens because its molecules vibrate so much that they break free from each other and the substance loses its shape. The energy supplied to melt a solid raises the potential energy of the molecules because they break free from each other.
- In a liquid, the molecules move about at random in contact with each other. The forces between the molecules are not strong enough to hold the molecules in fixed positions. The higher the temperature of a liquid, the faster its molecules move. The energy supplied to a liquid to raise its temperature increases the kinetic energy of the liquid molecules. Heating the liquid more and more causes it to vaporise. The molecules have sufficient kinetic energy to break free and move away from each other.
- In a gas or vapour, the molecules also move about randomly but much further apart on average than in a liquid. Heating a gas or a vapour makes the molecules speed up and so gain kinetic energy.

> **The internal energy of an object is the sum of the random distribution of the kinetic and potential energies of its molecules.**

Increasing the internal energy of a substance increases the kinetic and/or potential energy associated with the random motion and positions of its molecules.

10.1.3 How to change the energy of the molecules of a substance

1 Raising a substance increases the potential energy of all its molecules by the same amount.

2 Making the substance move faster increases the kinetic energy of all its molecules by the same amount.

3 Heating a substance changes the kinetic energy and/or potential energies of the individual molecules by amounts that **differ** and change at random.

In a liquid the particles are free to move around. A liquid therefore flows easily and has no fixed shape. There are still forces of attraction between the particles.
   When a liquid is heated, some of the particles gain enough energy to break away from the other particles. The particles which escape from the body of the liquid become a gas.

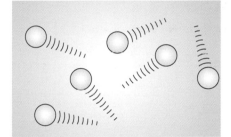

In a gas, the particles are far apart. There are almost no forces of attraction between them. The particles move about at high speed. Because the particles are so far apart, a gas occupies a very much larger volume than the same mass of liquid.
   The molecules collide with the container. These collisions are responsible for the pressure which a gas exerts on its container.

Fig 10.2 *Particles in a solid, a liquid and a gas*

QUESTIONS

1 Describe the energy transfers that occur when a low voltage heater connected to a battery is used to heat some water in a beaker.

2 **a** Explain why an electric motor becomes warm when it is used.

   b A battery is connected to an electric motor which is used to raise a weight at a steady speed. When in operation, the electric motor is at a constant temperature which is above the temperature of its surroundings. Describe the energy transfers that take place.

3 **a** State what is meant by internal energy.

   b Describe a situation in which the internal energy of an object is constant even though work is done on the object.

4 **a** State one difference between the motion of the molecules in a solid and the molecules in a liquid.

   b Describe how the motion of the molecules in a solid changes when the solid is heated.

The temperature of an object is a measure of the degree of hotness of the object. The hotter an object is, the more internal energy it has. Place your hand in cold water and it loses internal energy due to heat transfer. Place it in warm water and it gains internal energy due to heat transfer. If the water is at the same temperature as your hand, no overall heat transfer takes place. Your hand is in **thermal equilibrium** with the water. No overall heat transfer takes place between two objects at the same temperature.

The 'baby in the bath' rule

Before dipping the baby in the bath water, the parent tests the water by putting a hand (not the baby's hand!) in the water. If the baby is at the same temperature as the parent and the parent's hand is at the same temperature as the bath water, the baby will be at the same temperature as the bath water.

10.2.1 Practical temperature scales

A temperature scale is defined in terms of **fixed points** which are standard degrees of hotness which can be accurately reproduced.

- **The Celsius scale of temperature**, in °C, is defined in terms of:
  1. ice point, 0°C, which is the temperature of pure melting ice,
  2. steam point, 100°C, which is the temperature of steam at standard atmospheric pressure.

- **The thermodynamic (Kelvin) scale of temperature**, in kelvins (K) is defined in terms of:
  1. absolute zero, 0 K, which is the lowest possible temperature,
  2. the triple point of water, 273.16 K, which is the temperature at which ice, water and water vapour are in thermal equilibrium.

Because ice point on the absolute scale is 273.15 K and steam point is 100 K higher,

temperature in °C = absolute temperature in kelvins − 273.15

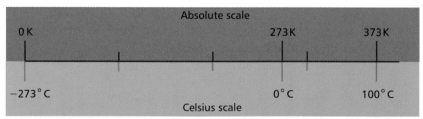

Fig 10.3 Temperature scales

10.2.2 About absolute zero

The thermodynamic scale of temperature, also referred to as the absolute or kelvin scale, is based on absolute zero, the lowest possible temperature. No object can have a temperature below absolute zero. **An object at absolute zero has minimum internal energy**, regardless of the substances the object consists of.

As explained on p. 125, the pressure of a fixed mass of gas in a sealed container of fixed volume decreases as the gas temperature is reduced. If the pressure measured at ice point and at steam point is plotted on a graph as shown in Figure 10.4, the line between the two points always cuts the temperature axis at −273°C, regardless of which gas is used or how much gas is used.

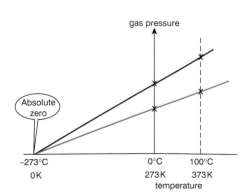

Fig 10.4 Absolute zero

The thermodynamic scale of temperature starts at absolute zero. Its unit, the kelvin, is defined so that a temperature change of 1 K is the same as a temperature change of 1°C. The kelvin scale depends on a fundamental feature of nature, namely the lowest possible temperature. In comparison, the Celsius scale depends on the properties of a substance, water, chosen for convenience rather than for any fundamental reason.

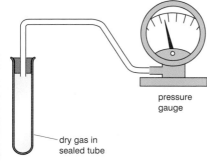

Fig 10.5 *A low temperature research laboratory*

The coldest places in the world

You don't need to travel to the South Pole to find the coldest places in the world. Go to the nearest University physics department that has a low temperature research laboratory. Substances have very strange properties at very low temperatures. For example, metals cooled to a few degrees within absolute zero become superconductors which means they have zero electrical resistance. Superfluids that can empty themselves out of containers have been discovered. Temperatures within a few microkelvins of absolute zero have been reached in these laboratories.

10.2.3 A thermometer test

Use a travelling microscope to measure the interval between adjacent graduations on the scale of an accurate liquid-in-glass thermometer. You may be surprised to find that the interval distance is not the same near the middle of the scale as it is near the ends of the scale. This is because the expansion of the liquid is not directly proportional to the change of temperature.

All thermometers are calibrated in terms of the temperature measured by a gas thermometer. This is a thermometer consisting of dry gas in a sealed container. The pressure of the gas is proportional to the absolute temperature of the gas. In other words, equal increases of temperature cause equal increases of gas pressure.

By measuring the gas pressure, p_{Tr}, at the triple point of water ($= 273.16$ K by definition) and at unknown temperature T/K, the unknown temperature, in kelvins, can be calculated using

(a) A resistance thermometer

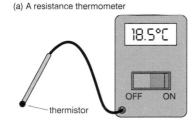

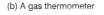

$$\frac{T}{273.16} = \frac{p}{p_{Tr}}$$

where p is the gas pressure at the unknown temperature.

(b) A gas thermometer

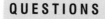

QUESTIONS

1 a Define the thermodynamic scale of temperature and state its unit.

  b State each of the following temperatures to the nearest degree on the thermodynamic scale:
    (i) the temperature of pure melting ice,
    (ii) 20°C,
    (iii) −196°C.

2 The pressure of a constant-volume gas thermometer was 100 kPa at a temperature of 273 K.

  a Calculate the temperature of the gas when its pressure was 120 kPa.

  b Calculate the pressure of the gas at 100°C.

3 Explain why the 50°C mark on the stem of a liquid-in-glass thermometer is not exactly midway between the 0 and 100°C marks.

4 Explain why a gas thermometer is used to calibrate other types of thermometers.

Fig 10.6 *Different types of thermometers*

10.3.1 Heating and cooling

Sunbathers on the hot sandy beaches of the Mediterranean Sea dive into the sea to cool off. Sand heats up much more readily than water does. Even when the sand is almost too hot to walk barefoot across, the sea water is refreshingly cool. The temperature rise of an object when it is heated depends on:

• the mass of the object,

• the amount of energy supplied to it,

• the substance or substances from which the object is made.

> **The specific heat capacity, c, of a substance is the energy needed to raise the temperature of unit mass of the substance by 1 K without change of temperature.**

The unit of c is $J\ kg^{-1}\ K^{-1}$.

Specific heat capacities of some common substances are shown in Table 10.1.

To raise the temperature of mass m of a substance from temperature T_1 to temperature T_2,

$$\text{the energy needed } \Delta Q = mc\ (T_2 - T_1)$$

For example, to calculate the heat that must be supplied to raise the temperature of 5.0 kg of water from 20°C to 100°C, using the above formula gives $\Delta Q = 5.0 \times 4200 \times (100 - 20) = 1.7 \times 10^6$ J.

> **The heat capacity, C, of an object is the heat supplied to raise the temperature of the object by 1 K.**

Therefore, for an object of mass m made of a single substance of specific heat capacity c, its heat capacity $C = mc$. For example, the heat capacity of 5.0 kg of water is 21 000 J K^{-1} = 5.0 kg × 4200 J $kg^{-1}\ K^{-1}$.

Table 10.1 Some specific heat capacities

Substance	Specific heat capacity/J $kg^{-1}\ K^{-1}$
Aluminium	900
Concrete	850
Copper	390
Iron	490
Lead	130
Oil	2100
Water	4200

10.3.2 The inversion tube experiment

In this experiment, the gravitational potential energy of an object falling in a tube is converted into internal energy when it hits the bottom of a tube. Figure 10.7 shows the idea. The object is a collection of tiny lead spheres.

The tube is inverted each time the spheres hit the bottom of the tube. The temperature of the lead shot is measured initially and after a certain number of inversions.

Let m represent the mass of the lead shot.

For a tube of length L, the loss of gravitational potential energy for each inversion = mgL

Therefore, for n inversions, the loss of gravitational potential energy = $mgLn$

The gain of internal energy of the lead shot = $mc\Delta T$, where c is the specific heat capacity of lead and ΔT is the temperature rise of the lead shot.

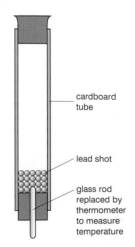

cardboard tube

lead shot

glass rod replaced by thermometer to measure temperature

Fig 10.7 The inversion tube experiment

Assuming all the gravitational potential energy lost is transferred to internal energy of the lead shot,

$$mc\,\Delta T = mgLn$$

$$\therefore \quad c = \frac{gLn}{\Delta T}$$

The experiment can therefore be used to measure the specific heat capacity of lead with no other measurements than the length of the tube, the temperature rise of the lead and the number of inversions.

10.3.3 Specific heat capacity measurements using electrical methods

1 Measurement of the specific heat capacity of a metal

A block of the metal of known mass m in an insulated container is used. A 12 V electrical heater is inserted into a hole drilled in the metal and used to heat the metal by supplying a measured amount of electrical energy. A thermometer inserted into a second hole drilled in the metal is used to measure the temperature rise ΔT ($=$ its final temperature $-$ its initial temperature).

The electrical energy supplied = heater current, $I \times$ heater p.d., $V \times$ heating time, t

$\therefore$ assuming no heat loss to the surroundings, $mc\Delta T = IVt$

$$\therefore \quad c = \frac{IVt}{m\Delta T}$$

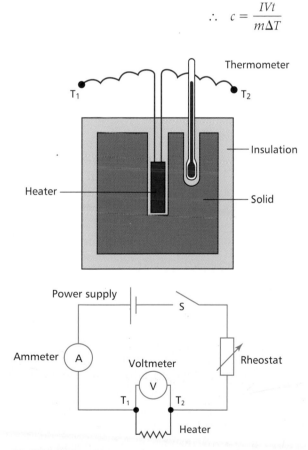

Fig 10.8 Measuring c

2 Measurement of the specific heat capacity of a liquid.

A known mass of the liquid is used in an insulated calorimeter of known mass and known specific heat capacity. A 12 V electrical heater is placed in the liquid and used to heat it directly. A thermometer inserted into the liquid is used to measure the temperature rise, ΔT. Assuming no heat loss to the surroundings:

- The electrical energy supplied = current I × voltage V × heating time t.

- The energy needed to heat the liquid =
  mass of liquid (m_l) × specific heat capacity of liquid (c_l) × temperature rise ΔT.

- The energy needed to heat the calorimeter =
  mass of calorimeter (m_{cal}) × specific heat capacity of calorimeter (c_{cal})
  × temperature rise ΔT

  $\therefore IVt = m_l c_l \Delta T + m_{cal} c_{cal} \Delta T.$

  Hence, c_l can be calculated from this equation as all the other quantities are known.

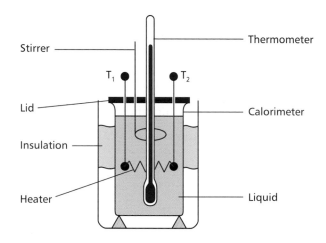

Fig 10.9 *Measurement of the specific heat capacity of a liquid*

10.3.4 Continuous flow heating

In an electric shower, water passes steadily through copper coils heated by an electrical heater. The water is hotter at the outlet than at the inlet. This is an example of continuous flow heating. For mass m of fluid passing through the heater in time t at a steady flow rate, assuming no heat loss.

$$\textbf{the electrical energy supplied per second } IV = \frac{mc\Delta T}{t}$$

where ΔT is the temperature rise of the water.

QUESTIONS

Use the data in Table 10.1 for the following calculations.

1 Calculate:

   a the energy needed to heat an aluminium pan of mass 0.30 kg from 15°C to 100°C,

   b the energy needed to heat 1.5 kg of water from 15°C to 100°C.

2 a Calculate the time taken to heat the water and pan in Question 1 from 15°C to 100°C using a 2.0 kW electric hot plate.

   b Calculate the energy needed to raise the temperature of 80 kg of water in an insulated copper tank of mass 20 kg from 20°C to 50°C.

3 In an inversion tube experiment, 0.50 kg of lead shot at an initial temperature of 18°C was inverted fifty times in a tube of length 1.30 m. The final temperature of the lead shot was 23°C. Calculate:

   a the total gravitational potential energy released by the lead,

   b the specific heat capacity of lead.

4 An electric shower is capable of heating water from 10°C to 40°C when the flow rate is 0.025 kg s^{-1}. Calculate the minimum power of the heater. The specific heat capacity of water = 4200 J kg^{-1} K^{-1}.

Change of state

When a solid is heated and heated, its temperature increases until it melts. If it is a pure substance, it melts at a well-defined temperature, its **melting point**. Once all the solid has melted, continued heating causes the temperature of the liquid to increase until the liquid boils. This occurs at a certain temperature, the **boiling point**. The substance turns to a vapour as it boils away.

The three physical states of a substance, solid, liquid and vapour, have different physical properties. For example:

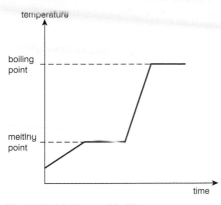

Fig 10.10 *Melting and boiling*

- The density of a gas is much less than the density of the same substance in the liquid or the solid state. This is because the molecules of a liquid and of a solid are packed together in contact with each other. In contrast, the molecules of a gas are, on average, separated from each other by relatively large distances.
- Liquids and gases can flow but solids cannot. This is because the atoms in a solid are locked together by strong force bonds which the atoms are unable to break free from. In a liquid or a gas, the molecules are not locked together because they have too much kinetic energy and the force bonds are not strong enough to keep the molecules fixed to each other.

10.4.1 Latent heat

When a solid or a liquid is heated so its temperature increases, its molecules gain kinetic energy. In a solid, the atoms vibrate more about their mean positions. In a liquid, the molecules move about faster, still keeping in contact with each other but free to move about.

1 **When a solid is heated at its melting point**, its atoms vibrate so much that they break free from each other. The solid therefore becomes a liquid due to energy being supplied at the melting point. The energy needed to melt a solid at its melting point is referred to as **latent heat of fusion**.

   Latent heat is released when a liquid solidifies. This happens because the liquid molecules slow down as the liquid is cooled; at the melting point, the molecules move slowly enough for the force bonds to lock the molecules together.
   - 'Latent' means 'hidden'; latent heat supplied to melt a solid may be thought of as hidden because no temperature change takes place even though the solid is being heated.
   - Fusion is used for the melting of a solid because the solid 'fuses' into a liquid as it melts.

2 **When a liquid is heated at its boiling point**, the molecules gain enough kinetic energy to overcome the bonds that hold them close together. The molecules therefore break away from each other to form bubbles of vapour in the liquid. The energy needed to vaporise a liquid is referred to as **latent heat of vaporisation**.

Latent heat is released when a vapour condenses. This happens because the vapour molecules slow down as the vapour is cooled; the molecules move slowly enough for the force bonds to pull the molecules together to form liquid.

Some solids vaporise directly when heated. This process is known as **sublimation**.

In general, much more energy is needed to vaporise a substance than to melt it. For example, 2.2 MJ is needed to vaporise 1 kg of water at its boiling point. In comparison, 0.34 MJ is needed to melt 1 kg of ice. The energy needed to change the state of 1 kg of a substance at its melting point (or its boiling point) is referred to as its specific latent heat of fusion (or vaporisation). Specific latent heat is not on the A2 specification.

CHAPTER SUMMARY

The internal energy of an object is the sum of the random distribution of the kinetic and potential energies of its molecules.

Absolute zero is the temperature at which an object has minimum internal energy.

Temperature in °C = absolute temperature in kelvins − 273.15.

Specific heat capacity, c, of a substance is the energy needed to raise the temperature of 1 kg of the substance by 1 K without change of temperature.

Energy needed to raise the temperature of mass m of a substance from T_1 to T_2 = $mc(T_2 - T_1)$, where c is the specific heat capacity of the substance.

Energy to melt a solid (latent heat of fusion) is used to break the bonds that lock the molecules of the solid into fixed positions.

Energy to boil a liquid (latent heat of vaporisation) is used to break the bonds that prevent molecules moving away from each other.

10.4.2 Temperature v. time graphs

If a pure solid is heated to its melting point and beyond, its temperature v. time graph will be as shown in Figure 10.11.

Assuming no heat loss occurs during heating,

- before the solid melts, the energy supplied each second = $mc_S \left(\dfrac{\Delta T}{\Delta t}\right)_S$ where $\left(\dfrac{\Delta T}{\Delta t}\right)_S$ is the rise of temperature per second of the solid and c_S is the specific heat capacity of the solid.

- at the melting point, the energy supplied = energy supplied per second × time taken to melt,

- after the solid melts, the energy supplied each second = $mc_L \left(\dfrac{\Delta T}{\Delta t}\right)_L$ where $\left(\dfrac{\Delta T}{\Delta t}\right)_L$ is the rise of temperature per second of the liquid and c_L is the specific heat capacity of the liquid.

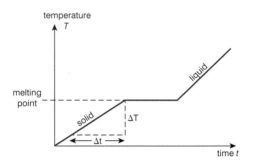

Fig 10.11 *Temperature v. time for a solid being heated*

QUESTIONS

1 a Explain why energy is needed to melt a solid.

  b Explain why the internal energy of the water in a beaker must be reduced to freeze the water.

2 Calculate the mass of water boiled away in a 3 kW electric kettle in 2 minutes, given that 2.2 MJ of energy must be supplied to boil away 1 kg of water at atmospheric pressure.

3 A plastic beaker containing 0.080 kg of water at 15°C was placed in a refrigerator and cooled to 0°C in 1200 s.

  a Calculate how much energy each second was removed from the water in this process. The specific heat capacity of water = 4200 J kg^{-1} K^{-1}.

  b Calculate how long the refrigerator would take to freeze the water in **a**, given that 340 kJ of energy must be removed from 1.0 kg of water at 0°C to freeze it.

4 The temperature v. time graph shown in Figure 10.12 was obtained by heating 0.12 kg of a substance in an insulated container. The specific heat capacity of the substance in the solid state is 1200 J kg^{-1} K^{-1}. Calculate:

  a the energy per second supplied to the substance in the solid state if its temperature increased from 60°C to its melting point at 78°C in 120 s,

  b the energy needed to melt the solid if it took 300 s to melt with energy supplied at the same rate as in **a**.

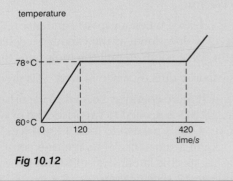

Fig 10.12

$g = 9.8\,\mathrm{m\,s^{-2}}$

1 a In terms of molecules, explain why:
  (i) a solid has its own shape,
  (ii) a liquid and a gas can flow,
  (iii) a gas is much less dense than a solid or a liquid.

b Describe the effect on the molecules of a solid of:
  (i) supplying energy to it to raise its temperature,
  (ii) supplying energy to it to melt it.

2 When a certain object is heated, its internal energy increases. Explain, in molecular terms:

a what is meant by internal energy,

b why increasing the internal energy of the object differs from increasing its kinetic energy.

3 A vehicle of mass 1200 kg is fitted with brake pads of total mass 23 kg. When the car is travelling at a speed of 30 m s^{-1}, the brakes are applied and the car stops in a distance of 110 m. The temperature of the brake pads increases by 7.5 K during this time.

a Calculate:
  (i) the initial kinetic energy of the car,
  (ii) the gain of internal energy of the brake pads, assuming no heat transfer from the brake pads occurs.

b Show that the frictional force on the car due to the brakes was at least 3.9 kN.

The specific heat capacity of the brake pad material = 2500 J kg^{-1} K^{-1}.

4 a An electric motor in prolonged use becomes hotter than its surroundings.
  (i) State two reasons why some of the electrical energy transferred to the motor is wasted as heat.
  (ii) Describe the energy transfers in the motor when it is in prolonged use at a constant temperature which is higher than the temperature of its surroundings.

b A 250 W electric winch raises a load of weight 110 N through a height of 4.0 m in 20 s.
  (i) Calculate the efficiency of the winch.
  (ii) The temperature of a pulley wheel in the winch increases by 2.0 K when the load in (i) is raised. The pulley wheel is made of steel and has a mass of 0.095 kg. Calculate the energy needed to raise the temperature of the wheel by 2.0 K and determine the increase of efficiency of the winch if friction at the pulley could be eliminated.

Specific heat capacity of steel = 460 J kg^{-1} K^{-1}

5 An insulated metal cylinder of mass 1.4 kg was heated by a 24 W electric heater placed in a slot in the cylinder, as shown in Figure 10.8. The temperature of the metal was measured using a thermometer placed in a different slot in the metal. The measurements were used to plot a graph of the temperature v. time, as shown in the diagram below.

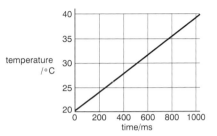

a Determine the temperature rise per second of the cylinder.

b Calculate the specific heat capacity of the metal.

6 A 3.0 kW electric kettle took 260 s to heat 1.8 kg of water from 18°C to 100°C.

a Calculate:
  (i) the electrical energy supplied to the kettle in this time,
  (ii) the internal energy gained by the water in the kettle.

b The mass of the kettle was 1.2 kg and it was made from aluminium.
  (i) Calculate the internal energy gained by the kettle.
  (ii) Account for the difference between the electrical energy supplied to the kettle and the internal energy gained by the water and the kettle.

specific heat capacity of water = 4200 J kg^{-1} K^{-1},
specific heat capacity of aluminium = 900 J kg^{-1} K^{-1}

7 A shower fitted with an electric heater raised the temperature of water passing through the shower from 12°C to 46°C when the flow rate was 0.050 kg s^{-1}.

a Calculate the power of the electric heater, assuming there is no heat loss to the surroundings.

b The shower is fitted with a thermostat that restricts the temperature of the outflowing water to 50°C. Calculate the flow rate that would give this outflow temperature when the temperature of the inflow is 12°C.

Specific heat capacity of water = 4200 J kg^{-1} K^{-1}

Hence, the combined gas law may be written as

$$pV_m = RT$$

where V_m = volume of 1 mole of ideal gas at pressure p and temperature T.

Therefore, for n moles of ideal gas,

$$pV = nRT$$

where V = volume of the gas at pressure p and temperature T.

This equation is known as the **ideal gas equation**.

Notes

1 T is the temperature in kelvins.

2 The unit of R is the joule per mol per kelvin (J mol^{-1} K^{-1}) which is the same as the unit of $\dfrac{\text{pressure} \times \text{volume}}{\text{temperature}}$. This is because the unit of pressure (the pascal = 1 N m^{-2}) $\times$ the unit of volume (m^3) is the joule (= 1 N m).

3 A graph of pV against temperature T is a straight line through absolute zero and has a gradient equal to nR.

4 The density of an ideal gas of molar mass M, $\rho = \dfrac{\text{mass}}{\text{volume}} = \dfrac{nM}{V} = \dfrac{pM}{RT}$.

Therefore, for an ideal gas at constant pressure, its density ρ is inversely proportional to its temperature T (as $\rho = \dfrac{pM}{RT} = \dfrac{\text{constant}}{T}$ for constant pressure).

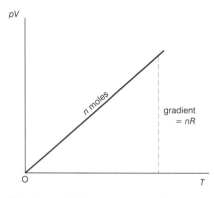

Fig 11.8 A graph of pV against T for an ideal gas

Worked example

$R = 8.31$ J mol^{-1} K^{-1}

Calculate the number of moles of air in a balloon when the air pressure in the balloon is 170 kPa, the volume of the balloon is 8.4×10^{-4} m^3 and the temperature of the air in the balloon is 17°C.

Solution

$T = 273 + 17 = 290$ K

Using $pV = nRT$ gives $n = \dfrac{pV}{RT} = \dfrac{170 \times 10^3 \times 8.4 \times 10^{-4}}{8.31 \times 290} = 5.9 \times 10^{-2}$ moles

QUESTIONS

1 A gas cylinder has a volume of 0.024 m^3 and is fitted with a valve designed to release the gas if the pressure of the gas reaches 125 kPa. Calculate:

  a the maximum number of moles of gas that can be contained by this cylinder at 50°C,

  b the pressure in the cylinder of this amount of gas at 10°C.

2 In an electrolysis experiment, 2.2×10^{-5} m^3 of a gas is collected at a pressure of 103 kPa and a temperature of 20°C. Calculate:

  a the number of moles of gas present,

  b the volume of this gas at 0°C and 101 kPa.

3 **a** Sketch a graph to show how the pressure of 2 moles of gas varies with temperature when the gas is heated from 20°C to 100°C in a sealed container of volume 0.050 m^3.

  b The molar mass of the gas in **a** is 0.032 kg. Calculate the density of the gas.

4 The molar mass of air is 0.029 kg.

  a Calculate the density of air at 20°C and a pressure of 101 kPa.

  b Calculate the number of molecules in 0.001 m^3 of air at 20°C and a pressure of 101 kPa.

The kinetic model of an ideal gas

The gas laws can be explained by assuming a gas consists of point molecules moving about at random, continually colliding with the container walls. Each impact causes a force on the container. The force of many impacts is the cause of the pressure of the gas on the container walls.

- Boyle's Law: the pressure of a gas is increased by reducing its volume because the gas molecules travel less distance between impacts at the walls due to the reduced volume. Hence, there are more impacts per second so the pressure is greater.
- Pressure law: the pressure of a gas is increased by raising its temperature. The average speed of the molecules is increased by raising the gas temperature so the impacts of the molecules on the container walls are harder and more frequent. Hence, the pressure is raised as a result.

11.3.1 Molecular speeds

The molecules in an ideal gas have a continuous spread of speeds, as shown in Figure 11.9. The speed of an individual molecule changes when it collides with another gas molecule but the distribution stays the same, provided the temperature does not change.

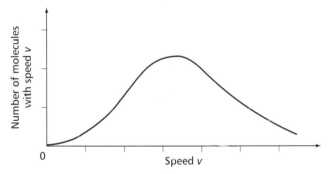

Fig 11.9 *Distribution of molecular speeds*

If the temperature of a gas is raised, its molecules move faster on average. The mean speed of the molecules increases. The distribution curve becomes flatter and broader as there are more molecules at higher speeds.

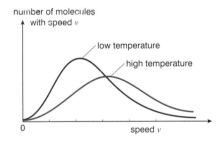

Fig 11.10 *The effect of temperature on the distribution of speeds*

11.3.2 Molecules and kinetic energy

Consider a gas consisting of N identical molecules with individual speeds c_1, c_2, c_3, ... c_N. The kinetic energy of the molecule with speed c_1 is $\frac{1}{2}mc_1^2$, where m is the mass of the molecule. The kinetic energy of every other molecule is given by a similar formula.

$$\text{The mean kinetic energy of a molecule of the gas} = \frac{\text{total kinetic energy of all the molecules}}{\text{total number of molecules}}$$

$$= \frac{\frac{1}{2}mc_1^2 + \frac{1}{2}mc_2^2 + ... \frac{1}{2}mc_N^2}{N}$$

For an ideal gas, it can be shown that the mean kinetic energy of a molecule is proportional to the absolute temperature, T, of the gas.

Mean kinetic energy of a gas molecule $\propto T$

1 The higher the temperature of a gas, the higher the mean kinetic energy of a molecule of the gas.

If the absolute temperature of an ideal gas is raised from T_1 to T_2,

$$\frac{\text{the mean kinetic energy of a gas molecule at temperature } T_2}{\text{the mean kinetic energy of a gas molecule at temperature } T_1} = \frac{T_2}{T_1}$$

2 The total kinetic energy of N molecules of a gas $= N \times$ the mean kinetic energy of a gas molecule.

Because the internal energy of an ideal gas is due only to the kinetic energy of its molecules, the internal energy of an ideal gas is proportional to its absolute temperature.

Therefore, for a fixed mass of an ideal gas

$$\frac{\text{its internal energy at temperature } T_2}{\text{its internal energy at temperature } T_1} = \frac{T_2}{T_1}$$

3 The average speed of a molecule of a gas can be estimated using the kinetic energy equation $E_K = \frac{1}{2}mv^2$ if the mean kinetic energy of a molecule of the gas is known.

Rearranging this equation gives $\left(\frac{2E_K}{m}\right)^{\frac{1}{2}}$ as an estimate of the average speed.

Notes

The proof of the relationship between the mean kinetic energy of a gas molecule and the temperature of the gas is not required in the A2 specification. The notes below are provided to aid understanding.

Step 1 It can be shown that the pressure of N identical gas molecules in a container of volume V is given by the equation $pV = \frac{1}{3}Nm <c^2>$ where $<c^2> = \dfrac{c_1^2 + c_2^2 + \ldots c_N^2}{N}$.

Knowledge or proof of this equation is not required in this module.

Step 2 Combining this equation with the ideal gas law $pV = nRT$ gives the mean kinetic energy of a gas molecule, $\frac{1}{2}m <c^2> = \dfrac{\frac{3}{2}pV}{N} = \dfrac{\frac{3}{2}nRT}{N}$

Step 3 As $\dfrac{nR}{N} = \dfrac{R}{N_A}$, then $\frac{1}{2}m <c^2> = \frac{3}{2}kT$, where $k = \dfrac{R}{N_A} = 1.38 \times 10^{-23}$ J mol^{-1} K^{-1}.

k is referred to as the Boltzmann constant.

Worked example

$N_A = 6.02 \times 10^{23}$ mol^{-1}

The average kinetic energy of an oxygen gas molecule at 0°C is 5.7×10^{-21} J.

a Calculate the speed of an oxygen molecule with kinetic energy of 5.7×10^{-21} J.

b Calculate the internal energy of 1 mole of oxygen gas at 0°C.

The molar mass of oxygen $= 0.032$ kg mol^{-1}

Solution

a The mass of an oxygen molecule, $m = \dfrac{0.032}{6.02 \times 10^{23}} = 5.3 \times 10^{-26}$ kg

Rearranging $E_K = \frac{1}{2}mv^2$ where v is the speed of the molecule and E_K is its kinetic energy gives

$$v^2 = \frac{2E_K}{m} = \frac{2 \times 5.7 \times 10^{-21}}{5.3 \times 10^{-26}} = 2.15 \times 10^5 \text{ m}^2 \text{ s}^{-2}$$

$$\therefore \quad v = (2.15 \times 10^5)^{\frac{1}{2}} = 464 \text{ m s}^{-1}$$

b The internal energy of 1 mole of gas $= N_A \times$ average kinetic energy of a molecule $= 6.02 \times 10^{23} \times 5.7 \times 10^{-21} = 3.4 \times 10^3$ J

QUESTIONS

$N_A = 6.02 \times 10^{23}\,\text{mol}^{-1}$, $R = 8.3\,\text{J mol}^{-1}\,\text{K}^{-1}$

1 a Explain in molecular terms why the pressure of a gas in a sealed container increases when its temperature is raised

b The molar mass of oxygen is 0.032 kg. A cylinder of volume $0.025\,\text{m}^3$ contains oxygen gas at a pressure of 120 kPa and a temperature of 373 K. Calculate:

  (i) the number of moles of oxygen in the cylinder,

  (ii) the mass of an oxygen molecule in the cylinder,

  (iii) the kinetic energy of an oxygen molecule that has a speed of $540\,\text{m s}^{-1}$.

2 Calculate:

a the mass of a hydrogen molecule,

b the kinetic energy of a hydrogen molecule that has a speed of $1800\,\text{m s}^{-1}$.

The molar mass of hydrogen gas = 0.002 kg.

3 a The average kinetic energy of a molecule of a gas at 273 K is 5.7×10^{-21} J. Calculate the average kinetic energy of a molecule of the gas at 373 K.

b Air consists mostly of nitrogen and oxygen. Show that the speed of a nitrogen molecule in air is $1.07 \times$ the speed of an oxygen molecule with the same kinetic energy.

The molar mass of nitrogen is 0.028 kg and the molar mass of oxygen is 0.032 kg.

4 An ideal gas of molar mass 0.028 kg in a container of volume $0.037\,\text{m}^3$ has a pressure of 100 kPa at a temperature of 300 K.

a Calculate:

  (i) the number of moles,

  (ii) the mass of gas present.

b The average kinetic energy of a molecule of the gas at 300 K is 6.2×10^{-21} J.

  (i) Calculate the average kinetic energy of a molecule of the gas at 373 K.

  (ii) Show that the gain of internal energy of the gas in the container is 1350 J when the gas is heated from 300 to 373 K.

CHAPTER SUMMARY

Absolute temperature, T, in kelvins = temperature in °C + 273(.15).

The ideal gas law $pV = nRT$, where n is the number of moles of gas, T is the absolute temperature and R is the molar gas constant.

The Avogadro constant, N_A is defined as the number of atoms in 12 grams of the carbon isotope $^{12}_{6}\text{C}$.

One mole of a substance consisting of identical particles is the quantity of substance that contains N_A particles of the substance.

The molar mass of a substance is the mass of one mole of that substance.

The mean kinetic energy of a molecule in a gas is proportional to the absolute temperature of the gas.

$N_A = 6.02 \times 10^{23} \, mol^{-1}$, $R = 8.3 \, J \, mol^{-1} \, K^{-1}$

1 a In molecular terms, explain why the pressure of a gas increases:
(i) if the temperature of the gas is raised at constant volume,
(ii) if the amount of gas is increased at constant volume.

b Sketch a graph to show how the pressure of a gas in a sealed cylinder increases with the absolute temperature of the gas if the cylinder contains:
(i) 1 mole of gas,
(ii) 2 moles of gas.

2 a Assuming that air at atmospheric pressure consists of 80% nitrogen and 20% oxygen, show that the molar mass of air is 0.029 kg.

molar mass of nitrogen = 0.028 kg,
molar mass of oxygen = 0.032 kg.

b A rectangular room has a length of 5.0 m, a width of 4.0 m and a height of 2.5 m. The air in the room has a pressure of 100 kPa and a temperature of 290 K. Calculate:
(i) the number of moles of air in the room,
(ii) the number of gas molecules in the room.

3 A vehicle air bag inflates rapidly when an impact causes the production and release of a large quantity of nitrogen in a chemical reaction. In a test of an air bag, the bag inflates to a volume of 1.2 m^3 and a pressure of 103 kPa at a final temperature of 280 K. Calculate:

a the number of moles of gas in the bag,

b the initial pressure of the gas if it was released from a container of volume 5.6×10^{-4} m^3 at the same temperature.

4 A hot air balloon rises from the ground because it is partly filled with helium which is lighter than air.

a A certain hot air balloon contains 370 m^3 of helium gas at a temperature of 300 K. Calculate:
(i) the number of moles of helium gas in the balloon when the pressure of the gas is 110 kPa,
(ii) the density of the gas.

b The helium gas in the balloon fills most of the balloon from the top down. Heating the gas causes it to expand and displace some of the air in the lower part of the balloon.
(i) Explain why heating the gas causes its density to decrease.
(ii) Explain why the balloon ascends when the helium gas is heated.

The molar mass of helium = 4.0×10^{-3} kg

5 A hollow steel cylinder fitted with a pressure gauge is used to store nitrogen gas. The cylinder has an internal volume of 5.0×10^{-3} m^3.

The molar mass of nitrogen = 0.028 kg

a (i) Calculate the mass of nitrogen gas that must be stored in the cylinder at 300 K to give a gas pressure of 150 kPa.
(ii) Describe how the mass of gas remaining in the cylinder could be estimated from the pressure reading of the pressure gauge.

b The cylinder is fitted with a valve that releases gas from the cylinder if the gas pressure exceeds 160 kPa.

Calculate the maximum mass of nitrogen that could be stored in the cylinder at 350 K.

6 Argon is an inert gas. The gas is composed of single atoms that do not combine with each other. A certain light bulb contains 8.0×10^{-5} m^3 of argon gas. When the light bulb was at a temperature of 300 K, the pressure of the gas in the light bulb was 15 kPa.

a (i) Calculate the number of moles of argon gas in the light bulb.
(ii) Calculate the number of argon atoms in the light bulb.
(iii) The mean kinetic energy of an argon atom at 300 K is 6.2×10^{-21} J. Calculate the speed of an argon atom which has 6.2×10^{-21} J of kinetic energy.

b When the light bulb was switched on, the temperature of the gas in the bulb increased to 350 K. Calculate:
(i) the pressure in the light bulb at this temperature,
(ii) the increase of kinetic energy of the gas molecules in the light bulb.

The molar mass of argon = 0.040 kg.

7 Helium gas released with oil from an oil well was collected and stored in a sealed underground cavern of volume 26 000 m^3 at a temperature of 280 K. As a result of storing the helium gas, the pressure of the gas in the cavern increased from 100 kPa to 125 kPa.

a Calculate:
(i) the mass of helium gas stored in the cavern,
(ii) the mass of a helium molecule.

b The mean kinetic energy of a helium gas molecule at 280 K is 5.8×10^{-21} J. Calculate:
(i) the speed of a helium gas molecule which has 5.8×10^{-21} J of kinetic energy,
(ii) the kinetic energy of all the helium gas molecules in the cavern at 280 K.

The molar mass of helium = 0.004 kg

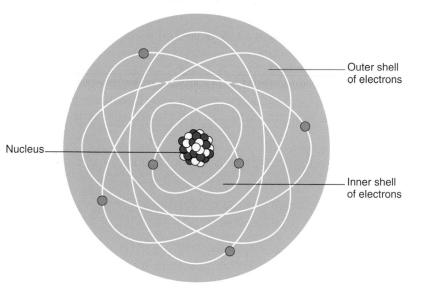

Nucleus

Outer shell of electrons

Inner shell of electrons

Fig 12.1 *The structure of an atom*

The nucleus was discovered by Ernest Rutherford in 1914. He knew from the work of J.J. Thomson that every atom contains one or more electrons. As outlined on p. 97, Thomson had shown that the electron is a negatively charged particle inside every atom but no one knew until Rutherford's discovery how the positive charge in the atom was distributed. Thomson thought the atom could be like a 'currant bun' – with electrons dotted in the atom like currants in a bun. In this model, the positive charge was supposedly spread throughout the atom like the dough of the bun.

Rutherford knew that the atoms of certain elements were unstable and emitted radiation. It had been shown that there were three types of such radiation, referred to as alpha radiation (symbol α), beta radiation (symbol β) and gamma radiation (symbol γ). Rutherford knew that α-radiation consisted of fast-moving positively charged particles. He used this type of radiation to probe the atom. He reckoned that a beam of the particles directed at a thin metal foil might be scattered slightly by the atoms of the foil if the positive charge was spread out throughout each atom. He was astonished when he discovered that some of the particles bounced back from the foil – in his own words 'as incredible as if you fired a 15-inch naval shell at tissue paper and it came back'. Let's consider Rutherford's experiment in more detail.

12.1.1 Rutherford's alpha scattering experiment

Rutherford used a narrow beam of alpha particles, all of the same kinetic energy, in an evacuated container to probe the structure of the atom. The diagram shows an outline of the arrangement he used. A thin metal foil was placed in the path of the beam. Alpha particles scattered by the metal foil were detected by a detector which could be moved round at a constant distance from the point of impact of the beam on the metal foil.

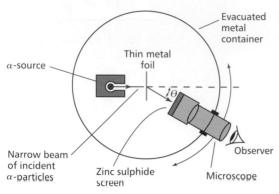

Fig 12.2 *Rutherford's α-scattering apparatus*

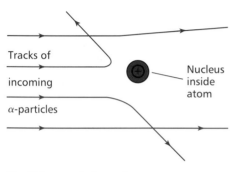

Fig 12.3 *α-scattering paths*

Rutherford used a microscope to observe the pinpoints of light emitted by alpha particles hitting a fluorescent screen. He measured the number of alpha particles reaching the detector per minute for different angles of deflection from zero to almost 180°. His measurements showed that:

1 most alpha particles pass straight through the foil with little or no deflection,

2 a small percentage of alpha particles deflect through angles of more than 90°.

Imagine throwing tennis balls at a row of vertical posts separated by wide gaps. Most of the balls would pass between the posts and therefore would not be deflected much. However, some would rebound as a result of hitting a post. Rutherford realised the alpha scattering measurements could be explained in a similar way by assuming every atom has a 'hard centre' much smaller than the atom. His interpretation of each result was that:

1 most of the atom's mass is concentrated in a small region, the nucleus, at the centre of the atom,

2 the nucleus is positively charged because it repels alpha particles (which carry positive charge) that approach it too closely.

Figure 12.3 shows the paths of some alpha particles which pass near a fixed nucleus. The closer an alpha track deflection passes to a nucleus, the greater its deflection is because the alpha particle and the nucleus repel each other as they carry the same type of charge. Using Coulomb's law of force (i.e. the law of force between charged objects) and Newton's laws of motion, Rutherford used his nuclear model to explain the exact pattern of the results. By testing foils of different metal elements, he also showed that the magnitude of the charge of a nucleus is $+Ze$, where e is the charge of the electron and Z is the atomic number of the element.

Notes

1 The alpha particles must have the same speed otherwise slow alpha particles would be deflected more than faster alpha particles on the same initial path.

2 The tube must be evacuated or the alpha particles would be stopped by air molecules.

3 The source of the alpha particles must have a long half-life, otherwise later readings would be lower than earlier readings due to radioactive decay of the source nuclei.

Ernest Rutherford 1871–1937

Ernest Rutherford arrived in Britain from New Zealand in 1895. By the age of 28, he was a professor. He made important discoveries about radioactivity and was awarded the Nobel Prize for chemistry in 1908 for his investigations into the disintegration of radioactive substances. He worked in the universities of Montreal, Manchester and Cambridge. He put forward the nuclear model of the atom and proved it experimentally using α-scattering experiments. He was knighted in 1914 and made Lord Rutherford of Nelson in 1931. His co-worker Otto Hahn described him as a 'very jolly man'. In 1915, he expressed the hope that 'no one discovers how to release the intrinsic energy of radium until man has learned to live at peace with his neighbour'. After his death in 1937, his ashes were placed close to Newton's tomb in Westminster Abbey.

Fig 12.4 *Ernest Rutherford*

12.1.2 Estimate of the size of the nucleus

About 1 in 10 000 alpha particles are deflected by more than 90° when they pass through a metal foil. The foil must be very thin otherwise alpha particles are scattered more than once. For such single scattering by a foil that has n layers of atoms, the probability of an alpha particle being deflected by a given atom is therefore about 1 in 10 000n. This probability depends on the effective area of cross-section of the nucleus to that of the atom. Therefore, for a nucleus of diameter d in an atom of diameter D, the area ratio is equal to $\dfrac{(\frac{1}{4}\pi d^2)}{(\frac{1}{4}\pi D^2)}$.

So, $d^2 = \dfrac{D^2}{10\,000n}$. A typical value of $n = 10^4$ gives $d = \dfrac{D}{10\,000}$. In other words, the size of a nucleus in an atom is about the same as a football in a football stadium!

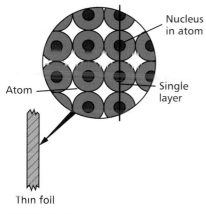

Fig 12.5 *Estimating nuclear size*

QUESTIONS

1 **a** In the Rutherford α-particle scattering experiment, most of the alpha particles passed straight through the metal foil. What did Rutherford deduce about the atom from this discovery?

   b A small fraction of the alpha particles were deflected through large angles. What did Rutherford deduce about the atom from this discovery?

2 In Rutherford's α-particle scattering experiment, why was it essential that:

   a the apparatus was in an evacuated chamber,

   b the foil was very thin,

   c the α-particles in the beam all had the same speed,

   d the beam was narrow?

3 An alpha particle collided with a nucleus and was deflected by it, as shown in Figure 12.6.

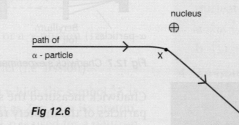

Fig 12.6

   a Copy the diagram and show on it:
   (i) the direction of motion of the alpha particle,
   (ii) the direction of the force on the alpha particle when it was at the position marked X.

   b Describe how:
   (i) the kinetic energy of the alpha particle, and
   (ii) the potential energy of the alpha particle changed during this interaction.

4 In the alpha scattering experiment, about 1 in 10 000 alpha particles are deflected by more than 90°.

   a For a metal foil which has n layers of atoms, explain why the probability of an alpha particle being deflected by a given atom is, therefore, about 1 in 10 000n.

   b Assuming this probability is equal to the ratio of the cross-sectional area of the nucleus to that of the atom, estimate the diameter of a nucleus for atoms of diameter 0.5 nm in a metal foil of thickness 10 μm.

Probing the atom

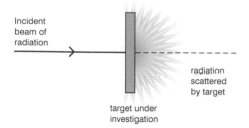

Incident
beam of
radiation

→

radiation
scattered
by target

target under
investigation

Fig 12.9 *Probing the atom*

Rutherford's α-scattering investigations showed how a beam of radiation can be used to probe the structure of matter. Since then, beams of different types of radiation have been used to probe matter at deeper and deeper levels inside the atom, to investigate the properties of different nuclides and to find out how atoms are arranged in different substances. In each of these investigations, a beam of a certain type of radiation is used to investigate structure on a scale far too small to see using an optical microscope.

Before considering different types of investigations, here are some key points about all these investigations.

1   The radiation consists of either matter particles (e.g. alpha particles, electrons, neutrons, etc.) or photons (e.g. X-rays).

2   The structures range from molecules (of the order of nanometres or more in size) and atoms (of the order of a nanometre or less) individually or in crystals, to nuclei (of the order of femtometres (10^{-15} m)).

3   The smaller the structure to be investigated, the higher the energy of the particles or photons needed to investigate it. The radiation is diffracted or scattered by the structure under investigation. For diffraction to be measurable, the wavelength of the radiation must be of the same order as the dimensions of the structures under investigation. For example, diffraction of electromagnetic radiation by a slit can be demonstrated using microwaves or using light. See Essential AS Physics, section 10.3 if necessary. However, the width of the slit in a microwave demonstration needs to be about the same as the wavelength of the microwaves used, which is of the order of centimetres. In comparison, to observe diffraction with light, the width of the slit needs to be much smaller than for the microwave demonstration because the wavelength of light is much less than the wavelength of microwaves. The smaller the structure, the shorter the wavelength of the radiation needed and, therefore, the higher the energy of the radiation particles or photons needed. Remember from your AS course that:

- the wavelength of a photon, $\lambda = \dfrac{c}{f}$ where f is its frequency and c is the speed of light in a vacuum. As the energy of a photon, $E = hf$, where h is the Planck constant, $\lambda = \dfrac{hc}{E}$

- the wavelength of a matter particle, $\lambda = \dfrac{h}{mv}$, in accordance with de Broglie's equation, where m is the mass of the particle and v is its speed.

4   In the case of α-scattering by nuclei, scattering is due to the electrostatic repulsion by the nucleus. The electrostatic force field of each nucleus prevents low-energy α-particles from approaching the nucleus close enough for diffraction to be significant. Electrons in a high-energy beam are also used to probe the nucleus because the de Broglie wavelength of a high-energy electron is of the order of the size of the nucleus so diffraction by the nucleus is significant.

12.3.1   X-ray diffraction and its use to probe crystal structure

When X-rays with a single precise wavelength are directed in a narrow beam at a single crystal, X-rays emerge from the crystal in certain directions only. A photographic film behind the crystal can record the directions of the emergent

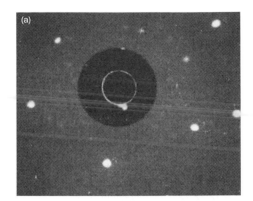

beams. The X-rays are diffracted by the layers of atoms in the crystal. This effect was discovered by Max Von Laue in 1912 and developed by William and Lawrence Bragg. The techniques were used about 50 years ago to unravel the structure of complicated molecules such as DNA and RNA which carry the genetic code in every living cell.

X-rays are electromagnetic waves with wavelengths less than about 1 nm. An optical diffraction grating consists of many regularly spaced parallel slits close together and is used to diffract a beam of monochromatic light in certain directions only. For each such direction, light diffracted by each slit is reinforced by light diffracted by adjacent slits. However, an optical diffraction grating would not diffract X-rays because its line spacing is much greater than the wavelength range of X-rays. The atoms in a crystal are regularly arranged in a lattice. The spacing between the atoms is of the same order of magnitude as the wavelength of X-rays. So a crystal with its regularly arranged atomic planes *does* diffract X-rays because it acts like a grating.

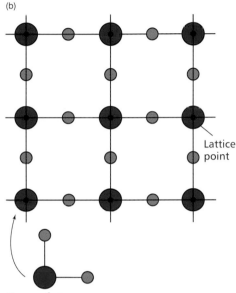

- Each plane of atoms in the crystal reflects some of the incident X-rays weakly as a result of the interaction between the electrons in each atom and the incident X-rays.
- The reflected beams from parallel planes of atoms reinforce each other at certain angles of incidence only. So, strong reflections occur in certain directions only. At all other angles, the reflected beams are not in phase and cancel each other out.
- By measuring the angle of diffraction of each beam, the arrangement and spacing of the atoms in the crystal can be worked out.

Note William Bragg showed that reinforcement occurs at angles θ between the incident beam and parallel planes of atoms given by the equation $m\lambda = 2d \sin \theta$. This is because the path difference between reflections at adjacent layers = $2d \sin \theta$. For reinforcement, this path difference must equal a whole number (m) of wavelengths. This equation is not required in the A2 specification.

X-ray diffraction by metals occurs because a metal has a crystalline structure. The atoms in each tiny crystal (referred to as a 'grain') in a metal are arranged the same but each arrangement is in a different direction. The layers of atoms at certain angles to the incident beam cause reinforcement. Because the grains are aligned at random to each other, each diffracted order of X-rays forms a cone, as shown in Figure 12.11. The half angle of each cone is 2θ, where θ is given by the Bragg equation. By measuring θ, the wavelength of the X-rays can be measured if distance d is known (using a crystal of known spacing) or distance d can be calculated if the wavelength is known.

Fig 12.10
(a) X-ray diffraction by a single crystal
(b) Atoms in a crystal

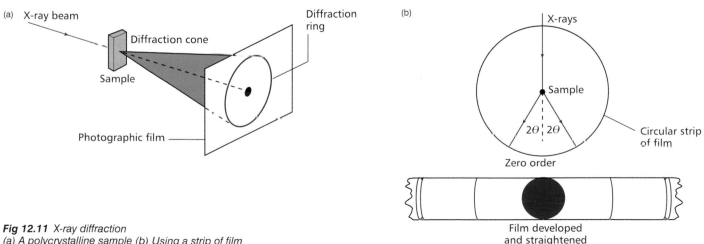

Fig 12.11 X-ray diffraction
(a) A polycrystalline sample (b) Using a strip of film

Energy from the nucleus

12.4.1 Energy and mass

In 1905, Einstein published the theory of special relativity in which he showed that moving clocks run slower than stationary clocks, fast-moving objects appear shorter than when stationary, the mass of a moving object changes with its speed and no material object can travel as fast as light. He also showed that the mass, m, of an object changes when it gains or loses energy E in accordance with the equation

$$E = mc^2, \text{ where } c \text{ is the speed of light in free space.}$$

The significance of this equation is that the mass of any object increases if it gains energy and decreases if it loses energy. For example:

- A sealed torch that radiates 10 W of light for 100 hours ($= 36\ 000$ s) would lose 0.36 MJ of energy ($= 10$ W $\times 36\ 000$ s). Its mass would therefore decrease by 4.0×10^{-12} kg, an insignificant amount compared with the mass of the torch.
- An unstable nucleus that releases a 5 MeV γ-photon would lose 8.0×10^{-13} J of energy. Its mass would therefore decrease by 8.9×10^{-30} kg which is not an insignificant amount compared with the mass of a nucleus.

$E = mc^2$ applies to all energy changes of any object. These two examples show that such changes are important in nuclear reactions but are not usually significant otherwise. A century after Einstein published his theory, the reason why the mass of an object changes when energy is transferred to or from it is still not clearly understood. However, it is known that for every type of particle, there is a corresponding antiparticle with the same mass and opposite charge (if charged). The link between energy and mass is even more direct where particles and antiparticles interact. For example:

- when a particle and its corresponding antiparticle meet, they annihilate each other and 2 gamma (γ) photons are produced, each of energy mc^2 where m is the mass of the particle or antiparticle;
- a single γ-photon of energy in excess of $2mc^2$ can produce a particle and an antiparticle, each of mass m, in a process known as pair production.

12.4.2 The strong nuclear force

The nucleus of any atom is composed of neutrons and protons, the only exception being the hydrogen nucleus $^1_1$H which is a single proton. In heavier nuclei, the protons try to repel each other because they have the same charge as each other. Most nuclei are stable and do not burst apart. What holds them together? There must be an attractive force between any two protons or neutrons in the nucleus. This force, referred to as **the strong nuclear force**, is responsible for holding the nucleus together. For example, the stable isotope of lead $^{208}_{92}$Pb has 82 protons and 126 neutrons in each nucleus. The strong nuclear force holding them all together must be strong enough to withstand the electrostatic force of 82 protons repelling one another.

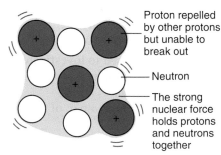

Proton repelled by other protons but unable to break out

Neutron

The strong nuclear force holds protons and neutrons together

Fig 12.16 *The strong nuclear force*

- The strength of the strong nuclear force can be estimated by working out the force of repulsion between two protons at a separation of 10^{-15} m, the approximate size of the nucleus. The strong nuclear force must be greater in magnitude than this force of repulsion. Prove for yourself, using Coulomb's law of force (see p. 68), that the force of repulsion between 2 protons at a separation of 10^{-15} m is of the order of 200 N. So the strong nuclear force is at least 200 N.

- The range of the strong nuclear force is no more than about 2 to 3×10^{-15} m. The diameter of a nucleus can be measured from high-energy electron scattering experiments (see p. 142). The results show that nucleons are evenly spaced at about 10^{-15} m in the nucleus and therefore the strong nuclear force acts only between nearest neighbour nucleons.
  (**Note** 1 femtometre (fm) = 10^{-15} m.)

- The energy needed to pull a nucleon out of the nucleus is of the order of millions of electron volts (MeVs). This can be deduced because the strong nuclear force is at least about 200 N and it acts over a distance of about 2–3×10^{-15} m. The work done by the strong nuclear force over this distance is therefore about 5×10^{-13} J ($= 200$ N $\times 2$–3×10^{-15} m) which is 3 MeV as 1 MeV $= 1.6 \times 10^{-13}$ J.

- The strong nuclear force between two nucleons must become repulsive at separations of about 0.5 fm or less, otherwise nucleons would pull each other closer and closer together and the nucleus would be much smaller than it is.

12.4.3 Binding energy

Suppose all the nucleons in a nucleus were separated from one another, removing each one from the nucleus in turn. Work must be done to overcome the strong nuclear force and separate each nucleon from the others. The potential energy of each nucleon is therefore increased when it is removed from the nucleus.

> **The binding energy of the nucleus is the work that must be done to separate a nucleus into its constituent neutrons and protons.**

When a nucleus **forms** from separate neutrons and protons, energy is released as the strong nuclear force does work pulling the nucleons together. The energy released is equal to the binding energy of the nucleus. Because energy is released when a nucleus forms from separate neutrons and protons, the mass of a nucleus is less than the mass of the separated nucleons.

> **The mass defect Δm of a nucleus is defined as the difference between the mass of the separated nucleons and the combined mass of the nucleus.**

- Calculation of the mass defect of a nucleus of known mass; a nucleus of an isotope $^{A}_{Z}X$ is composed of Z protons and $(A - Z)$ neutrons. Therefore, for a nucleus $^{A}_{Z}X$ of mass M_{NUC},

$$\text{its mass defect } \Delta m = Zm_{p} + (A - Z)\, m_{n} - M_{NUC}$$

where m_{p} is the mass of a proton and m_{n} is the mass of a neutron.

- Calculation of the binding energy of a nucleus; the mass defect Δm is due to energy released when the nucleus formed from separate neutrons and protons. The energy released in this process is equal to the binding energy of the nucleus. Therefore,

$$\text{the binding energy of a nucleus} = \Delta m\, c^{2}$$

Worked example
The mass of a nucleus of the bismuth isotope $^{212}_{83}Bi$ is 3.518×10^{-25} kg. Calculate the binding energy of this nucleus in MeV.

The mass of a proton, $m_{p} = 1.673 \times 10^{-27}$ kg; the mass of a neutron, $m_{n} = 1.675 \times 10^{-27}$ kg

The speed of light in free space, $c = 3.00 \times 10^{8}$ m s^{-1}

Solution

Mass defect $\Delta m = 83\, m_{\mathrm{p}} + (212 - 83)\, m_{\mathrm{n}} - M_{\mathrm{NUC}} = 3.13 \times 10^{-27}$ kg

$\therefore$ binding energy $= \Delta m\, c^2 = 2.821 \times 10^{-10}$ J

As 1 MeV $= 1.60 \times 10^{-13}$ J, the binding energy $= 1762$ MeV

Notes on mass

1 The mass of an atom of an isotope $^A_Z X$ is measured using a mass spectrometer. See p. 98. The mass of a nucleus can then be calculated by subtracting the mass of Z electrons from the atomic mass.

2 The unified atomic mass constant, 1 u $= 1.661 \times 10^{-27}$ kg. This is defined as $\frac{1}{12}$th of the mass of an atom of the carbon isotope $^{12}_{6}C$.

3 The energy corresponding to a mass of 1 u $= 1.661 \times 10^{-27} \times (3.00 \times 10^8)^2$ J $= 931.3$ MeV.

12.4.4 Nuclear stability

The binding energy of each nuclide is different. **The binding energy per nucleon** of a nucleus is the work done to remove a nucleon from a nucleus; it is therefore a measure of the stability of a nucleus. For example, the binding energy per nucleon of the $^{212}_{83}$Bi nucleus is 8.3 MeV per nucleon ($= 1762$ MeV/212 nucleons).

If the binding energies per nucleon of two different nuclides are compared, the nucleus with more binding energy per nucleon is the more stable of the two nuclei. Figure 12.17 shows a graph of the binding energy per nucleon v. mass number A for all the known nuclides. This graph is a curve which has a maximum value of 8.7 MeV per nucleon between $A = 50$ and $A = 60$. Nuclei with mass numbers in this range are the most stable nuclei. As explained below, energy is released in:

- **nuclear fission**, the process in which a large unstable nucleus splits into two fragments which are more stable than the original nucleus. The binding energy per nucleon increases in this process, as shown in Figure 12.17.

- **nuclear fusion**, the process of making small nuclei fuse together to form a larger nucleus. The product nucleus has more binding energy per nucleon than the smaller nuclei. So, the binding energy per nucleon also increases in this process, provided the nucleon number of the product nucleus is no greater than about 50.

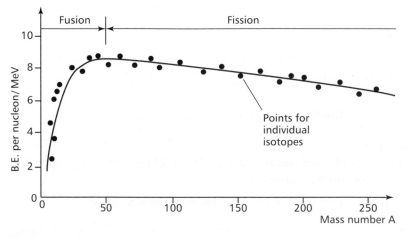

Fig 12.17 *Binding energy per nucleon for all known nuclides*

12.4.5 Nuclear fission

Fission of a nucleus occurs when a nucleus splits into two approximately equal fragments. This happens when the uranium isotope $^{235}_{92}U$ is bombarded with neutrons, a discovery made by Hahn and Strassmann in 1938. The process is known as **induced fission**. The plutonium isotope, $^{239}_{94}Pu$, is the only other isotope that is fissionable. This isotope is an artificial isotope formed by bombarding nuclei of the uranium isotope $^{238}_{92}U$ with neutrons.

Hahn and Strassmann knew that bombarding different elements with neutrons produces radioactive isotopes. Uranium is the heaviest of all the naturally occurring elements; scientists thought that neutron bombardment could turn uranium nuclei into even heavier nuclei. Hahn and Strassmann undertook the difficult work of analysing chemically the products of uranium after neutron bombardment to try to discover any new elements heavier than uranium. Instead, they discovered that many lighter elements such as barium were present after bombardment, even though the uranium was pure before. The conclusion could only be that uranium nuclei were split into two approximately equal fragment nuclei as a result of neutron bombardment.

Further investigations showed that each fission event releases energy and two or three neutrons.

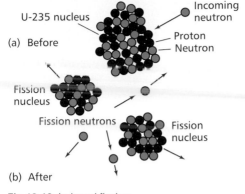

Fig 12.18 Induced fission

- **Fission neutrons**, the neutrons released in a fission event, are each capable of causing a further fission event as a result of a collision with another $^{235}_{92}U$ nucleus. A **chain reaction** is therefore possible in which fission neutrons produce further fission events which release fission neutrons and cause further fission events, and so on. If each fission event releases 2 neutrons on average, after n 'generations' of fission events, the number of fission neutrons would be 2^n. Prove for yourself that fission of 6×10^{23} $^{235}_{92}U$ nuclei (i.e. 235 g of the isotope) would happen in 79 generations. As explained below, each fission event releases about 200 MeV of energy. As each generation takes no more than a fraction of a second, a huge amount of energy is released in a very short time. Using the above figures, complete fission of 235 g of $^{235}_{92}U$ would release about 10^{13} J ($= 6.0 \times 10^{23} \times 200$ MeV). This is about a million times more than the energy released as a result of burning a similar mass of fossil fuel.

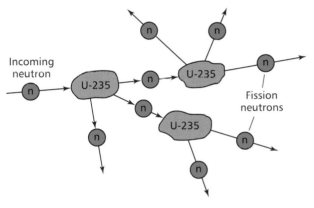

Fig 12.19 A chain reaction

- **Energy is released** when a fission event occurs because the fragments repel each other (as they are both positively charged) with sufficient force to overcome the strong nuclear force trying to hold them together. The fragment nuclei and the fission neutrons therefore gain kinetic energy. The two fragment nuclei are smaller and therefore more tightly bound than the original $^{235}_{92}U$ nucleus. In other words, they have more binding energy so they are more stable than the original nucleus. The energy released is equal to the change of binding energy. The binding energy of each nucleon increases from about 7.5 MeV to about 8.5 MeV as a result of the fission event. As there are about 200 nucleons in the original nucleus, the energy released in a fission event is of the order of 200 MeV ($= 200 \times$ about 1 MeV).

- Many fission products are possible when a fission event occurs. For example, the equation below shows a fission event in which a $^{235}_{92}U$ nucleus is split into a barium nucleus ($^{144}_{56}Ba$) and a krypton nucleus ($^{90}_{36}Kr$) and two neutrons are released.

$$^{235}_{92}U + {}^{1}_{0}n \rightarrow {}^{144}_{56}Ba + {}^{90}_{36}Kr + 2\,{}^{1}_{0}n + \text{energy released, } Q$$

- The energy released, Q, can be calculated using $E = mc^2$ in the form $Q = \Delta mc^2$, where Δm is the difference between the total mass before and after the event.

In the above equation, the mass difference $\Delta m = M_{\text{U-235}} - M_{\text{Ba-144}} - M_{\text{Kr-90}} - m_{\text{n}}$, where M represents the appropriate nuclear mass and m_{n} is the mass of the neutron.

Notes

1 For a chain reaction to occur, the mass of the fissile material (i.e. $^{235}_{92}\text{U}$ or $^{239}_{94}\text{Pu}$) must be greater than a minimum mass, referred to as the **critical mass**. This is because some fission neutrons escape from the fissile material without causing fission and some are absorbed by other nuclei without fission. If the mass of fissile material is less than the critical mass needed, too many of the fission neutrons escape because the surface area to mass ratio of the material is too high.

2 Natural uranium contains about 1% of uranium 235. The other 99% is uranium 238 which absorbs neutrons without fission. In a nuclear reactor, the fuel rods contain enriched uranium which contains about 2–3% uranium 235. The probability of fission is increased by slowing the fission neutrons down. This is achieved using a moderator. For a steady chain reaction, one fission neutron per fission event on average should go on to produce further fission. Control rods inserted in the reactor core are used to absorb surplus neutrons and so maintain a steady chain reaction in the reactor.

12.4.6 Nuclear fusion

Fusion takes place when two nuclei combine to form a bigger nucleus. The binding energy curve, Figure 12.17, shows that if two light nuclei are combined, the individual nucleons become more tightly bound together. The binding energy per nucleon of the product nucleus is greater than of the initial nuclei. In other words, the nucleons become even more trapped in the nucleus when fusion occurs. As a result, energy is released equal to the increase of binding energy.

Nuclear fusion can only take place if the two nuclei that are to be combined collide at high speed. This is necessary to overcome the electrostatic repulsion between the two nuclei so they can become close enough to interact through the strong nuclear force. Some examples of nuclear fusion reactions are given below:

1 The fusion of two protons produces a nucleus of deuterium, the hydrogen isotope ^2_1H and a positron ($^0_{+1}\beta$), the antiparticle corresponding to the electron (see p. 157).

$$^1_1\text{p} + ^1_1\text{p} \rightarrow ^2_1\text{H} + ^0_{+1}\beta + 0.4\,\text{MeV}$$

2 The fusion of a proton and a deuterium nucleus ^2_1H produces a nucleus of the helium isotope ^3_2He and 5.5 MeV of energy.

$$^2_1\text{H} + ^1_1\text{p} \rightarrow ^3_2\text{He} + 5.5\,\text{MeV}$$

3 The fusion of two nuclei of the helium isotope, ^3_2He, produces a nucleus of the helium isotope ^4_2He, two protons are released and 12.9 MeV of energy.

$$^3_2\text{He} + ^3_2\text{He} \rightarrow ^4_2\text{He} + 2^1_1\text{p} + 12.9\,\text{MeV}$$

In each case, the energy released in the reaction is calculated using $E = mc^2$ in the form $Q = \Delta mc^2$, where Δm is the difference between the total mass before and after the event.

Solar energy is produced as a result of fusion reactions inside the Sun. The temperature at the centre of the Sun is thought to be 10^8 K or more. At such temperatures, atoms are stripped of their electrons. Matter in this state is referred to as 'plasma'. The nuclei of the plasma move at very high speeds because of the enormous temperature. When two nuclei collide, they fuse together because they overcome the electrostatic repulsion due to their charge and approach each other closely enough to interact through the strong nuclear force. Protons (i.e. hydrogen nuclei) inside the Sun's core fuse together in stages

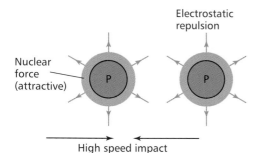

Electrostatic repulsion

Nuclear force (attractive)

High speed impact

Fig 12.20 *Fusion of two protons*

(corresponding to equations **1**, **2** and **3** above) to form helium $_2^4$He nuclei. For each helium nucleus formed, 25 MeV of energy is released. This corresponds to 7 MeV per proton, considerably more than the energy released per nucleon in a fission event.

Prototype fusion reactors such as JET, the Joint European Torus, in the United Kingdom have produced large amounts of power but only for short periods of time. This is achieved by fusing nuclei of deuterium $_1^2$H and tritium $_1^3$H to produce nuclei of the helium isotope $_2^4$He and neutrons, as below.

$$_1^2\text{H} + {}_1^3\text{H} \rightarrow {}_2^4\text{He} + {}_0^1\text{n} + 17.6\,\text{MeV}$$

The neutrons are absorbed by a 'blanket' of lithium surrounding the reactor vessel. The reaction between the neutrons and the lithium nuclei, as shown below, produces tritium which is then used in the main reaction. Deuterium occurs naturally in water as it forms 0.01% of naturally occurring hydrogen.

$$_3^6\text{Li} + {}_0^1\text{n} \rightarrow {}_2^4\text{He} + {}_1^3\text{H} + 4.8\,\text{MeV}$$

The plasma is contained in a doughnut-shaped steel container and is heated by passing a very large current through it. A magnetic field is used to confine the plasma so it does not touch the sides of its steel container, otherwise it would lose its energy. In theory, the energy released per second should be more than is needed to heat the plasma so the reactor ought to give a continuous output of power. However, at the present time, power can only be produced for a short time as the plasma becomes unstable at such high temperatures.

Fig 12.21 *The JET fusion reactor*

QUESTIONS

1 u is equivalent to 931.3 MeV

1 a Explain why the protons in a nucleus do not leave the nucleus even though they repel each other.

b Explain why the mass of a nucleus is less than the mass of the separated protons and neutrons from which the nucleus is composed.

2 a What is meant by nuclear fission?

b (i) Complete the equation below that represents a reaction that takes place when a neutron collides with a nucleus of the uranium isotope $_{92}^{235}$U.

$$_{92}^{235}\text{U} + {}_0^1\text{n} \rightarrow {}_{?}^{136}\text{Xe} + {}_{36}^{?}\text{Kr} + 2{}_0^1\text{n} + \text{energy released, } Q$$

   (ii) Calculate the energy, in MeV, released in this fission reaction.

   Mass of $_{92}^{235}$U nucleus = 234.992 u

   Mass of $_{?}^{136}$Xe nucleus = 135.877 u

   Mass of $_{36}^{?}$Kr nucleus = 97.886 u

   mass of neutron = 1.0087 u

   1 u is equivalent to 931.3 MeV

3 a What is meant by nuclear fusion?

b Hydrogen nuclei fuse together to form helium nuclei in the Sun. One stage in this process is represented by the following equation:

$$_1^2\text{H} + {}_1^1\text{p} \rightarrow {}_2^3\text{He} + Q$$

   (i) Describe the reaction that this equation represents.

   (ii) Calculate the energy released in this stage.
   The mass of the proton = 1.00728 u
   The mass of the $_1^2$H nucleus = 2.01355 u
   The mass of the $_2^3$He nucleus = 3.01493 u

4 a Explain why light nuclei do not fuse when they collide unless they are moving at a sufficiently high speed.

b Calculate the energy released in the following fusion reaction:

$$_1^3\text{H} + {}_1^2\text{H} \rightarrow {}_2^4\alpha + {}_0^1\text{n} + Q$$

Masses/u; neutron 1.00867, $_1^3$H nucleus 3.0155; $_1^2$H nucleus 2.01355; α-particle 4.00150

149

CHAPTER SUMMARY

Isotopes of an element are atoms which have the same number of protons in each nucleus but different numbers of neutrons.

A nuclide of an isotope $^A_Z X$ is a nucleus composed of Z protons and $(A - Z)$ neutrons, where Z is the proton number (and also the atomic number of element X) and A is the number of protons and neutrons in a nucleus.

Rutherford's α-particle scattering experiment demonstrated that every atom contains a positively charged nucleus which is much smaller than the atom and where all the positive charge and most of the mass of the atom is located.

Probing the atom

Beam	Target	Result	Cause
α-scattering	Atomic nucleus	Scattering decreases with angle of scatter, some α-particles rebound	Force of electrostatic repulsion between nucleus and α-particles
X-ray diffraction	Planes of atoms in a crystal, molecules	Strong diffraction in certain directions only	Weak reflections from planes of atoms reinforce one another in certain directions only
Neutron diffraction	Planes of atoms in a crystal, molecules, alloys, magnetic materials	Strong diffraction in certain directions only	
Low-energy electron diffraction	Planes of atoms in thin polycrystalline materials (e.g. metal foils), spacing between atoms	Strong diffraction in certain directions only	
High-energy electron scattering	Nuclear diameter, charge distribution in the nucleus	Intensity minimum at certain angles to direction of incident beam	Diffraction by the nucleus superimposed on Rutherford-type scattering

Energy from the nucleus

Strong nuclear force holds the nucleons together

Binding energy of a nucleus is the work that must be done to separate a nucleus into its constituent neutrons and protons.

Binding energy = mass defect $\times c^2$

Binding energy per nucleon is greatest for nuclei of mass number 57

Fission is the splitting of a $^{235}_{92} U$ nucleus or a $^{239}_{94} Pu$ nucleus into two approximately equal fragments. Induced fission is fission caused by an incoming neutron colliding with a $^{235}_{92} U$ nucleus or a $^{239}_{94} Pu$ nucleus.

Fusion is the fusing together of light nuclei to form a heavier nucleus.

$c = 3.00 \times 10^8 \, \mathrm{m \, s^{-1}}$, $e = 1.60 \times 10^{-19} \, \mathrm{C}$,
$h = 6.63 \times 10^{-34} \, \mathrm{J \, s}$, $1 \, \mathrm{u} = 1.66 \times 10^{-27} \, \mathrm{kg} = 931.3 \, \mathrm{MeV}$

1 A beam of α-particles was directed at normal incidence towards a thin metal foil. A detector was used to measure the number of α-particles per second scattered by different angles.

  a Explain why:
    (i) most α-particles passed through the metal foil with little or no deflection,
    (ii) some α-particles were scattered through very large angles.

  b The figure below shows the path of two α-particles moving at the same speed in the same direction as they approached a nucleus of an atom. Copy the diagram and complete the paths of these particles.

2 An α-particle collided head-on with a nucleus, as shown below.

  a Describe and explain how the kinetic energy of the α-particle changed as it approached then moved away from the nucleus.

  b (i) Discuss the factors that determine how closely the α-particle can approach the nucleus.
    (ii) Explain why an α-particle with more kinetic energy on such a track might not rebound from the nucleus.

3 **a** Explain what is meant by the binding energy of a nucleus.

  b Calculate the binding energy per nucleon, in MeV, of:
    (i) an α-particle,
    (ii) a deuterium $^2_1$H nucleus.

Masses: neutron = 1.00866 u, proton = 1.00728 u,
$^2_1$H nucleus = 2.01355 u, α-particle = 4.00150 u

  c Discuss why an α-particle does not break up into two $^2_1$H nuclei.

4 **a** Describe how the size of the nucleus is investigated using a beam of high-energy electrons.

  b Why is it necessary in **a** that the electrons in the beam should have:
    (i) the same kinetic energy,
    (ii) sufficiently high kinetic energy?

5 **a** A beam of X-rays from an X-ray tube is directed at a single crystal, as shown below.

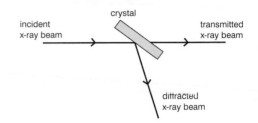

    (i) Explain why X-rays are diffracted by the crystal in certain directions only.
    (ii) Explain why the X-rays diffracted in a certain direction consist of photons with the same energy whereas the X-rays from the X-ray tube consist of photons with a continuous spread of energies.

  b The structure of a crystal can be investigated using a beam of X-ray photons of the same energy or using a beam of monoenergetic neutrons.
    (i) State one advantage of using X-rays and one advantage of using neutrons.
    (ii) Calculate the kinetic energy of a neutron that has the same wavelength as a photon of energy 6.5 keV. The mass of a neutron = 1.67×10^{-27} kg.

6 **a** In a nuclear reaction, a neutron collided with a nucleus of the lithium isotope $^6_3$Li. A tritium nucleus $^3_1$H and another nucleus X was formed as a result.

  Write down an equation that represents this reaction and identify the nucleus X.

  b The mass loss in the above reaction was 0.00514 u.
    (i) Calculate the energy released, in J, in this reaction.
    (ii) Calculate the mass of X, given the masses of the other nuclei are as follows: $^3_1$H 3.0155 u, $^6_3$Li 6.01348 u, neutron 1.00866 u

7 **a** (i) State two properties of the strong nuclear force.
    (ii) Explain why energy is released when a $^{235}_{92}$U nucleus undergoes induced fission.

  b (i) Copy and complete the induced fission equation below:
$$^{235}_{92}\mathrm{U} + {}^1_0\mathrm{n} \rightarrow {}^{140}_{?}\mathrm{Xe} + {}^{93}_{38}\mathrm{Sr} + ? \, {}^1_0\mathrm{n}$$
    (ii) Calculate the energy released, in J, in the above reaction.

Masses: $^{235}_{92}$U 235.0430 u, $^1_0$n 1.00866 u,
$^{140}_{?}$Xe 139.9216 u, $^{93}_{38}$Sr 92.9140 u

13 Radioactivity

13.1 The properties of α, β and γ radiation

Fig 13.2 *Marie Curie (1867–1934)*

Marie Curie established the nature of radioactive materials. She showed how radioactive compounds could be separated and identified. She and her husband Pierre won the 1903 Nobel Prize for their discovery of two new elements, polonium and radium. After Pierre's death in 1906 she continued her painstaking research and was awarded a second Nobel Prize in 1911 – an unprecedented honour.

13.1.1 The discovery of radioactivity

In 1896, Henri Becquerel was investigating materials that glow when placed in an X-ray beam. He wanted to find out if strong sunlight could make uranium salts glow. He prepared a sample and placed it in a drawer on a wrapped photographic plate, ready to test the salts on the next sunny day. When he developed the film, he was amazed to see the image of a key. He had put the key on the plate in the drawer and then put the uranium salts on top of the key. He realised that uranium salts emit radiation which can penetrate paper and blacken a photographic film. The uranium salts were described as being radioactive. The task of investigating radioactivity was passed on by Becquerel to one of his students, Marie Curie. Within a few years, Marie Curie discovered other elements which are radioactive. One of these elements, radium, was found to be over a million times more radioactive than uranium.

Photographic plate

Fig 13.1 *Becquerel's key*

13.1.2 Rutherford's investigations into radioactivity

Rutherford wanted to find out what the radiation emitted by radioactive substances was and what caused it. He found that the radiation:

- Ionised air, making it conduct electricity. He made a detector which could measure the radiation from its ionising effect.

- Was of two types. One type which he called **alpha** (α) radiation was easily absorbed. The other type which he called **beta** (β) radiation was more penetrating. A third type of radiation, called **gamma** (γ) radiation, even more penetrating than β radiation, was discovered a year later.

Further tests showed that a magnetic field deflects α and β radiation in opposite directions and has no effect on γ radiation. From the deflection direction, it was concluded that α radiation consists of positively charged particles and β radiation consists of negatively charged particles. γ radiation was later shown to consist of high-energy photons.

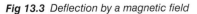

Fig 13.3 *Deflection by a magnetic field*

Magnetic field into diagram

Beam of radioactive particles

α (+charged)

γ (uncharged)

β (–charged)

1 Ionisation

The ionising effect of each type of radiation can be investigated using an ionisation chamber and a picoammeter, as shown in Figure 13.4. The chamber contains air at atmospheric pressure. Ions created in the chamber are attracted to the oppositely charged electrode where they are discharged. Electrons pass through the picoammeter as a result of ionisation in the chamber. The current is proportional to the number of ions per second created in the chamber.

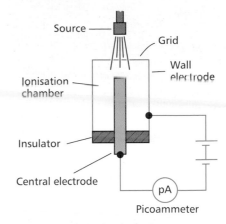

Fig 13.4 Investigating ionisation

- α radiation causes strong ionisation. However, if the source is moved away from the top of the chamber, ionisation ceases beyond a certain distance. This is because α radiation has a range in air of no more than a few centimetres.

- β radiation has a much weaker ionising effect than air. Its range in air varies up to a metre or more. A β-particle, therefore, produces fewer ions per millimetre along its path than an α-particle does.

- γ radiation has a much weaker ionising effect than either α or β radiation. This is because photons carry no charge so they have less effect than α- or β-particles do.

2 Cloud chamber observations

A cloud chamber contains air saturated with a vapour at a very low temperature. Due to ionisation of the air, an α- or a β-particle passing through the cloud chamber leaves a visible track of minute condensed vapour droplets. This is because the air space is supersaturated. When an ionising particle passes through the supersaturated vapour, the ions produced trigger the formation of droplets.

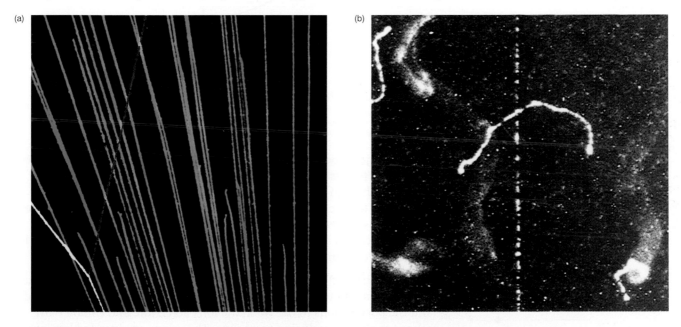

Fig 13.5 Cloud chamber photographs (a) α-particle tracks (b) β-particle tracks

- α-particles produce straight tracks that radiate from the source and are easily visible. The tracks from a given isotope are all of the same length, indicating that the α-particles have the same range.

- β-particles produce wispy tracks that are easily deflected as a result of collisions with air molecules. The tracks are not as easy to see as α-particle tracks because β-particles are less ionising than α-particles.

3 Absorption tests

Figure 13.6 shows how a Geiger tube and a counter may be used to investigate absorption by different materials. Each particle of radiation that enters the tube is registered by the counter as a single count. The number of counts in a given

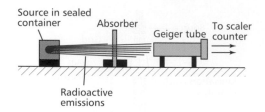

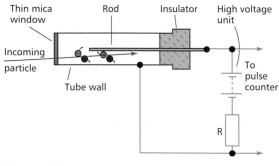

Fig 13.6 *Investigating absorption*

time is measured and used to work out the count rate which is the number of counts divided by the time taken. Before the source is tested, the count rate due to background radioactivity must be measured. This is the count rate without the source present.

- The count rate is then measured with the source at a fixed distance from the tube without any absorber present. The background count rate is then subtracted from the count rate with the source present to give the **corrected (i.e. true) count rate** from the source.
- The count rate is then measured with the absorber in a fixed position between the source and the tube. The corrected count rates with and without the absorber present can then be compared.

By using absorbers of different thicknesses of the same material, the effect of the absorber thickness can be investigated. Figure 13.7 shows a typical set of measurements for the absorption of β radiation by aluminium.

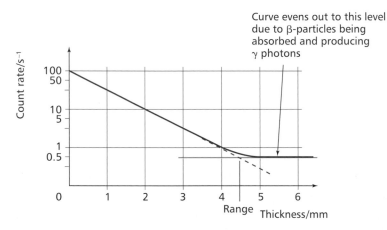

Fig 13.7 *Count rate v. absorber thickness*

4 The Geiger tube

The Geiger tube is a sealed metal tube that contains argon gas at low pressure. The thin mica window at the end of the tube allows α- and β-particles to enter the tube. γ-photons can enter the tube through the tube wall as well. A metal rod down the middle of the tube is at a positive potential as shown in Figure 13.8. The tube wall is connected to the negative terminal of the power supply and is earthed.

When a particle of ionising radiation enters the tube, the particle ionises the gas atoms along its track. The negative ions are attracted to the rod and the positive ions to the wall. The ions accelerate and collide with other gas atoms, producing more ions. These ions produce further ions in the same way so that within a very short time, many ions are created and discharged at the electrodes. A pulse of charge passes round the circuit through resistor R, causing a voltage pulse across R which is recorded as a single count by the pulse counter.

Fig 13.8 *A Geiger tube*

The **dead time** of the tube, the time taken to regain its non-conducting state after an ionising particle enters it, is typically of the order of 0.2 ms. Another particle that enters the tube in this time will not cause a voltage pulse. Therefore, the count rate should be no greater than about 5000 s^{-1} ($= \frac{1}{0.2\,\text{ms}}$)

5 Range in air

The arrangement in Figure 13.6 without the absorbers may be used to investigate the range of each type of radiation in air. The count rate is measured for different distances between the source and the tube, starting with the source close to the tube. The background count rate must also be measured in the absence of the source so the corrected count rate can be calculated for each distance.

- α radiation has a range of several centimetres in air. The count rate decreases sharply once the tube is beyond the range of the α-particles. This can be seen in Figure 13.5 as the tracks from the source are the same length indicating that the particles from a given source have the same range and, therefore, the same initial kinetic energy. The range differs from one source to another indicating that the initial kinetic energy differs from one source to another.

- β radiation has a range in air of up to a metre or so. The count rate gradually decreases with increasing distance until it is the same as the background count rate at a distance of about 1 metre. The reason for the gradual decrease of count rate as the distance increases is that the β-particles from any given source have a range of initial kinetic energies up to a maximum. Faster β-particles travel further in air than slower β-particles as they have greater initial kinetic energy.

- γ radiation has an unlimited range in air. The count rate gradually decreases with increasing distance because the radiation spreads out in all directions so the proportion of the γ-photons from the source entering the tube decreases.

Note The number of γ-photons per second entering the tube when it is at distance r from the source is proportional to $\dfrac{1}{r^2}$. This is because all the photons emitted from the source are spread over a total area of $4\pi r^2$ (the surface area of a sphere of radius r) at the tube. If the tube area facing the radiation is A, the proportion of photons entering the tube from the source is $\dfrac{A}{4\pi r^2}$. So, the number of photons per second entering the tube is proportional to $\dfrac{1}{r^2}$.

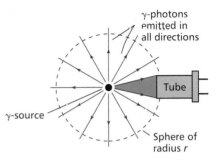

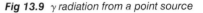

Fig 13.9 γ radiation from a point source

QUESTIONS

1 A beam of radiation from a radioactive substance passes through paper and is then stopped by an aluminium plate of thickness 5 mm.

   a What type of particles are in this beam?

   b Describe a further test you could do to check your answer in **a**.

2 a (i) What type of radioactivity was responsible for the image of the key seen by Becquerel in the effect described on p. 152?
   (ii) Explain why an image of the key was produced on the photographic plate.

   b Which type of radiation from a radioactive source is:
   (i) least ionising, (ii) most ionising?

   c When an α emitting source above an ionisation chamber grid was moved gradually away from the grid, the ionisation current suddenly dropped to zero. Explain why the current suddenly dropped to zero.

3 In an absorption test as shown in Figure 13.5 using a β-emitting source and a Geiger counter, a count rate of 8.2 counts per second was obtained without the absorber present and a count rate of 3.7 counts per second was obtained with the absorber present. The background count rate was 0.4 counts per second. What percentage of the β-particles hitting the absorber:

   a pass through it,

   b are stopped by the absorber?

4 In an investigation to find out the type of radiation emitted by a radioactive source, a Geiger tube was placed near the source and its count rate was significantly more than the background count rate. When an aluminium plate was placed between the source and the tube, the count rate was reduced but it was still significantly more than the background count rate.

   a What can be concluded from these observations?

   b When the distance from the source to the tube was doubled with the aluminium plate still present, the corrected count rate decreased to about 25%. What conclusion can be drawn from this observation?

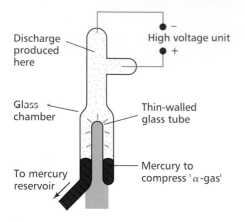

Discharge produced here

High voltage unit

Glass chamber

Thin-walled glass tube

To mercury reservoir

Mercury to compress 'α-gas'

Fig 13.10 *Identifying α-particles*

13.2.1 The nature of α, β and γ radiation

Alpha radiation consists of positively charged particles. Each α-particle is composed of two protons and two neutrons, the same as the nucleus of a helium atom. Rutherford devised an experiment in which α-particles were collected as a gas in a glass tube fitted with two electrodes. When a voltage was applied to the electrodes, the gas conducted electricity and emitted light. Using a spectrometer, he proved that the spectrum of light from the tube was the same as from a tube filled with helium gas.

Rutherford made the discovery that neutralised α-particles are the same as helium some years before his discovery that every atom contains a nucleus. After he established the nuclear model of the atom, it was realised that the nucleus of the hydrogen atom, the lightest known atom, was a single positively charged particle which became known as the **proton**. Rutherford realised that other nuclei contain protons and he predicted the existence of neutral particles of similar mass, **neutrons**, in the nucleus. For example, the helium nucleus carries twice the charge of the hydrogen nucleus and therefore contains two protons. However, its mass is four times the mass of the hydrogen nucleus so Rutherford predicted that it contained two neutrons as well as two protons. The existence of the neutron was established in 1932 by James Chadwick, one of Rutherford's former students (see p. 136).

β radiation consists of fast-moving electrons. This was proved by measuring the deflection of a beam of β-particles using electric and magnetic fields. The measurements were used to work out the specific charge (which is the charge/mass) of the particles. This was shown to be the same as the specific charge of the electron. An electron is created and emitted from a nucleus with too many neutrons as a result of a neutron suddenly changing into a proton.

A nucleus with too many protons is also unstable and emits a **positron**, the antiparticle of the electron, when a proton changes to a neutron. Such unstable nuclei are not present in naturally occurring radioactive substances. They are created when high-energy protons collide with nuclei. The theory that for every type of particle, there is a corresponding antiparticle was put forward by Paul Dirac in 1928. The first antiparticle to be discovered, the positron, was discovered by Carl Anderson four years later (see p. 144).

γ radiation consists of photons with a wavelength of the order of a fraction of a nanometre or less. This discovery was made by using a crystal to diffract a beam of γ radiation in a similar way to the diffraction of light by a diffraction grating.

13.2.2 The equations for radioactive change

A nuclide $^A_Z X$ contains Z protons and $A - Z$ neutrons. In terms of:

- the magnitude of the charge of an electron, e, its charge $= Z$,
- atomic mass units, u, its mass $= A$ approximately.

Note The mass of a proton is 1.00728 u and the mass of a neutron is 1.00866 u, where $1\text{ u} = \frac{1}{12}$ of the mass of a $^{12}_6 C$ atom.

1 α-emission
An α-particle is represented by the symbol $^4_2\alpha$ as its charge $= +2e$ so $Z = 2$ and it consists of 2 neutrons and 2 protons so $A = 4$.

When a nucleus $_Z^A X$ emits an α-particle, it loses two protons and two neutrons. Therefore, its proton number (Z) is reduced by 2 and its mass number (A) is reduced by 4.

$$_Z^A X \rightarrow {}_2^4\alpha + {}_{Z-2}^{A-4}Y$$

2 β^--emission

A negative β-particle (i.e. electron) is represented by the symbol $_{-1}^{0}\beta$ as its charge $= -e$ and it is not a neutron or a proton.

When a nucleus $_Z^A X$ emits a negative β-particle (i.e. an electron), a neutron in the nucleus changes into a proton. Therefore, the proton number of the nucleus increases by 1 and the mass number is unchanged. An uncharged particle called an antineutrino (symbol $\bar{\nu}$) is also emitted.

$$_Z^A X \rightarrow {}_{-1}^{0}\beta + {}_{Z+1}^{A}Y + \bar{\nu}$$

3 β^+-emission

A positive β-particle (i.e. positron) is represented by the symbol $_{+1}^{0}\beta$ as its charge $= +e$ and it is not a neutron or a proton.

When a nucleus $_Z^A X$ emits a positive β-particle (i.e. a positron), a proton in the nucleus changes into a neutron. Therefore, the proton number of the nucleus decreases by 1 and the mass number is unchanged. An uncharged particle called a neutrino (symbol ν) is also emitted.

$$_Z^A X \rightarrow {}_{+1}^{0}\beta + {}_{Z-1}^{A}Y + \nu$$

4 γ-emission

No change occurs in the number of protons or neutrons of a nucleus when it emits a γ-photon.

A γ-photon is emitted if a nucleus has excess energy after it has emitted an α- or a β-particle.

Note the positron and the decay equation for positron emission is not part of the specification for this module and is discussed here as background material.

QUESTIONS

1 Copy and complete each of the following equations representing α-emission.

a $_{92}^{238}U \rightarrow {}_{90}Th +$

b $_{90}Th \rightarrow {}_{88}^{224}Ra +$

2 Copy and complete each of the following equations representing β-emission

a $_{29}^{64}Cu \rightarrow {}_{30}Zn + {}^{0}\beta$

b $_{15}P \rightarrow {}^{32}S + {}_{-1}^{0}\beta$

3 The bismuth isotope $_{83}^{213}Bi$ decays by emitting a β^--particle to form an unstable isotope of polonium (Po) which then decays by emitting an α-particle to form an unstable isotope of lead (Pb). This isotope then decays by emitting a β^--particle to form a stable isotope of bismuth.

a Write down the symbol for each of the three product nuclides in this sequence.

b Write down the number of protons and the number of neutrons in a nucleus of:
   (i) the bismuth isotope $_{83}^{213}Bi$,
   (ii) the stable bismuth isotope.

4 A point source of γ radiation is placed 200 mm from the end of a Geiger tube. The corrected count rate was measured at 12.7 counts per second. Calculate:

a the corrected count rate if the source was moved to a distance of 400 mm from the tube,

b the distance between the source and the tube for a corrected count rate of 20 counts per second.

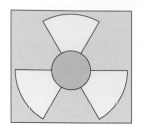

Fig 13.11 *A radioactive warning sign*

13.3.1 The hazards of ionising radiation

Ionising radiation is hazardous because it damages living cells. Ionising radiation is any form of radiation that creates ions in substances it passes through. Such radiation includes X-rays, protons and neutrons as well as α, β and γ radiation. Ionising radiation affects living cells because:

- it can destroy cell membranes which causes cells to die, or
- it can damage vital molecules such as DNA directly or indirectly by creating 'free radical' ions which react with vital molecules. Normal cell division is affected and nuclei become damaged. Damaged DNA can cause cells to divide and grow uncontrollably, causing a tumour which may be cancerous. Damaged DNA in a sex cell (i.e. an egg or a sperm) can cause a mutation which might be passed on to future generations.

As a result of exposure to ionising radiation, living cells die or grow uncontrollably or mutate, affecting the health of the affected person (somatic effects) and possibly affecting future generations (genetic effects). High doses of ionising radiation kill living cells. Cell mutation and cancerous growth occur at low doses as well as at high doses. There is no evidence of the existence of a threshold level of ionising radiation below which living cells would not be damaged.

13.3.2 Radiation monitoring

Anyone using equipment that produces ionising radiation must wear a film badge to monitor his or her exposure to ionising radiation. The badge contains a strip of photographic film in a light-proof wrapper. Different areas of the wrapper are covered by absorbers of different materials and different thicknesses. When the film is developed, the amount of exposure to each form of ionising radiation can be estimated from the blackening of the film. If the badge is overexposed, the wearer is not allowed to continue working with the equipment.

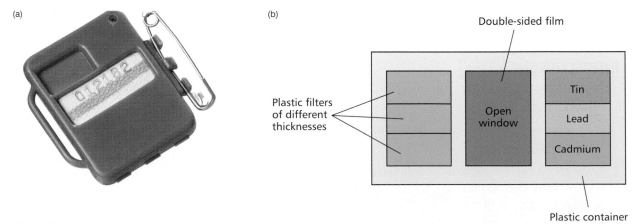

Fig 13.12 *(a) A film badge (b) Inside a film badge*

The biological effect of ionising radiation depends on the dose received and the type of radiation. The dose is measured in terms of the energy absorbed per unit mass of matter from the radiation. The same dose of different types of ionising radiation has different effects. For example, α radiation produces far more ions per millimetre than γ radiation in the same substance so it is far more damaging.

For any dose of ionising radiation, its dose equivalent, measured in sieverts (Sv), is the dose due to 250 kV X-rays that would have the same effect. For example, 1 millisievert of α radiation has the same biological effect as 10 millisieverts of 250 kV X-rays.

- **Maximum permissible exposure limits** are recommended safety limits for the annual dose equivalent which a radiation worker should not exceed. The recommended limit is 15 mSv per year, although the average dose due to occupation is much lower at 2 mSv per year. This is based on the death rates of survivors of the atomic bombs dropped on Hiroshima and Nagasaki which is estimated at 3 deaths per 100 000 survivors for each millisievert of radiation. Thus, the risk of death to a radiation worker exposed to 2 mSv per year for 5 years would be 3 in 10 000.

- **Background radioactivity** occurs naturally due to cosmic radiation and from radioactive materials in rocks, soil and in the air. Everyone is exposed to background radioactivity which does vary with location due to local geological features. In addition, radon gas which is radioactive can accumulate in poorly ventilated areas of buildings in such locations. Figure 13.13 shows the sources of background radioactivity in the UK.

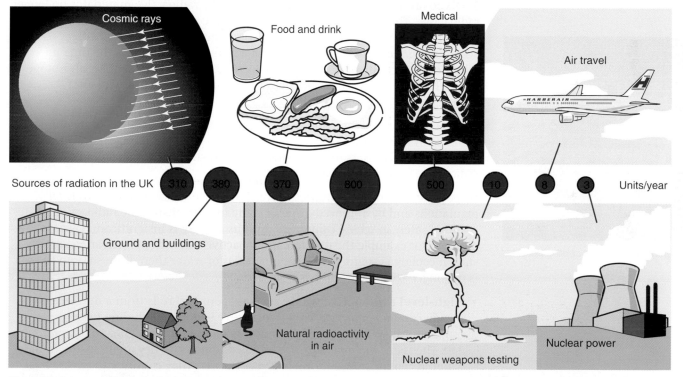

Fig 13.13 *Sources of background radioactivity in the UK*

The unit is the microsievert, a measure of the effect of radioactivity on cells

13.3.3 Safe use of radioactive materials

Because radioactive materials produce ionising radiation, they must be stored and used with care. In addition, disposal of a radioactive substance must be done in accordance with specific regulations. Only approved institutions are allowed to use radioactive materials. Approval is subject to regular checks and approved institutions are categorised according to purpose.

1 Storage of radioactive materials should be in lead-lined containers. Most radioactive sources produce γ radiation as well as α or β radiation so the lead lining of a container must be thick enough to absorb all the γ radiation from the sources in the container. In addition, regulations require that the containers are under 'lock and key' and a record of the sources is kept.

2 When using radioactive materials, established rules and regulations must be followed. No source should be allowed to come into contact with the skin.

- Solid sources should be transferred using handling tools such as tongs or a glove-box or using robots. The handling tools ensure the material is as far from the user as practicable so the intensity of the γ radiation from the source at the user is as low as possible and the user is beyond the range of α or β radiation from the source.
- Liquid and gas sources and solids in powder form should be in sealed containers. This is to ensure radioactive gas cannot be breathed in and radioactive liquid cannot be splashed on the skin or drunk.

Note A typical radioactive source used in a school might produce of the order of 10^5 radioactive particles per second, each typically of energy of the order of MeV. Show for yourself that the energy transfer per second from such a source is of the order of 10^{-8} J s^{-1}. In 15 minutes or so, the source would transfer 10^{-5} J to its surroundings. If this amount of energy were to be absorbed by about 10 kg of living tissue, the dose would be about 10^{-6} Sv ($=1\ \mu$Sv) which is not insignificant.

3 Disposal requires long-term storage until the radioactive material is no longer radioactive. The key aim is to ensure that people and the environment are not put at risk. As explained in the next section, radioactive half-lives differ according to the isotope. The half-life of a radioactive isotope is the time it takes for the activity of the isotope to decrease to half. For example, an isotope with a half-life of 5 years would decay to 0.1% of its initial activity after 50 years.

Radioactive waste is categorised according to its activity as high- or medium- or low-level waste. Most high-level radioactive waste is from nuclear power stations or from specialist users in universities and industry, or from hospitals that use radioactive isotopes for diagnosis or therapy.

Disposal of any form of radioactive waste must be in accordance with legal regulations and by approved disposal companies to ensure the radioactive waste is stored safely in secure containers until its activity is insignificant. Disposal by dilution, for example the dilution of radioactive water from nuclear power station cooling systems with large quantities of water then dispersal into the sea, is no longer acceptable and has been banned.

Fig 13.14 Spent fuel rods in a cooling pond

- **High-level radioactive waste** such as spent fuel rods from a nuclear power station contains many different radioactive isotopes, including fission fragments as well as unused uranium-235 and uranium-238 and plutonium-239. The spent fuel rods must be handled remotely. They are first stored under water in cooling ponds for up to a year because they continue to release heat due to radioactive decay. The unused uranium and plutonium is then removed and stored in sealed containers for further possible use. The radioactive waste is stored in sealed containers in deep trenches or in underground caverns which are geologically stable. Such waste must be stored safely for centuries as it contains long-lived radioactive isotopes which must be prevented from contaminating food and water supplies. The long-term safe storage of high-level radioactive waste remains a major issue in Britain because no one wants such storage in their own locality, nor do people want radioactive waste to be carried through their own locality to storage facilities elsewhere. At present, radioactive waste from Britain's nuclear power stations is stored and reprocessed at Sellafield in Cumbria.
- **Intermediate-level waste** such as the radioactive materials with low activity and containers of radioactive materials are sealed in drums that are encased in concrete and stored in specially constructed buildings with walls of reinforced concrete.

• **Low-level waste** such as laboratory equipment and protective clothing is sealed in metal drums and buried in large trenches.

Fig 13.15 *Burial of low-level waste*

QUESTIONS

1 a What is meant by ionisation?

b Explain why a source of α radiation is not as dangerous as a source of β radiation provided the sources are outside the body.

2 a Discuss the reasons why ionising radiation is hazardous to a person exposed to the radiation.

b (i) What is the purpose of a film badge worn by a radiation worker?

(ii) With the aid of a diagram, describe what is in a film badge and how the film badge is tested.

3 a Explain why a radioactive source should be:

(i) kept in a lead-lined storage box when not in use,

(ii) transferred using a pair of tongs with long handles.

b Discuss the precautions you would take when carrying out an experiment using a source of γ radiation.

4 a Why is it necessary for radioactive waste from spent fuel rods to be stored securely and safely for many centuries?

b Outline how high-level radioactive waste can be stored securely and safely until it is no longer radioactive.

Radioactive decay

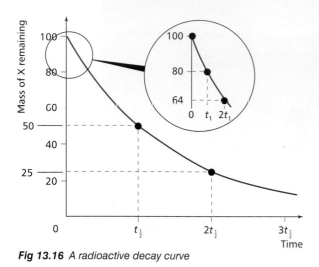

Fig 13.16 *A radioactive decay curve*

13.4.1 Half-life

When a nucleus of a radioactive isotope emits an α-or a β-particle, it becomes a nucleus of a different isotope because its proton number changes. The number of nuclei of the initial radioactive isotope therefore decreases. The mass of the initial isotope decreases gradually as the number of nuclei of the isotope decreases. Figure 13.16 shows how the mass decreases with time. The curve is referred to as a decay curve. The mass of the isotope decreases at a slower and slower rate. Measurements show that the mass decreases exponentially which means that the mass drops by a constant factor (e.g. $\times 0.8$) in equal intervals of time. For example, if the initial mass of the radioactive isotope is 100 g and the mass decreases by a factor of $\times 0.8$ every 1000 seconds, then:

- after 1000 s, the mass remaining = 80 g ($= 0.8 \times 100$ g),
- after 2000 s, the mass remaining = 64 g ($= 0.8 \times 0.8 \times 100$ g),
- after 3000 s, the mass remaining = 51 g ($= 0.8 \times 0.8 \times 0.8 \times 100$ g).

A convenient measure for the rate of decrease is the time taken for a decrease by half. This is the half-life of the process.

> **The half-life, $t_{\frac{1}{2}}$, of a radioactive isotope is the time taken for the mass of the isotope to decrease to half the initial mass**.

This is the same as the time taken for the number of nuclei of the isotope to decrease to half the initial number.

Consider a sample of a radioactive isotope X which initially contains 100 g of the isotope.

- After 1 half-life, the mass of X remaining = $0.5 \times 100 = 50$ grams
- After 2 half-lives from the start, the mass of X remaining = $0.5^2 \times 100$
  = 25 grams
- After 3 half-lives from the start, the mass of X remaining = $0.5^3 \times 100$
  = 12.5 grams
- After n half-lives from the start, the mass of X remaining = $0.5^n\, m_0$, where m_0 = the initial mass

The mass of X decreases exponentially. This is because radioactive decay is a **random** process and the number of nuclei that decay in a certain time is in proportion to the number of nuclei of X remaining. To understand this idea, consider a game of dice where there are 1000 dice, each representing a nucleus of X. The throw of a dice is a random process in which each face has an equal chance of being uppermost.

- 1st throw; when the dice are all thrown, you would expect $\frac{1}{6}$ of the dice to show the same figure on the upper surface. Let all the dice that show '1' uppermost represent nuclei that have disintegrated, an expected total of 167 ($= \frac{1000}{6}$). If these are removed, then 833 dice remain.
- 2nd throw; the remaining dice are thrown to give $\frac{1}{6}$ of 833 as the expected number of '1' s. So 694 dice ($= 833 - \frac{833}{6}$) remain.
- 3rd throw; the remaining dice are thrown to give $\frac{1}{6}$ of 694 as the expected number of '1' s. So 578 dice ($= 694 - \frac{694}{6}$) remain.
- 4th throw; the remaining dice are thrown to give $\frac{1}{6}$ of 578 as the expected number of '1' s. So 482 dice ($= 578 - \frac{578}{6}$) remain.

The analysis shows that 4 throws are needed to reduce the number of dice to less than half the initial number. Prove for yourself that a further 4 throws would reduce the number of dice to 25% of the initial number. Figure 13.17 shows how the number of dice remaining decreases with time. The curve has the same shape as Figure 13.16. The half-life of the process is 3.8 'throws'.

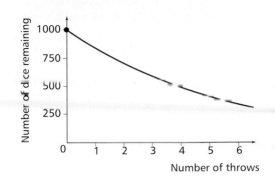

Fig 13.17 *Exponential decrease*

Reminder about molar mass and the Avogadro constant
As explained on page 127 for an element with a mass number A,

* its molar mass M is its mass number in grams,
* one mole of the element contains N_A atoms where N_A is the Avogadro constant,
* mass m of the element contains $\left(\dfrac{m}{M}\right) N_A$ atoms.

13.4.2 Activity

The activity A of a radioactive isotope is the number of nuclei of the isotope that disintegrate per second. In other words, it is the rate of change of the number of nuclei of the isotope. The unit of activity is the **becquerel (Bq)**, where 1 Bq = 1 disintegration per second.

The activity of a radioactive isotope is proportional to the mass of the isotope. Because the mass of a radioactive isotope decreases with time due to radioactive decay, the activity decreases with time. Figure 13.18 shows an experiment in which the activity of a radioactive isotope of protoactinium $^{234}_{91}$Pa is measured and recorded using a Geiger tube and a counter. This isotope is a β-emitter produced by the decay of the radioactive isotope of thorium $^{234}_{90}$Th. In this experiment, an organic solvent in a sealed bottle is used to separate protoactinium from thorium to enable the activity of the protoactinium to be monitored.

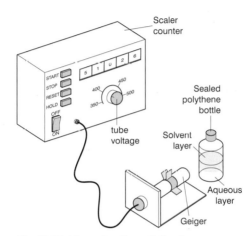

Fig 13.18 *Measuring the activity of protoactinium*

Before the experiment is carried out, the background count rate is measured without the bottle present. The bottle is then shaken to mix the aqueous and solvent layers and then placed near the end of the Geiger tube. The layers are allowed to separate as shown in Figure 13.18. The protoactinium is collected by the solvent and the thorium by the aqueous layer. The Geiger tube detects β-particles emitted by the decay of the protoactinium nuclei in the solvent layer.

The counter is used to measure the number of counts every 10 seconds. The count rate is the number of counts in each ten-second interval divided by 10 s. The background count rate is subtracted to give the corrected count rate. Since the activity is proportional to the corrected count rate, a graph of the corrected count rate against time, as in Figure 13.19, shows how the activity of the protoactinium decreases with time.

13.4.3 Activity and power

For a radioactive source of activity A that emits particles (or photons) of the same energy E, the energy per second released by radioactive decay in the source by the radiation is the product of its activity and the energy of each particle. In other words, the power of the source = AE.

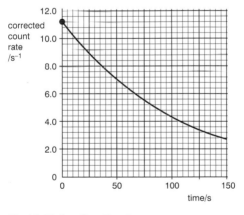

Fig 13.19 *A radioactive decay curve*

> **The energy transfer per second from a radioactive source = AE**

If the source is in a sealed container and emits only α-particles which are all absorbed by the container, the container gains thermal energy from the absorbed radiation equal to the energy transferred from the source. For example, for a source that has an activity of 30 MBq and emits particles of energy 2.5 MeV, the energy transfer per second from the source is given by

$$30 \times 10^6 \text{ Bq} \times 2.5 \text{ MeV} = 7.5 \times 10^7 \text{ MeV s}^{-1} = 1.2 \times 10^{-5} \text{ J s}^{-1}.$$

QUESTIONS

$N_A = 6.02 \times 10^{23}$ mol^{-1}, 1 MeV = 1.6×10^{-13} J

1 Figure 13.20 shows how the mass of a certain radioactive isotope decreases with time. Use the graph to work out:

a the half-life of this isotope,

b the mass of the isotope remaining after 120 s.

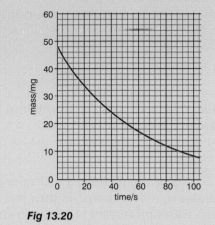

Fig 13.20

2 A freshly prepared sample of a radioactive isotope X contains 1.8×10^{15} atoms of the isotope. The half-life of the isotope is 8.0 hours. Calculate:

a the number of atoms of this isotope remaining after:
   (i) 8 hours,
   (ii) 24 hours.

b the number of atoms of X that would have decayed after:
   (i) 8 hours,
   (ii) 24 hours.

c the energy transfer from the sample in 24 hours if the isotope emits α-particles of energy 5 MeV.

3 $^{131}_{53}$I is a radioactive isotope of iodine which has a half-life of 8.0 days. A sample of this isotope has an initial activity of 38 kBq. Calculate the activity of this sample:

a 8.0 days later,

b 32 days later.

4 $^{137}_{55}$Cs is a radioactive isotope of caesium which has a half-life of 35 years. A sample of this isotope has a mass of 1.0×10^{-3} kg.

a Calculate the number of atoms in 1.0×10^{-3} kg of this isotope.

b Calculate the number of atoms of the isotope remaining in the sample after 70 years.

The theory of radioactive decay

13.5.1 The random nature of radioactive decay

An unstable nucleus becomes stable by emitting an α- or a β-particle or a γ-photon. This is an unpredictable event. Every nucleus of a radioactive isotope has an equal probability of becoming stable in any given time interval. Therefore, for a large number of nuclei of a radioactive isotope, the number of nuclei that disintegrate in a certain time interval depends only on the total number of nuclei present. The same idea was considered in the dice experiment. The greater the number of dice used, the more likely it is that 1 in every 6 dice show a particular number on the upper face.

Consider a sample of a radioactive isotope X that initially contains N_0 nuclei of the isotope.

Let N represent the number of nuclei of X remaining at time t after the start.

Suppose in time Δt, the number of nuclei that disintegrate is ΔN.

Because radioactive disintegration is a random process, ΔN is proportional to:

1 N, the number of nuclei of X remaining at time t,

2 the duration of the time interval Δt.

Therefore, $\Delta N = -\lambda N \Delta t$, where λ is a constant referred to as the **decay constant**. The minus sign is necessary because ΔN is a decrease.

So, the rate of disintegration, $\dfrac{\Delta N}{\Delta t} = -\lambda N$

For a given radioactive isotope, its activity is the rate of disintegration $\dfrac{\Delta N}{\Delta t}$

Therefore, the activity A of N atoms of a radioactive isotope is given by

$$A = \lambda N$$

The solution of the equation $\dfrac{\Delta N}{\Delta t} = -\lambda N$ is $N = N_0 e^{-\lambda t}$

where e^x is the exponential function. See 14.4.

Figure 13.21 shows that a graph of N against t gives a decay curve. The number of nuclei N decreases exponentially with time. In other words,

Fig 13.21 $N = N_0 e^{-\lambda t}$

- in one half-life, the remaining number of nuclei $N_1 = 0.5\,N_0$
- in two half-lives, the remaining number of nuclei $N_2 = 0.25\,N_0$
- in n half-lives, the remaining number of nuclei $N = 0.5^n\,N_0$

The graph of the number of nuclei N against time t as represented by the equation $N = N_0\,e^{-\lambda t}$ is shown in Figure 13.21 above. It is a curve with exactly the same shape as Figure 13.16.

The mass, m, of a radioactive isotope decreases from initial mass, m_0, in accordance with the equation $m = m_0 e^{-\lambda t}$ because the mass, m, is proportional to the number of nuclei, N, of the isotope.

The activity, A, of a sample of N nuclei of an isotope decays in accordance with the equation

$$A = A_0 e^{-\lambda t}$$

This is because the activity, A = the magnitude of the number of disintegrations per second = λN. Hence, $A = \lambda N_0 e^{-\lambda t} = A_0 e^{-\lambda t}$ where $A_0 = \lambda N_0$.

The **count rate, C**, due to a sample of a radioactive isotope at a fixed distance from a Geiger tube is proportional to the activity of the source. Therefore, the count rate decreases with time in accordance with the equation $C = C_0 e^{-\lambda t}$, where C_0 is the count rate at time $t = 0$.

The above equations for the number of nuclei, N, the activity, A, and the count rate, C, are all of the same general form, namely $x = x_0 e^{-\lambda t}$, where x represents N or A or C and x_0 represents the initial value.

Notes The following notes are not part of the A2 specification and are provided to help students gain a deeper understanding of the topic.

1 The exponential function appears in any situation where the rate of change of a quantity is in proportion to the quantity itself. This is because the rate of change of each term in the function sequence is equal to the previous term in the sequence.

2 The exponential function, $e^x = 1 + x + \dfrac{x^2}{2!} + \dfrac{x^3}{3!} + \dots$ (See 14.4.)

Differentiating e^x with respect to x gives e^x $\left(\text{i.e. } \dfrac{d(e^x)}{dx} = e^x\right)$ because

differentiating each term in the expression for e^x gives the previous term.

The exponential function is indicated on a calculator as 'exp' or 'e^x' or 'inv ln'. (See 14.3.)

3 The natural logarithm function, $\ln x$, is the inverse exponential function. In other words, if $y = e^x$, then $\ln y = x$. Therefore, $N = N_0 e^{-\lambda t}$ may be written $\ln N = \ln N_0 - \lambda t$.

The graph of $\ln N$ against t is therefore a straight line with
- a gradient $= -\lambda$, and
- a y-intercept $= \ln N_0$.

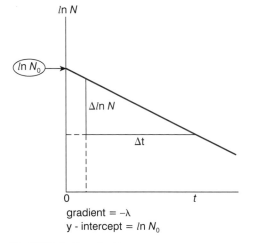

gradient = –λ
y - intercept = ln N₀

Fig 13.22 ln N against t

4 The exponential decrease formula is also used in the theory of capacitor discharge. (See 7.4.)

Worked example

A sample of a radioactive isotope initially contains 1.2×10^{20} atoms of the isotope. The decay constant for the isotope is 3.6×10^{-3} s^{-1}. Calculate:

a the number of atoms of the isotope remaining after 1000 s,

b the activity of the sample after 1000 s.

Solution

a $N_0 = 1.2 \times 10^{20}$, $\lambda = 3.6 \times 10^{-3}$ s^{-1}, $t = 1000$ s,

$\lambda t = 3.6 \times 10^{-3}$ s$^{-1} \times 1000$ s $= 3.6$

$\therefore N = N_0 e^{-\lambda t} = 1.2 \times 10^{20} e^{-3.6} = 1.2 \times 10^{20} \times 2.7 \times 10^{-2} = 3.2 \times 10^{18}$

b Activity, $A = \lambda N = 3.6 \times 10^{-3} \times 3.2 \times 10^{18} = 1.2 \times 10^{16}$ Bq

13.5.2 The decay constant

The decay constant λ is the probability of an individual nucleus decaying per second. If there are 10 000 nuclei present and 300 decay in 20 seconds, the

decay constant is 0.0015 s^{-1} $\left(= \dfrac{\left(\frac{300}{10\,000}\right)}{20 \text{ s}}\right)$.

In general, if the change of the number of nuclei ΔN in time Δt is given by

$\Delta N = -\lambda N \Delta t$, then, the probability of decay, $\dfrac{\Delta N}{N} = \lambda \Delta t$ (the minus sign is not needed here as reference is made to decay).

So, the probability per unit time $= \dfrac{\frac{\Delta N}{N}}{\Delta t} = \lambda$

As explained on p. 165, the **half-life**, $t_{\frac{1}{2}}$, of a radioactive isotope is the time taken for half the initial number of nuclei to decay. The longer the half-life, the smaller the decay constant because the probability of decay per second is smaller.

The half-life $t_{\frac{1}{2}}$ is related to the decay constant λ according to the equation

$$t_{\frac{1}{2}} = \frac{\ln 2}{\lambda}$$

As $\ln 2 = 0.693$, this equation may be written as $t_{\frac{1}{2}} = \dfrac{0.693}{\lambda}$

13.5.3 Proof of $t_{\frac{1}{2}} = \dfrac{\ln 2}{\lambda}$

The proof of this equation is not part of the A2 specification. It is provided below to help students develop a better understanding of the topic.

Let the number of nuclei $N = N_0$ at time $t = 0$, so at time $t = t_{\frac{1}{2}}$, $N = 0.5\,N_0$

Inserting $t = t_{\frac{1}{2}}$, $N = 0.5\,N_0$ into $N = N_0 e^{-\lambda t}$ gives $0.5\,N_0 = N_0 e^{-\lambda t_{\frac{1}{2}}}$

Cancelling N_0 and taking the natural logarithm (ln) of each side gives $\ln 0.5 = -\lambda t_{\frac{1}{2}}$

Because $\ln 0.5 = -\ln 2$, then $\ln 2 = \lambda t_{\frac{1}{2}}$.

Rearranging this equation gives $t_{\frac{1}{2}} = \dfrac{\ln 2}{\lambda}$

Note To calculate N at time t, given values of N_0 and $t_{\frac{1}{2}}$,

- **either** calculate λ using $\lambda = \dfrac{\ln 2}{t_{\frac{1}{2}}}$ then use the equation $N = N_0 e^{-\lambda t}$,

- **or** calculate the number of half-lives, n, using $n = \dfrac{t}{t_{\frac{1}{2}}}$ then use $N = 0.5^n N_0$

QUESTIONS

$N_A = 6.02 \times 10^{23}\ \text{mol}^{-1}$, $1\ \text{MeV} = 1.6 \times 10^{-13}\ \text{J}$

1 $^{131}_{53}\text{I}$ is a radioactive isotope of iodine which has a half-life of 8.0 days. A fresh sample of this isotope contains 4.2×10^{16} atoms of isotope. Calculate:

a the decay constant of this isotope,

b the number of atoms of this isotope remaining after 24 hours.

2 A radioactive isotope has a half-life of 35 years. A fresh sample of this isotope has an activity of 25 kBq. Calculate:

a the decay constant in s^{-1},

b the activity of the sample after 10 years.

3 a Calculate the number of atoms present in 1.0 kg of $^{226}_{88}\text{Ra}$.

b The isotope $^{226}_{88}\text{Ra}$ has a half-life of 1620 years. For an initial mass of 1.0 kg of this isotope, calculate:
   (i) the mass of this isotope remaining after 1000 years,
   (ii) how many atoms of the isotope will remain after 1000 years.

4 A fresh sample of a radioactive isotope has an initial activity of 40 kBq. After 48 hours, its activity has decreased to 32 kBq. Calculate:

a the decay constant of this isotope,

b its half-life.

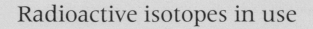

13.6 Radioactive isotopes in use

Radioactive isotopes are used for many purposes. The choice of an isotope for a particular purpose depends on its half-life and on the type of radiation it emits. For some uses, the choice also depends on how the isotope is obtained and on whether or not it produces a stable decay product. The following examples are intended to provide a wider awareness of important uses of radioactive substances and to set contexts in which knowledge and understanding of radioactivity is developed further.

13.6.1 Radioactive tracers

A radioactive tracer is used to follow the path of a substance through a system, as illustrated below.

Fig 13.23 *Using tracers*

- **Environmental uses**; for example, the detection of leaks in underground pipes that carry water or oil. Such a leak can be detected by injecting a radioactive tracer into the flow. Geiger tubes on the surface above the pipeline can then be used to detect leakage. The radioactive isotope used should have a half-life short enough so it decays quickly after use and long enough so the test can be completed before its activity becomes too low. In addition, it should be a β-emitter as α-radiation would be absorbed by the pipes and γ radiation would pass through the pipes without absorption.

- **Geological uses**; for example, to improve the recovery of oil from an underground reservoir. Water containing a radioactive tracer is injected into an oil reservoir at high pressure, forcing some of the oil out. Detectors at the production wells monitor breakthrough of the radioactive isotope. The results are used to build up a model of the reservoir to improve and control recovery. Because the time from injection to breakthrough can be many months, the tracer must have a suitably long half-life. A suitable tracer is 'tritiated' water ^3H_2O, a β-emitter with a half-life of 12 years.

- **Medical uses**; for example, to monitor the uptake of iodine by the thyroid gland. The thyroid gland absorbs iodine to maintain its function of producing a hormone. The rate of uptake is measured by giving the patient a solution containing sodium iodide which includes a small quantity of the radioactive isotope of iodine, $^{131}_{53}I$, which is a β-emitter with a half-life of 8 days. The activity of the patient's thyroid and the activity of an identical sample prepared at the same time are measured 24 hours later. The percentage uptake by the patient is then calculated from (the corrected count rate of the thyroid/the corrected count rate of the identical solution) $\times$ 100%. A normal thyroid has a percentage uptake of 20–50% after 24 hours.

- **Agricultural research**; for example, to investigate the uptake of fertilisers by plants. This can be done by using a fertiliser which contains the radioactive isotope of phosphorus, $^{32}_{15}P$, which is a β-emitter with a half-life of 14 days. By measuring the radioactivity of the leaves, the amount of fertiliser reaching them can be determined.

13.6.2 Radioactive dating

- **Carbon dating**; living plants and trees contain a small percentage of the radioactive isotope of carbon, $^{14}_6C$, which is formed in the atmosphere as a result of cosmic rays knocking out neutrons from nuclei. These neutrons then collide with nitrogen nuclei to form carbon-14 nuclei.

$$^1_0n + {}^{14}_7N \rightarrow {}^{14}_6C + {}^1_1p$$

Carbon dioxide from the atmosphere is taken up by living plants as a result of photosynthesis. So a small percentage of the carbon content of any plant is carbon-14. This isotope has a half-life of 5570 years so there is negligible decay during the life-time of a plant. Once a tree has died, no further carbon is taken in so the proportion of carbon-14 in the dead tree decreases as the carbon-14 nuclei decay. Because activity is proportional to the number of atoms still to decay, measuring the activity of the dead sample enables its age to be calculated, provided the activity of the same mass of living wood is known.

Worked example

A certain sample of dead wood is found to have an activity of 0.28 Bq. An equal mass of living wood is found to have an activity of 1.3 Bq. Calclulate the age of the sample.

The half-life of carbon-14 is 5570 years.

Solution

The half-life, $t_{\frac{1}{2}}$, in seconds $= 5570 \times 365 \times 24 \times 3600 \text{ s} = 1.76 \times 10^{11} \text{ s}$

$\therefore$ the decay constant of carbon-14, $\lambda = \dfrac{0.693}{t_{\frac{1}{2}}} = \dfrac{0.693}{1.76 \times 10^{11}} = 3.95 \times 10^{-12} \text{ s}^{-1}$

Using activity $A = A_0 e^{-\lambda t}$ where $A = 0.28$ Bq and $A_0 = 1.30$ Bq gives

$$0.28 = 1.3 e^{-\lambda t} \quad \text{so} \quad e^{-\lambda t} = \left(\dfrac{0.28}{1.30}\right) = 0.215$$

$$\therefore \quad \lambda t = 1.535$$

$$t = \dfrac{1.535}{\lambda} = \dfrac{1.535}{3.95 \times 10^{-12} \text{ s}} = 3.88 \times 10^{11} \text{ s} = 12\,300 \text{ years}$$

Note A useful check is to estimate the number of half-lives needed for the activity to decrease from 1.30 Bq to 0.28 Bq. You should find that just over 2 half-lives are needed, corresponding to about 11 000 years.

• **Argon dating**; ancient rocks contain trapped argon gas as a result of the decay of the radioactive isotope of potassium, $^{40}_{19}\text{K}$ into the argon isotope $^{40}_{18}\text{Ar}$. This happens when its nucleus captures an inner shell electron. As a result, a proton in the nucleus changes into a neutron and a neutrino is emitted. The equation for the change is

$$^{40}_{19}\text{K} + \,^{0}_{-1}\text{e} \rightarrow \,^{40}_{18}\text{Ar} + \nu$$

The potassium isotope $^{40}_{19}\text{K}$ also decays by β-emission to form the calcium isotope $^{40}_{20}\text{Ca}$. This process is 8 times more probable than electron capture.

$$^{40}_{19}\text{K} \rightarrow \,^{0}_{-1}\beta + \,^{40}_{20}\text{Ca} + \bar{\nu}$$

The effective half-life of the decay of $^{40}_{19}\text{K}$ is 1250 million years. The age of the rock (i.e. the time from when it solidified) can be calculated by measuring the proportion of argon-40 to potassium-40. For every n potassium-40 atoms now present, if there is 1 argon-40 atom present, there must have been originally $n + 9$ potassium atoms. (i.e. 1 that decayed into argon-40 + 8 that decayed into calcium-40 + n remaining). The radioactive decay equation $N = N_0 e^{-\lambda t}$ can then be used to find the age of the sample. For example, suppose for every 4 potassium-40 atoms now present, a certain rock now has 1 argon-40 atom. Therefore, $N = 4$ and $N_0 = 13$. Substituting these values into the equation $N = N_0 e^{-\lambda t}$ gives $4 = 13 e^{-\lambda t}$.

Therefore, $e^{-\lambda t} = \dfrac{4}{13} = 0.308$ which gives $t = \dfrac{-\ln 0.308}{\lambda}$. Substituting $\dfrac{0.693}{t_{\frac{1}{2}}}$ for λ into this equation gives $t = \left(\dfrac{-\ln 0.308}{0.693}\right) t_{\frac{1}{2}} = 1.70\, t_{\frac{1}{2}}$. The age of the sample is therefore 2120 million years.

Note A useful check is to estimate the number of half-lives needed for N to decrease from 13 to 4. You should find that between 1 and 2 half-lives are needed, corresponding to an age of between 1250 and 2500 million years.

Fig 13.24 *Measuring engine wear*

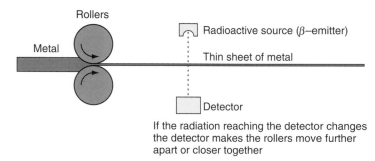

Fig 13.25 *The manufacture of metal foil*

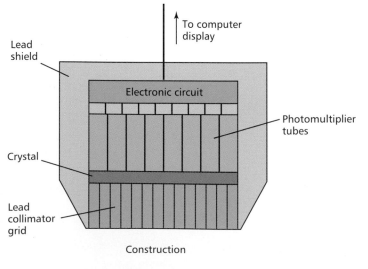

Fig 13.26 *The gamma camera*

13.6.3 Industrial uses

The examples below are just two of a wide range of applications of radioactivity in industry.

- **Engine wear**
  The rate of wear of a piston ring in an engine can be measured by fitting a ring that is radioactive. As the ring slides along the piston compartment, radioactive atoms transfer from the ring to the engine oil. By measuring the radioactivity of the oil, the mass of radioactive metal transferred from the ring can be determined and the rate of wear calculated. A metal ring can be made radioactive by exposing it to neutron radiation in a nuclear reactor. Each nucleus that absorbs a neutron becomes unstable and disintegrates by β-emission.

- **Thickness monitoring**
  Metal foil is manufactured by using rollers to squeeze plate metal on a continuous production line. A detector measures the amount of radiation passing through the foil. If the foil is too thick, the detector reading drops. A signal from the detector is fed back to the control system to make the rollers move closer together and so make the foil thinner. The source used is a β-emitter with a long half-life. α radiation would be absorbed completely by the foil and γ radiation would pass straight through without absorption.

- **Power for remote devices** such as satellites and weather sensors can be obtained using a radioactive isotope in a thermally insulated sealed container which absorbs all the radiation emitted by the isotope. A thermocouple attached to the container produces electricity as a result of the container becoming warm through absorbing radiation. For mass, m, of the isotope, its activity, $A = \lambda N$ where N is the number of radioactive atoms present in mass m. If each disintegration of a nucleus releases energy E, the energy transfer per second from the source $= \lambda NE$. The source needs to have a reasonably long half-life so it does not need to be replaced frequently but a very long half-life would require too much mass to generate the necessary power.

13.6.4 Medical and health uses

As explained earlier, radioactive isotopes are used as medical tracers. Further uses of radioactive isotopes in medicine include the gamma camera used to form images of joints and organs, the PET scanner and gamma therapy to destroy cancerous tissues.

- **The gamma camera** is designed to detect γ radiation from sites inside the body where a γ-emitting isotope is located. For example, bone deposits can be located using a phosphate tracer containing the radioactive isotope of technetium, $^{99}_{52}\text{Te}$ which is a γ-emitter that has a half-life of 6 hours.

The γ-photons from inside the body are absorbed by a lead collimator grid unless they travel parallel to narrow channels through the collimator. Each γ-photon that passes through the grid strikes a large sodium iodide crystal, causing a flash of light which is detected by a photomultiplier tube in an array of tubes. The tubes are connected to a computer which displays an image of the γ-emitting sources in the body.

- **Gamma therapy** is used to destroy tumours inside the body. A narrow beam of γ radiation from the radioactive isotope of cobalt, $^{60}_{27}$Co, is directed at the tumour from different directions by moving the source or by moving the patient. This movement is necessary to ensure healthy tissue in the path of the beam is exposed much less than the target tissue. The cobalt-60 source has a half-life of 5.3 years and emits γ-photons of energies 1.17 MeV and 1.33 MeV. The source is enclosed in a thick lead container. When the source is to be used, it is rotated to the inner end of an exit channel so that a beam of γ radiation emerges after passing along the exit channel. When the source is not in use, it is rotated away from the inner end of the exit channel so no γ radiation can emerge from the container.

- **Food preservation** can be achieved by irradiating food with γ radiation. About 20% of the world's food is lost through spoilage. The major cause is bacteria, moulds and yeast which grow on food. Some bacteria produce toxic waste products that cause food poisoning. Irradiation of food with γ radiation kills 99% of the disease-carrying organisms in the food, such as *Salmonella* which infects poultry and *Clostridium*, the cause of botulism. The treatment is not suitable for all foods. Red meat turns brown and develops an unpleasant taste, eggs develop a smell and tomatoes go soft.

QUESTIONS

$N_A = 6.02 \times 10^{23}$ mol^{-1}, 1 MeV = 1.6×10^{-13} J

1 **a** Explain why living wood is slightly radioactive.

b A sample of ancient wood of mass 0.5 g is found to have an activity of 0.11 Bq. A sample of living wood of the same mass has an activity of 0.13 Bq. Calculate the age of the sample of wood.

The half-life of radioactive carbon $^{14}_{6}$C is 5570 years.

2 The radioactive isotope of iodine, $^{131}_{53}$I, is used for medical diagnosis of the kidneys. The isotope has a half-life of 8 days. A sample of the isotope is given to a patient in a glass of water. The passage of the isotope through each kidney is then monitored using two detectors outside the body. The isotope is required to have an activity of 800 kBq at the time it is given to the patient.

a Calculate:
  (i) the activity of the sample 24 hours after it was given to the patient,
  (ii) the activity of the sample when it was prepared 24 hours earlier,
  (iii) the mass of $^{131}_{53}$I in the sample when it was prepared.

b The reading from the detector near one of the patient's kidneys rises then falls. The reading from the other detector which is near the other kidney rises and does not fall. Discuss the conclusions that can be drawn from these observations.

3 **a** (i) In the manufacture of metal foil, describe how the thickness of the foil is monitored using a radioactive source and a detector.
  (ii) Explain why the source needs to be a β-emitter, not an α-emitter or a γ-emitter.

b (i) Explain why a cobalt-60 source used for γ-therapy is enclosed in a thick lead lined container.
  (ii) Explain why a beam of γ radiation used to destroy a tumour inside a patient is directed at the tumour from different directions during treatment.

4 **a** A cardiac pacemaker is a device used to ensure that a faulty heart beats at a suitable rate. The required electrical energy in one type of pacemaker is obtained from the energy released by a radioactive isotope. The radiation is absorbed inside the pacemaker. As a result, the absorbing material gains thermal energy and heats a thermocouple attached to the absorbing material. The voltage from the thermocouple provides the source of electrical energy for the pacemaker.
  (i) Discuss whether the radioactive source should be an α-emitter or a β-emitter or a γ-emitter.
  (ii) The radioactive source needs to have a reasonably long half-life, otherwise it would need to be replaced frequently. Discuss the disadvantages of using a radioactive source with a very long half-life.

b The energy source for a remote weather station is the radioactive isotope of strontium, $^{90}_{38}$Sr which has a half-life of 28 years. It emits β-particles of energy 0.40 MeV. For a mass of 10 g of this isotope, calculate:
  (i) its activity,
  (ii) the energy released per second.

Trigonometry

14.1.1 The radian

The radian (rad) is a unit used to express or measure angles. It is defined such that

$$2\pi \text{ radians} = 360°$$

When using a calculator to work out sines, cosines, tangents or the corresponding inverse functions, always check that the calculator is in the correct 'angle' mode. This is usually indicated on the display by 'deg' for degrees or 'rad' for radians. Your calculations will be incorrect if you work in one mode when you should be working in the other mode. For example, check for yourself that $\sin 30° = 0.5$ whereas $\sin 30 \text{ rad} = -0.988$. You also need to know how to change from one mode to the other; read your calculator manual or ask your teacher if you can't do this.

14.1.2 Arcs and segments

Consider an arc of length s on the circumference of a circle of radius r, as shown in Figure 14.1. The angle θ, in degrees, subtended by the arc to the centre of the circle is given by the equation

$$\theta/\text{degrees} = \left(\frac{s}{2\pi r}\right) \times 360$$

Applying this conversion factor to the above equation for θ gives

$$\theta/\text{radians} = \frac{s}{r}$$

Rearranging this equation gives

the arc length $s = r\theta$, where θ is the angle subtended in radians.

Note that for $s = r$, $\theta = 1$ rad $\left(= \dfrac{360}{2\pi} = 57.3°\right)$

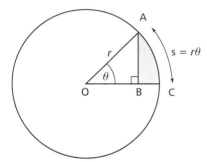

Fig 14.1 *Arcs and segments*

14.1.3 The small angle approximation

For angle θ less than about 10°,

$$\sin\theta \approx \tan\theta \approx \theta \text{ in radians, and}$$
$$\cos\theta \approx 1$$

To explain these approximations, consider Figure 14.1 again. If angle θ is sufficiently small, then the segment OAC will be almost the same as triangle OAB, as shown in Figure 14.2.

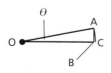

Fig 14.2 *The small angle approximation*

- AB $\approx$ arc length s so $\sin\theta = \dfrac{AB}{OA} \approx \dfrac{s}{r} = \theta$ in radians. $\therefore$ **$\sin\theta \approx \theta$ in radians,**

- OB $\approx$ radius r, so $\tan\theta = \dfrac{AB}{OB} \approx \dfrac{s}{r} = \theta$ in radians. $\therefore$ **$\tan\theta \approx \theta$ in radians,**

and $\cos\theta = \dfrac{OB}{OA} \approx \dfrac{r}{r} = 1$. $\therefore$ **$\cos\theta \quad 1$**

Use a calculator to prove for yourself that sin 10° = 0.1736, tan 10° = 0.1763 and 10 ° = 0.1745 rad. Also, cos 10° = 0.9848. So, the small angle approximation is almost 99% accurate up to 10°. Figure 14.3 shows how sin θ and cos θ change as θ increases.

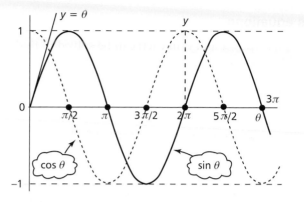

Fig 14.3 Sine and cosine curves

14.1.4 The cosine rule

For any triangle,

$$a^2 = b^2 + c^2 - 2bc \cos A$$

where a, b and c represent the lengths of its sides and angle A is opposite the side of length a, as shown in Figure 14.4. If A = 90°, then cos A = 0 so $a^2 = b^2 + c^2$ in accordance with Pythagoras' theorem.

Note The AS specification includes the **sine rule**. Applying the sine rule to the triangle in Figure 14.4 gives $\dfrac{a}{\sin A} = \dfrac{b}{\sin B} = \dfrac{c}{\sin C}$.

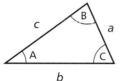

Fig 14.4 The cosine rule

QUESTIONS

1 a Convert the following angles from degrees into radians and express your answer to 3 significant figures:
(i) 30°, (ii) 50°, (iii) 120°, (iv) 230°, (v) 300°.

b Convert the following angles from radians into degrees and express your answer to 3 significant figures:
(i) 0.10 rad, (ii) 0.50 rad, (iii) 1.20 rad, (iv) 2.50 rad, (v) 6.00 rad.

2 a Measure the diameter of a 1p coin to the nearest mm. Calculate the angle subtended at your eye, in degrees, by a 1p coin held at a distance of 50 cm from your eye.

b (i) Estimate the angular width of the Moon, in degrees, at your eye by holding a millimetre scale at 50 cm from your eye and measuring the distance on the scale covered by the lunar disc.
(ii) The diameter of the Moon is 3500 km. The average distance to the Moon from the Earth is 380 000 km. Calculate the angular width of the Moon as seen from the Earth and compare the calculated value with your estimate in **b**(i).

3 a Use the small angle approximation to calculate sin θ for:
(i) $\theta = 2.0°$,
(ii) $\theta = 8.0°$.

b Show that the small angle approximation for sin θ is more than 99% accurate for $\theta = 10°$.

4 A triangle has sides of lengths a, b, and c and internal angles A, B and C opposite sides a, b and c respectively.

a Sketch each of the following triangles and use the cosine rule to calculate a for:
(i) $b = 80$ mm, $c = 60$ mm and A = 60°,
(ii) $b = 75$ mm, $c = 40$ mm and A = 70°,
(iii) $b = 120$ mm, $c = 45$ mm and A = 120°.

b For each triangle in **a**, use the sine rule as appropriate to calculate B and C.

14.2 Algebra

14.2.1 Linear simultaneous equations

Two equations with two variable quantities, x and y, in each can be solved to find the values of x and y. Such a pair of equations is referred to as **simultaneous equations** because they have the same solution. They are described as **linear** because they contain terms in x and y and do not contain any higher order terms such as x^2 or y^2.

The general equation for a straight-line graph is $y = mx + c$, as explained in section 12.4 of the AS book. Two straight lines on a graph can be represented by two such equations. Provided the two lines are not parallel to one another, they cross each other at a single point. The coordinates of this point are the values of x and y that fit both equations. In other words, these coordinates are the solution of a pair of simultaneous equations representing the two straight lines. See 12.4 in the AS book.

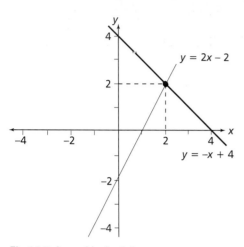

Fig 14.5 *A graphical solution*

The graph approach to finding the solution of a pair of simultaneous equations is shown in Figure 14.5 and is described in section 12.4 in the AS book. However, plotting graphs takes time and is not as accurate as a systematic algebraic method. This method can best be explained by considering an example, as follows

$$2x - y = 2 \qquad \text{(equation 1)}$$
$$x + y = 4 \qquad \text{(equation 2)}$$

Make the coefficient of x the same in both equations by multiplying one or both equations by a suitable number. In the above equation, this is most easily achieved by multiplying equation 2 throughout by 2 to give $2x + 2y = 8$.

The two equations to be solved are now

$$2x - y = 2 \qquad \text{(equation 1)}$$
$$2x + 2y = 8 \qquad \text{(modified equation 2)}$$

Subtracting modified equation 2 from equation 1 gives

$$(2x - y) - (2x + 2y) = 2 - 8$$
$$\therefore -y - 2y = -6$$
$$-3y = -6$$
$$y = \frac{-6}{-3} = 2$$

Substituting this value into equation 1 or equation 2 enables the value of x to be determined. Using equation 2 for this purpose gives $x + 2 = 4$ hence, $x = 4 - 2 = 2$.

The solution of the two equations is, therefore, $x = 2$, $y = 2$

Linear simultaneous equations with two unknown quantities can arise in several parts of the A level physics course, for example:

• $v = u + at$ in kinematics (see AS 12.4)
• $V = \varepsilon - Ir$ in electricity (see AS 12.4)
• $E_{Kmax} = hf - \varphi$ (see AS 12.4)

14.2.2 The quadratic equation

Any quadratic equation can be written in the form $ax^2 + bx + c = 0$, where a, b and c are constants. The general solution of the quadratic equation $ax^2 + bx + c = 0$ is

$$x = -b \pm \frac{\sqrt{(b^2 - 4ac)}}{2a}$$

Note that every quadratic equation has two solutions, one given by the $+$ sign before the square root sign in the above expression, and the other given by the $-$ sign. For example, consider the solution of the equation $2x^2 + 5x - 3 = 0$.

As $a = 2$, $b = 5$ and $c = -3$, the solution is

$$x = \frac{-5 \pm \sqrt{(5^2 - (4 \times 2 \times -3))}}{4} = \frac{-5 \pm \sqrt{49}}{4} = \frac{-5 \pm 7}{4} = +0.5 \text{ or } -3$$

A graph of $y = 2x^2 + 5x - 3$ is shown in Figure 14.6. Note that the two solutions above are the values of the x-intercepts which is where $y = 0$.

Quadratic equations arise in A level physics where a formula contains the square of a variable. The equation $s = ut + \frac{1}{2}at^2$ for displacement at constant acceleration is a direct example. Other examples can arise indirectly. For example, suppose the p.d. across a certain type of component varies with current I according to the equation $V = kI^2$. In a circuit with a battery of negligible internal resistance and a resistor of resistance R, the battery p.d., $V_0 = IR + kI^2$. Given values of R, k and V_0, the current could be calculated using the solution for the quadratic equation with $a = k$, $b = R$ and $c = -V_0$. Such a question is more likely on an A level extension paper (formerly special papers) rather than at AS or A2 and it would probably be structured in stages to lead up to the quadratic equation in small steps.

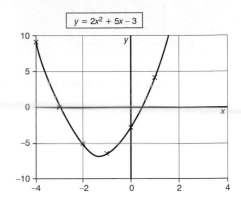

Fig 14.6 $y = 2x^2 + 5x - 3$

QUESTIONS

1 Solve each of the following pairs of simultaneous equations.

   a $3x + y = 6$; $2y = 5x + 1$

   b $3a - 2b = 8$; $a + b = 2$

   c $5p + 2q = 18$; $q = 2p$

2 Use the data and the given equation to write down a pair of simultaneous equations and so determine the unknown quantities in each case:

   a For $v = u + at$, when $t = 3.0$ s, $v = 8.0$ m s^{-1} and when $t = 6.0$s, $v = 2.0$ m s^{-1}. Determine the values of u and a.

   b For $\varepsilon = IR + Ir$, when $R = 5.0$ Ω, $I = 1.5$ A and when $R = 9.0$ Ω, $I = 0.9$ A. Determine the values of ε and r.

3 Solve each of the following quadratic equations.

   a $2x^2 + 5x - 3 = 0$

   b $x^2 - 7x + 8 = 0$

   c $3x^2 + 2x - 5 = 0$

4 Use the data and the given equation to write down a quadratic equation and so determine the unknown quantity in each case:

   a $s = ut + \frac{1}{2}at^2$, where $s = 20$ m, $u = 4$ m s^{-1} and $a = 6$ m s^{-2}; find t.

   b $P = \dfrac{V^2R}{(R + r)^2}$, where $P = 16$ W, $V = 12$ V, $r = 2.0$ Ω; find R.

Logarithms

Any number can be expressed as any other number raised to a particular power. You can use the y^x key on a calculator to show, for example that $8 = 2^3$ and $9 = 2^{3.17}$ In these examples, 2 is referred to as the base number and is raised to a different power in each case to generate 8 or 9. The power is defined as the **logarithm** of the number generated.

In general, for a number $n = b^p$ where b is the base number, then $p = \log_b n$ where $\log_b$ means a logarithm using b as the base number.

Note that $\log_b (b^p) = p$ as $b^p = n$ and $\log_b n = p$.

Applying the general definition above gives the following rules to remember when working with logs:

1 **For any two numbers m and n,**

$$\log (nm) = \log n + \log m$$

Let $p = \log n$ and let $q = \log m$ so $n = b^p$ and $m = b^q$.

$\therefore nm = b^p b^q = b^{p+q}$ so $\log (nm) = p + q = \log m + \log n$

2 **For any two numbers m and n,**

$$\log \left(\frac{n}{m}\right) = \log n - \log m$$

Let $p = \log n$ and let $q = \log m$ so $n = b^p$ and $m = b^q$. Therefore $\dfrac{1}{m} = \dfrac{1}{b^q} = b^{-q}$

$\therefore \dfrac{n}{m} = b^p b^{-q} = b^{p-q}$ so $\log \left(\dfrac{n}{m}\right) = p - q = \log n - \log m$.

3 **For any number m raised to a power p,**

$$\log (m^p) = p \log m$$

This is because $m^p = m$ multiplied by itself p times.

$$\overset{\longleftarrow \text{ p terms } \longrightarrow}{\text{Therefore, } \log m^p = \{\log m + \log m + \dots + \log m\} = p \log m}$$

The following particular bases are used extensively in physics.

1 Base 10 logs, written as $\log_{10}$ or lg

For example,

- $100 = 10^2$ so $\log_{10} 100 = 2$,
- $50 = 10^{1.699}$ so $\log_{10} 50 = 1.699$,
- $10 = 10^1$ so $\log_{10} 10 = 1$,
- $5 = 10^{0.699}$ so $\log_{10} 5 = 0.699$

The above examples illustrate the product rule for logs (i.e. $\log (nm) = \log n + \log m$)) since $\log_{10} 50 = \log_{10} 5 + \log_{10} 10 = 0.699 + 1 = 1.699$.

Uses of base 10 logs

In graphs where a logarithmic scale is necessary to show the full range of a variable that covers a very wide range, as shown in Figure 14.7. Notice in Figure 14.7 that the frequency increases by $\times 10$ in equal intervals along the horizontal axis.

In data analysis where a relationship between two variables is of the form $y = kx^n$ and k and n are unknown constants. Applying the above rules to an equation of the form $y = kx^n$,

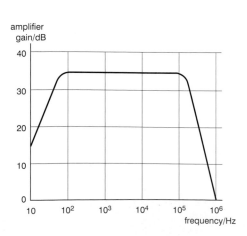

Fig 14.7 *Logarithmic scales*

$$\log_{10} y = \log_{10} k + \log_{10} x^n = \log_{10} k + n \log_{10} x$$

The graph of $\log_{10} y$ (on the vertical axis) against $\log_{10} x$ is, therefore, a straight line of gradient n with an intercept equal to $\log k$.

In certain formulas where a $\times 10$ scale is used. For example, the gain of an amplifier in decibels (dB) is a $\times 10$ scale defined by the formula

voltage gain/dB $= 10 \log_{10} \left(\dfrac{V_{\text{out}}}{V_{\text{in}}} \right)$,

where V_{out} and V_{in} are the output and input voltages respectively.

If $V_{\text{out}} = 50 \, V_{\text{in}}$, the gain of the amplifier is 17 dB ($= 10 \log_{10} 50$).

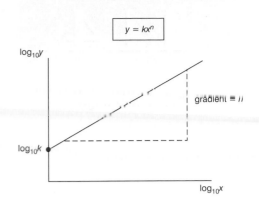

Fig 14.8 *Using logs to test* $y = kx^n$

2 Natural logs, written as $\log_e$ or $\ln$

Here, e is the exponential number used as the base of natural logarithms and is equal to 2.718. For example,

- $2.718 = e^1$ so $\ln 2.718 = 1$
- $7.389 = e^2$ so $\ln 7.389 = 2$
- $20.009 = e^3$ so $\ln 20.009 = 3$
- In general, for any number n, if p is such that $n = e^p$, then $\ln n = p$.

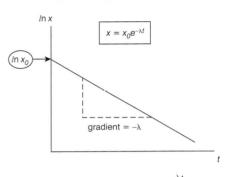

Fig 14.9 *Using logs to test* $x = x_0 e^{-\lambda t}$

Uses of natural logarithms

Natural logs are used in the equations for radioactive decay (p. 165) and capacitor discharge (p. 84) or any other process where the rate of change of a quantity is proportional to the quantity itself. For example, the rate of decrease of p.d. across a capacitor discharging through a resistor is proportional to the p.d. across the capacitor. This type of change is described as an exponential decrease because the quantity decreases by the same factor in equal intervals of time.

Applying the general rule (that if p is such that $n = e^p$, then $p = \ln n$) to the equation $x = x_0 e^{-\lambda t}$ gives $\ln x = \ln x_0 - \lambda t$.

Therefore, a graph of $\ln x$ (on the vertical axis) against t is a straight line with a gradient equal to $-\lambda$ and a y-intercept equal to $\ln x_0$.

Comparing the equation for capacitor discharge $Q = Q_0 \, e^{-t/RC}$ with the equation for radioactive decay $N = N_0 \, e^{-\lambda t}$

- for capacitor discharge, $\ln Q = \ln Q_0 - t/RC$ so a graph of $\ln Q$ (on the vertical axis) against t is a straight line which has a gradient $-1/RC$ and $\ln Q_0$ as its y-intercept,
- for radioactive decay, $\ln N = \ln N_0 - \lambda t$ so a graph of $\ln N$ (on the vertical axis) against t is a straight line which has a gradient $-\lambda$ and $\ln N_0$ as its y-intercept.

QUESTIONS

1 a Use your calculator to work out:
  (i) $\log_{10} 3$,   (ii) $\log_{10} 15$.

  b Use your answers in **a** to work out:
  (i) $\log_{10} 45$,   (ii) $\log_{10} 5$.

2 The gain of an amplifier, in decibels, is given by the formula $10 \log_{10} \left(\dfrac{V_{\text{out}}}{V_{\text{in}}} \right)$

  a Calculate the gain, in decibels (dB), for:
  (i) $V_{\text{out}} = 12 \, V_{\text{in}}$,   (ii) $V_{\text{out}} = 5 \, V_{\text{in}}$.

  b Show that the gain, in decibels, of an amplifier for which $V_{\text{out}} = 60 \, V_{\text{in}}$ is equal to the sum of the gain in (i) and the gain in (ii) above.

3 Write down the gradient and the y-intercept of a line on a graph representing the equation $\log_{10} y = n \log_{10} x + \log_{10} k$ for:

  a $y = 3 x^5$,

  b $y = \frac{1}{2} x^3$,

  c $y = x^2$.

4 a Use your calculator to work out.
  (i) $\ln 3$,
  (ii) $\ln 15$.

  b Use your answers in **a** to work out:
  (i) $\ln 45$,
  (ii) $\ln 5$.

14.4   Exponential decrease

14.4.1 Rates of change

Consider a variable quantity y that changes with respect to a second quantity x as shown in Figure 14.10. The gradient of the curve at any point is the rate of change of y with respect to x at that point. This can be worked out from the graph by drawing a tangent to the curve at that point and measuring the gradient of the tangent. Figure 14.10 shows the idea. The rate of change of y with respect to x at point P is equal to the gradient of the tangent to the curve at P which is $\dfrac{\Delta y}{\Delta x}$.

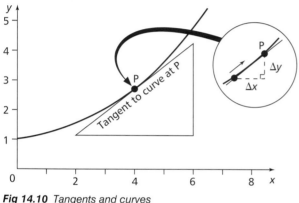

Fig 14.10 *Tangents and curves*

The rate of change of y with respect to x can be worked out algebraically if the equation relating y and x is known. This process is known as differentiation. For example:

- For $y = x^2$, then increasing x to $x + \Delta x$ increases y to $y + \Delta y$ where $y + \Delta y = (x + \Delta x)^2$.

  Multiplying out $(x + \Delta x)^2$ gives $y + \Delta y = x^2 + 2\Delta x + \Delta x^2$

  Subtracting $y = x^2$ from this equation gives $\Delta y = 2\Delta x + \Delta x^2$

  Dividing by Δx therefore gives $\dfrac{\Delta y}{\Delta x} = \dfrac{2\Delta x + \Delta x^2}{\Delta x} = 2x + \Delta x$

  Therefore, as $\Delta x \to 0$, $\dfrac{\Delta y}{\Delta x} \to 2x$ which is therefore the formula for the gradient at x.

  This is written $\dfrac{dy}{dx} = 2x$, where $\dfrac{dy}{dx}$ is the mathematical expression for the rate of change of y with respect to x.

- For the general expression $y = x^n$, it can be shown

  that $\dfrac{dy}{dx} = nx^{n-1}$

  For example, if $y = 3x^5$, then $\dfrac{dy}{dx} = 15x^4$.

Note that differentiation of functions is not required in the AS or the A2 specification. The information on differentiation is provided to help you develop your understanding of exponential change in the next section.

Exponential change happens when the change of a quantity is proportional to the quantity itself. Such a change can be an increase (i.e. exponential growth) or a decrease (i.e. exponential decay). In both cases, the quantity changes by a fixed proportion in equal intervals of time. The A2 specification requires knowledge and understanding of exponential decrease but not of exponential growth. The notes below will, therefore, concentrate on exponential decrease.

In your studies of capacitor discharge (p. 84) and of radioactive decay (p. 165), you will have met and used the equation $\dfrac{dx}{dt} = -\lambda x$ and the solution of this equation $x = x_0 e^{-\lambda t}$.

- Let's consider why the equation $\dfrac{dx}{dt} = -\lambda x$ represents an exponential decrease which is a change where the variable quantity x decreases with time at a rate in proportion to the quantity.

  If x decreases by Δx in time Δt, the rate of change is $\dfrac{\Delta x}{\Delta t}$. This is written as $\dfrac{dx}{dt}$ in the limit $\Delta t \to 0$.

  For an exponential decrease, the rate of change is negative and is proportional to x, therefore, $\dfrac{dx}{dt} = -\lambda x$, where λ is referred to as the decay constant.

- Now consider why the solution of this equation is $x = x_0 e^{-\lambda t}$, where x_0 is a constant.

  Applying the rules of differentiation to the function

  $$x = x_0 \left(1 + t + \frac{t^2}{2 \times 1} + \frac{t^3}{3 \times 2 \times 1} + \frac{t^4}{4 \times 3 \times 2 \times 1} + \right.$$

  similar higher order terms) gives

  $$\frac{dx}{dt} = x_0 \left(0 + 1 + t + \frac{t^2}{2 \times 1} + \frac{t^3}{3 \times 2 \times 1} + \right.$$

  similar higher order terms) which is the same as x.

  So, $\dfrac{dx}{dt} = x$ if x is the above function.

  It can be shown that the function in brackets may be written as e^t, where e is referred to as the exponential number.

Therefore,

$$e^t = 1 + t + \frac{t^2}{2 \times 1} + \frac{t^3}{3 \times 2 \times 1} + \frac{t^4}{4 \times 3 \times 2 \times 1} + \text{similar higher order terms} \dots$$

The value of e, the exponential number, can be worked out by substituting $t = 1$ in the above expression for e^t, giving $e = 1 + 1 + \frac{1}{2} + \frac{1}{6} +$ etc. $= 2.718$ to 4 significant figures.

To show that the solution of the equation $\frac{dx}{dt} = -\lambda x$ is $x = x_0 e^{-\lambda t}$, divide both sides of the equation by $-\lambda$ to give $\frac{1}{-\lambda} \frac{dx}{dt} = x$.

Substituting z for $-\lambda t$ therefore gives $\frac{dx}{dz} = x$ which has the solution $x = x_0 e^z = x_0 e^{-\lambda t}$

The half-life, $t_{\frac{1}{2}}$ of an exponential decrease is the time taken for x to decrease from x_0 to $\frac{x_0}{2}$.

Substituting $x = \frac{x_0}{2}$ and $t = t_{\frac{1}{2}}$ into $x = x_0 e^{-\lambda t}$ gives $\frac{x_0}{2} = x_0 e^{-\lambda t_{\frac{1}{2}}}$.

Applying logs to both sides gives $\ln x_0 - \ln 2 = \ln x_0 - \lambda t_{\frac{1}{2}}$ which simplifies to $\lambda t_{\frac{1}{2}} = \ln 2$

$$\therefore t_{\frac{1}{2}} = \frac{\ln 2}{\lambda} = \frac{0.693}{\lambda}$$

The time constant, τ of an exponential decrease is the time taken for x to decrease from x_0 to $\frac{x_0}{e}$ ($= 0.368 x_0$ as $1/e = 0.368$).

Substituting $x = \frac{x_0}{e}$ and $t = \tau$ into $x = x_0 e^{-\lambda t}$ gives $\frac{x_0}{e} = x_0 e^{-\lambda \tau}$.

Applying logs to both sides gives $\ln x_0 - \ln e = \ln x_0 - \lambda \tau$ which simplifies to $\tau = \frac{1}{\lambda}$ (as $\ln e = 1$)

For capacitor discharge, $\lambda = \frac{1}{CR}$ therefore $\tau = \frac{1}{\lambda} = CR$.

Note

As explained on p. 179, $\ln (e^{-\lambda t}) = -\lambda t$.

Therefore, $\ln x = \ln (x_0 e^{-\lambda t}) = \ln x_0 + \ln (e^{-\lambda t}) = \ln x_0 - \lambda t$.

QUESTIONS

1 **a** For each exponential decrease equation, write down the initial value at $t = 0$ and the decay constant:
  (i) $x = 2 e^{-3t}$,
  (ii) $x = 12 e^{-t/5}$,
  (iii) $x = 4 e^{-0.02 t}$.

  b For each exponential decrease equation above, work out the half-life.

2 A radioactive isotope has a half-life of 720 s and it decays to form a stable product. A sample of the isotope is prepared with an initial activity of 12.0 kBq. Calculate the activity of the sample after:

  a 1 minute,

  b 5 minutes,

  c 1 hour.

3 A capacitor of capacitance 22 μF discharged from a p.d. of 12.0 V through a 100 kΩ resistor.

  a Calculate:
    (i) the time constant of the discharge circuit,
    (ii) the half-life of the exponential decrease.

  b Calculate the capacitor p.d.:
    (i) 2.0 s,
    (ii) 5.0 s after the discharge started.

4 A certain exponential decrease process is represented by the equation $x = 1000 e^{-5t}$.

  a (i) Calculate the half-life of the process.
    (ii) Calculate N when $t = 0.5$ s.

  b Show that the above equation can be rearranged as an equation of the form $\ln x = a + bt$ and determine the values of a and b.

CHAPTER SUMMARY

Trigonometry

- 1 radian $= \dfrac{360}{2\pi}$ degrees.

- Arc length $s = r\,\theta$ where θ is the angle in radians.

- For small angles (i.e. $\theta <$ about $10°$) $\sin\theta \approx \tan\theta \approx \theta$ in radians, and $\cos\theta \approx 1$.

- The cosine rule; $a^2 = b^2 + c^2 - 2bc\cos A$

- The sine rule; $\dfrac{a}{\sin A} = \dfrac{b}{\sin B} = \dfrac{c}{\sin C}$.

Algebra

- Linear simultaneous equations; to solve a pair of simultaneous equations with two unknown variables, x and y,

   1 make the coefficient of x the same in both equations by multiplying one or both equations by a suitable number, then

   2 combine the two equations to eliminate x and so find y, then

   3 substitute the value of y into either equation to find x.

- The general solution of the quadratic equation $ax^2 + bx + c = 0$
   is $x = \dfrac{-b \pm \sqrt{(b^2 - 4ac)}}{}$

Logarithms

- For a number $n = b^p$ where b is the base number, then $p = \log_b n$.

- $\log(nm) = \log n + \log m$.

- $\log(n/m) = \log n - \log m$.

- $\log(m^p) = p\log m$.

- For $y = k\,x^n$, $\log_{10} y = \log_{10} k + n\log_{10} x$;
   the graph of $\log_{10} y$ (on the vertical axis) against $\log_{10} x$ is, therefore, a straight line of gradient n with an intercept equal to $\log k$.

- For $n = e^p$, $\ln n = p$.

- For $x = x_0 e^{-\lambda t}$, $\ln x = \ln x_0 - \lambda t$;
   the graph of $\ln x$ (on the vertical axis) against t is a straight line with a gradient equal to $-\lambda$ and a y-intercept equal to $\ln x_0$.

Exponential decrease

- Exponential change happens when the change of a quantity is proportional to the quantity itself.

- For an exponential decrease, the rate of change is negative and is proportional to x,
   therefore, $\dfrac{dx}{dt} = -\lambda x$, where λ is referred to as the decay constant.

- The solution of this equation is $x = x_0 e^{-\lambda t}$, where x_0 is a constant.

- Half-life, $t_{\frac{1}{2}} = \dfrac{0.693}{\lambda}$ ($=$ time for x to decrease from x_0 to $\dfrac{x_0}{2}$)

- Time constant, $\tau = \dfrac{1}{\lambda}$ ($=$ time for x to decrease from x_0 to $\dfrac{x_0}{e}$)

Synoptic assessment

Synoptic assessment is about testing how well you can draw together (i.e. synthesise) your knowledge, understanding and skills from different parts of the whole A level course. In the module tests for AS level and the A2 module 'Forces, Fields and Energy' and in AS practical assessment, you will have been, or will be, tested on the module specification but not on the links between modules or the links with practical work. Synoptic assessment is left until the last part of your course by which time you ought to be able to bring together your knowledge and skills from different parts of the course so you can apply them in other contexts.

Synoptic assessment contributes 20% of the total marks for A level. It is in three parts, each of which is considered in more detail in this chapter.

1 Data analysis and comprehension is tested by means of a common question attached to the option paper (module 2825) and by common features such as graph work on other questions in the option papers. Synoptic assessment here is worth one-third of the mark for this module so is worth 5% of the total A level mark.

2 Synoptic knowledge, understanding and skills are tested through the written paper 'Unifying Concepts in Physics' (component 01 of module 2826). This paper is worth 10% of the total A level mark. It tests synthesis (i.e. bringing together) of knowledge, understanding and skills from the compulsory modules of the course (i.e. AS modules 'Forces and Motion', 'Electrons and Photons' and component 01 'Wave Properties' of the third AS module + the A2 module 'Forces, Fields and Energy'.)

3 Synoptic knowledge, understanding and skills in the context of practical work are tested in coursework (component 02 of module 2826) and in the practical examination (component 03 of module 2826). The coursework criteria in skill P (Planning) and Skill A (Analysing) include additional A2 coursework criteria intended to test synoptic experimental skills as well as the AS coursework criteria. The other two skills (skill I (Implementing) and skill E (Evaluating)) consist only of the AS criteria. The A2 practical examination includes questions that test these additional criteria. Synoptic assessment here is worth one-half of the mark for the assessment of experimental skills so is worth 5% of the total A level mark.

Data analysis and comprehension

Throughout your course, you will have rearranged formulas, carried out calculations, plotted and used graphs, interpreted graphs, charts and diagrams and used the standard scientific conventions such as unit symbols and labelling of graphs. Given a set of measurements and a formula, you should know how to use the formula, the measurements and your knowledge of straight-line graphs to plot a graph and find out if the measurements fit the formula. All these skills are to do with using data and are referred to as data analysis skills. You should also have developed your comprehension skills through reading about physics in this book and in scientific magazines.

Data analysis skills and comprehension skills are tested directly in the option paper. Regardless of which option you have chosen, there will be one common question worth 20 marks in each option paper. In addition, parts of the other questions which test knowledge and understanding of the option topics, test

Unifying concepts in physics

A unifying concept in physics is an idea or a principle that is used in more than one part of the subject. For example, a conservation law is about a quantity such as momentum or energy that is unchanged when objects interact. You will have met conservation of charge as an explanation of Kirchhoff's 1st Law and you will have learned how to use the idea of conservation to work out the equations for nuclear reactions. Table 15.2 lists the unifying concepts that feature in your A level course and it shows you the topics where each concept is used.

Unifying concepts are tested by means of a written paper (module 2826, Component 01) which all candidates must take. This is part of the scheme of synoptic assessment in the A level specification. All questions on the paper are compulsory. The questions require candidates to draw together knowledge, understanding and skills from the AS modules 'Forces and Motion', 'Electrons and Photons' and 'Wave Motion' and the A2 module 'Forces, Fields and Energy'. The questions require candidates to show connections between different aspects of physics and be able to apply knowledge and understanding of more than one area to a particular situation or context.

This section of the book should help you to prepare for the questions in the 'Unifying Concepts in Physics' paper. It isn't sensible or realistic to try to cover every conceivable combination of topics from different modules so you need to concentrate on what the questions are aiming to do which is to test your understanding of physics by seeing if you can apply physics knowledge and skills to contexts or situations that bring together different aspects of physics. Table 15.3 shows the main links between A2 module 2824 and the AS modules.

To succeed on the 'Unifying Concepts in Physics' paper, you need to:

- Understand the concepts in the compulsory modules, particularly those that are in different modules. Table 15.2 provides a summary of the main concepts and where they appear in the compulsory modules.

- Appreciate key ideas from experimental physics such as accuracy, errors of measurement and graph work. A summary of the main points is provided in the next section, 15.3 Synoptic practical skills.

- Carry out calculations clearly, correctly and in logical order. These aspects of numeracy should be second-nature by now.

- Describe and explain ideas and topics in physics clearly and logically, using appropriate specialist vocabulary. Questions (or parts of questions) that require extended writing are included in the paper. These questions usually require an essay-style answer. Many marks can be lost on such questions through failure to develop written communication skills. Practise your skills of extended writing through homework and questions from past papers. The essay question itself may be no more than two or three lines of text followed by a page or so in which to write your answer. Time spent on the question should be in proportion to the number of marks which will be indicated in the margin. So a question worth 6 marks out of a total of 60 marks for the paper should take less than 10 minutes as the time for the whole paper is 75 minutes. In the limited amount of time for the question:

1 Read the question carefully, taking note of instructive words and phrases such as 'explain' or 'describe' or 'discuss' and of technical words. As you read through the question, underline these key words to reinforce what you read.

2 Decide on the key points of your answer and the order in which these points should be presented. If necessary, jot the key points down and number them in the order you intend to present them.

3 Write your answer in the space available. Don't pad your sentences out as you would be wasting time and space. Remember that the question is testing your ability to write about physics concisely and logically. Ask for extra writing paper if necessary but remember that the space available is an indication of how much to write. Don't waste time writing a 2-page answer if only one page is allocated.

4 Read your answer through to check you have covered all the points you wanted to cover in your answer. Check for spelling, punctuation and grammar.

Table 15.2 Concept connections

Concept		Topics	AS 2821	AS 2822	AS 2823/01	A2 2824
Conservation of	1. Charge	Current and charge; $I = \dfrac{\Delta Q}{\Delta t}$			✓	✓
		Capacitors				✓
		Charge of the electron		✓		✓
	2. Energy	Energy transfers in mechanics	✓			✓
		Energy transfers in circuits			✓	✓
		Energy transfer in thermal physics				✓
		Energy transfer by photons		✓		✓
	3. Momentum	Force, momentum and $F = ma$	✓			✓
		Conservation of momentum				✓
	4. Nucleon number	Equations for α, β and γ decay				✓
Circular motion		Velocity and speed	✓			✓
		Satellite motion				✓
		Charged particles in a magnetic field				✓
Equilibrium	1. Mechanical	Balanced forces	✓			✓
		Principle of moments	✓			
	2. Thermal	Temperature, specific heat capacity, change of state				✓
						✓
Exponential decay		Capacitor discharge				✓
		Radioactive decay				✓
Fields	1. Uniform	Electric field between parallel plates				✓
		Gravitational field near the Earth	✓			✓
		Magnetic field in a solenoid				✓
	2. Radial	Electric field near a point charge				✓
		Gravitational field near a spherical mass				✓
Inverse square law		Newton's law of gravitation				✓
		Coulomb's Law				✓
		Intensity of γ radiation				✓
Logarithmic functions		Half-life $= \dfrac{\ln 2}{\lambda}$ or $RC \ln 2$				✓
		$\ln x - \ln x_0 = -\lambda t$ or $= -\dfrac{t}{RC}$				✓
Probing matter	1. Atoms in solids	X-ray diffraction			✓	✓
		Low energy electron diffraction		✓	✓	✓
	2. The nucleus	Neutron diffraction			✓	✓
		α-scattering	✓			✓
		High-energy electron diffraction		✓	✓	✓
Rates of change		Of velocity and of displacement	✓			✓
		Of momentum				✓
		Of charge			✓	✓
		Of activity				✓
Randomness		Radioactive decay				✓
		Kinetic model of a gas				✓
Resonance		Vibrating system			✓	✓
Vectors and scalars		Resolving a vector	✓			✓
		Vector addition	✓			✓
		Multiplying 2 vectors; $W = Fs$	✓			✓

Table 15.3 *Topic links*

Topic links between A2 module 2824 and the AS modules

Module 2824	AS module 2821	AS module 2822	AS module 2823 (01)
Dynamics			
Force and momentum	$F = \dfrac{m(v - u)}{t}$		
Conservation of momentum	Action and reaction		
Work and energy			
Conservation of energy		Photoelectric equation	
Energy conversions		Photon energy $= hf$	
Work done $W = Fs \cos \theta$	$W = Fs$		
Potential and kinetic energy	$\Delta E_p = mg\Delta h$, $E_k = \frac{1}{2}mv^2$		
Circular motion			
Angular displacement	Speed $= \dfrac{2\pi r}{T}$		Phase difference
Centripetal acceleration	Vectors		
Centripetal force $= \dfrac{mv^2}{r}$	$F = ma$ unbalanced forces		
Oscillations/s.h.m.			
Terms	Displacement		Displacement, amplitude, frequency, period, phase difference
$a = -(2\pi f)^2 x$ $x = A \cos (2\pi ft)$, $A \sin (2\pi ft)$ $v = \pm 2\pi f (A^2 - x^2)^{\frac{1}{2}}$	Graphs of displacement v. time velocity v. time acceleration v. time		Frequency Phase difference, amplitude
Practical examples of oscillating systems	Hooke's Law ($F = kx$) for mass on a spring		
Free + forced vibrations Energy changes Resonance and damping	E_k and E_p changes		Amplitude Stationary waves
Gravitation			
Newton's Law $F = -\dfrac{Gm_1m_2}{r^2}$	Vector nature of force		
$g = F/m = -\dfrac{GM}{r^2}$	g, vectors		
Orbits $T^2 = \dfrac{4\pi^2 r^3}{GM}$	Speed		
Electric fields			
Coulomb's Law $F = \dfrac{Q_1Q_2}{4\pi\varepsilon_0 r^2}$	Force, vectors	Charge, electrons	
$E = \dfrac{F}{Q}$	Force, vectors	Charge	
$E = \dfrac{V}{d}$ (uniform field)	Comparison with g	$\dfrac{V}{L}$ along a wire	
$E = \dfrac{Q}{4\pi\varepsilon_0 r^2}$ (radial field)	Vectors		
E and G fields compared			

Module 2824	AS module 2821	AS module 2822	AS module 2823 (01)
Capacitors			
$C = \dfrac{Q}{V}$		$I = \dfrac{\Delta Q}{\Delta t}$	
$E = \frac{1}{2}QV$		$V = \dfrac{W}{Q}$	
Capacitor combinations		Components in series and in parallel	
Capacitor discharge		Use of $V = IR$ and $I = \dfrac{\Delta Q}{\Delta t}$	
Magnetic fields			
$F = BI\ell \sin\theta, F = BQv$	Force, vectors	$F = BI\ell$, left hand rule	
Circular orbits of charged particles	Force at right angles to velocity		
Electromagnetic induction			
Magnetic flux $\Phi = BA$, flux linkage $= N\Phi$		Magnetic flux density B	
Faraday's and Lenz's laws	Energy conversion	Current and e.m.f.	
Induced e.m.f. $\varepsilon = -\dfrac{N\Delta\Phi}{\Delta t}$			
Graphs; Φ v. t; ε v. t	Comparison with displacement v. time and velocity v. time graphs		
Thermal physics			
Internal energy and temperature	Energy transfers		
Specific heat capacity	Energy transfers	Electric heating	
Change of state	Density		
Ideal gas law	Pressure		
Mean k. e. of a gas molecule	Kinetic energy		
Nuclear atom			
α-scattering experiment	Force, energy, momentum		
Isotopes, moles			
X-ray diffraction			Diffraction
Neutron diffraction		de Broglie wavelength	Diffraction
Electron diffraction		de Broglie wavelength	Diffraction
High-energy electron scattering		de Broglie wavelength	Diffraction
Nuclear equations		Charge in units of e	
$\Delta E = \Delta mc^2$			
$1\ u = 931.3\ \text{MeV}$	Conservation of energy	Electron volt	
Fission and fusion	Energy transfer		
Radioactivity			
Nature of radioactive decay			
α, β, γ radiation		Electrons	γ-photons
Safety			
Activity, half-life			

189

15.3 Synoptic practical skills

Experimental and investigative skills are assessed in the A2 specification through either coursework (component 02 of module 2826) or a practical examination (component 03 of module 2826). The same skills are assessed in coursework as in the practical examination. Assessment of experimental and investigative skills at A2 includes synoptic requirements based on:

- the use of knowledge and understanding from the other compulsory units of the specification for planning experimental and investigative skills and for analysing evidence and drawing conclusions,
- experience of experimental and investigative skills during the whole course, including assessment of these skills at AS level.

The features of each skill area are listed below. These are the same for A2 and AS level. However, the demands at A2 are higher than at AS level because of the synoptic requirements outlined above. The mark schemes for the practical examination and the mark descriptors for coursework incorporate these demands, as explained in pp. 192–194.

15.3.1 The skills

Skill P Planning

- Identify and define the nature of a problem using scientific knowledge and available information.
- Choose effective and safe procedures, select appropriate apparatus and materials and decide on measurements and observation that are likely to produce reliable and useful results.

Skill I Implementing

- Use apparatus and materials appropriately and safely.
- Carry out practical work safely in a methodical and organised way.
- Make and record detailed observations suitably and make measurements with appropriate precision, using ICT where appropriate.

Skill A Analysing evidence and drawing conclusions

- Communicate scientific evidence and ideas appropriately, including tables, graphs, written reports and diagrams, using ICT where appropriate.
- Recognise and comment on patterns and trends in data.
- Understand what is meant by statistical significance.
- Draw valid conclusions by applying scientific knowledge and understanding.

Skill E Evaluating evidence and procedures

- Assess the reliability and precision of experimental data and the conclusions drawn from it.
- Evaluate experimental techniques and recognise their limitations.

The supporting CD-Rom for A2 Essential Physics includes a summary of the advice on practical skills given in Chapter 13 of the AS book (13.2 Planning, 13.3 Making careful measurements, 13.4 Everyday physics instruments, 13.5 Data analysis, 13.6 Report writing). These practical skills are assessed again at A2 in the A2 Practical Examination and in the assessment of A2 coursework. The notes below on the A2 Practical examination and on Coursework outline the synoptic features of the assessment of experimental and investigative skills.

15.3.2 The A2 Practical Examination (1 hour 30 minutes)

This consists of a Planning Exercise and a Practical Test.

1 The Planning Exercise is worth about a quarter of the total mark for the Practical Examination. As at AS level, the exercise is a task set by OCR but is in the context of the A2 module 'Forces, Fields and Energy' and the requirements of the A2 examination paper 'Unifying Concepts in Physics'. The exercise is to be carried out by the candidates over about 7 to 10 days in the period of two months before the Practical Test. Sufficient work must be carried out under direct supervision to allow the teacher to authenticate (i.e. confirm) the work of each candidate as that of the candidate. The Planning Exercise is collected from candidates on or before the day of the Practical Test. The Planning Exercise and the Practical Test are marked by an external examiner.

The mark scheme for the A2 Planning Exercise matches the A2 mark criteria for the coursework assessment of Skill P (Planning). At A2, the Planning Exercise requires research to provide a satisfactory solution to a problem that can be tackled in more than one way. The underlying knowledge, understanding and skills will be drawn from several parts of the AS and A2 specification, not just from one part.

The Planning Exercise is intended to be completed within 7 to 10 days of being issued to candidates. This time can be used to research the topic using library and other resources and to carry out any preliminary work. At A2, researching the topic is likely to be harder than at AS level as it will involve aspects of physics from different parts of the specification. You might find there are several different approaches to the problem and you need to consider and decide on which approach is best. The description of the exercise itself is likely to offer less guidance than at AS level which means that you will need to make more decisions for yourself. For example, if you are asked to investigate the variation of magnetic flux density with position along the axis of a solenoid, you will need to think about the circuit needed to produce the magnetic field and how to measure the magnetic flux density at different positions. Your AS studies on electric circuits and magnetic fields will be important, as well as what you know about magnetic fields and electromagnetic induction from your A2 course. You could use a Hall probe with a steady current passing through the solenoid or you could use a small secondary coil in the solenoid to pick up an induced e.m.f. when an alternating current is passed through the solenoid. In the latter case, you will need to decide how to measure the induced e.m.f. You will need to think about the procedure to follow, what the variables are and how to control them and the precautions you would take to ensure accuracy. You need to describe how you would use your measurements, perhaps using formulas and/or plotting graphs. Some preliminary work in the laboratory would be necessary to make sure your plans are realistic.

Notes for guidance, as summarised below, are issued with the Planning Exercise. Many centres require the plan to be written under supervision in a particular lesson.

Summary of notes for guidance

- The plan should have a clear structure. Diagrams, tables and graphs should be labelled and positioned appropriately.

- Technical and scientific terms should be used correctly and written in clear and correct English.

- The plan should be about 500 words on A4 paper. It can be hand-written or word-processed.

- The plan should be based on the use of standard equipment, apparatus and other materials available in a school or college science laboratory.

• You should show that you have consulted an appropriate range and variety of sources. These sources should be listed at the end of the plan. The list should not be included in the word count. References to these sources should be included in the plan where appropriate.

2 The Practical Examination is designed to test skills I (Implementing), A (Analysing) and E (Evaluating). The test consists of two compulsory practical questions. The mark scheme for both questions matches the coursework mark descriptors for the three skills. These are the same as at AS level except for skill A (Analysing evidence and drawing conclusions) which includes additional descriptors that require candidates to use underlying knowledge, understanding and skills drawn from different parts of the AS and A2 specification, not just from one part.

One question in the Practical Examination is longer than the other question and is set in the same general context as the planning exercise but will not be the same task. The questions are structured in several parts. Instructions are given in each part and candidates are expected to carry out each part and write an answer in the space provided in the question paper.

One of the questions may include making a set of measurements and using the measurements to plot a graph. The question might then require some feature of the graph such as its gradient to be linked to a given equation. Part of one of the questions will require a lengthy written evaluation. Thus, the Practical Examination is a test not just of practical skills but, also, it requires rapid and accurate reading skills as well as the ability to write coherent and fluent prose.

15.3.3 Coursework

The mark descriptors (i.e. criteria used to judge the mark for A2 coursework are outlined below. The descriptors highlighted in bold print are not used at AS level. These are the extra descriptors used for synoptic assessment at A2. Note that the additional descriptors appear only in Skill P (Planning) and Skill A (Analysing). In effect, these extra descriptors relate to how well a candidate uses scientific knowledge and understanding drawn from different parts of the AS and A2 specifications in planning and analysing his/her coursework.

As at AS level, to be awarded the mark at a certain level, all the criteria up to and including that level must be met. An intermediate mark is awarded if only one of the criteria at a certain level is met, provided all the lower criteria are met. If just one lower criteria is not met, your mark plummets to the level of the corresponding lower level.

Skill P; Planning (8 marks maximum)

1 mark

a Define a problem, make a prediction where relevant and plan a fair test or a practical procedure.

b Choose appropriate equipment.

3 marks

a Define a problem using scientific knowledge or understanding **drawn from more than one module of the specification**, and identify the key factors to vary or control or take into account.

b Decide on a suitable number and range of observations or measurements to be made.

5 marks

a Make an appropriate plan, using detailed scientific knowledge and understanding **drawn from more than one module of the specification**, and information from preliminary work or a secondary source, taking account of the need for safe working; justify any prediction and produce a clear account using appropriate specialist terms.

b Describe the plan, including choice of equipment and how to produce precise and reliable evidence.

7 marks

a Evaluate and use information from a variety of sources to develop a plan with logical steps linked to underlying scientific knowledge and understanding **drawn from different parts of the AS and A2 specifications;** use spelling, punctuation and grammar accurately.

b Justify the plan, including choice of equipment, in terms of the need for precision and reliability.

8 marks

The plan is exceptional in terms of originality, depth, flair and the use of novel or innovative methods.

Skill I Implementing (7 marks maximum)

1 mark

a Demonstrate competence and safety awareness in simple techniques.

b Make and record observations and measurements which are adequate for the activity.

3 marks

a Demonstrate competence in practical techniques and manipulate materials and equipment with precision.

b Make and record clearly and accurately systematic and accurate observations and/or measurements.

5 marks

a Demonstrate competence and confidence in practical techniques and adopt safe working practices throughout.

b Make observations and/or measurements with precision and skill, and record them in an appropriate format. Recognise systematic and random errors that affect the reliability and accuracy of the results.

7 marks

a Demonstrate skilful and proficient use of all techniques and equipment.

b Make and record all observations and/or measurements in appropriate detail with the maximum precision possible; respond to serious systematic and random errors by modifying procedures where appropriate.

Skill A Analysing evidence and drawing conclusions (8 marks maximum)

1 mark

a Process some experimental evidence.

b Identify trends or patterns in the evidence and draw simple conclusions.

3 marks

a Process and present experimental evidence, including graphs and calculations as appropriate.

b Link conclusions drawn from processed evidence with associated scientific knowledge and understanding, **drawn from more than one area of the specification.**

5 marks

a Process and analyse evidence in detail, including where appropriate, the use of statistics and the calculation of gradients and plotting of intercepts of graphs.

b Draw conclusions, linked to detailed scientific knowledge and **understanding drawn from more than one module of the specification**, consistent with the processed evidence; produce a clear account with appropriate use of specialist vocabulary.

7 marks

a Make deductions from the processed evidence, using detailed scientific knowledge and understanding **drawn from different parts of the AS and A2 specifications**, with due regard to terminology and use of significant figures.

b Draw conclusions that are appropriate, well-structured, concise, comprehensive and accurate, and linked coherently to underlying scientific knowledge and understanding **drawn from different parts of the AS and A2 specifications.**

8 marks

The work is exceptional in terms of originality, depth, flair and the use of novel or innovative methods.

Skill E Evaluating evidence and procedures (7 marks maximum)

1 mark

a Make relevant comments on the suitability of experimental procedures.

b Recognise any anomalous results.

3 marks

a Recognise how limitations in the experimental procedures or plan may result in sources of error.

b Comment on the accuracy of the observations and/or measurements, suggesting reasons for any anomalous results.

5 marks

a Indicate significant limitations of experimental procedures and/or plan and suggest improvements.

b Comment on the reliability of the evidence and evaluate the main sources of error.

7 marks

a Justify proposed improvements to the procedures and/or plan that would improve the reliability of the evidence and minimise significant sources of error.

b Assess the significance of the uncertainties in the evidence in terms of their effect on the validity of the final conclusions drawn.

Reference section

Data and formulae

Useful data

acceleration of free fall	$g = 9.81 \text{ m s}^{-2}$
the Avogadro constant	$N_A = 6.02 \times 10^{23} \text{ mol}^{-1}$
gravitational constant	$G = 6.67 \times 10^{-11} \text{ N m}^2 \text{ kg}^{-2}$
magnitude of the charge of the electron	$e = 1.60 \times 10^{-19} \text{ C}$
molar gas constant	$R = 8.31 \text{ J K}^{-1} \text{ mol}^{-1}$
permittivity of free space	$\varepsilon_0 = 8.85 \times 10^{-12} \text{ F m}^{-1}$
the Planck constant	$h = 6.63 \times 10^{-34} \text{ J s}$
rest mass of the electron	$m_e = 9.11 \times 10^{-31} \text{ kg}$
rest mass of the proton	$m_p = 1.67 \times 10^{-27} \text{ kg}$
speed of light in free space	$c = 3.00 \times 10^8 \text{ m s}^{-1}$
unified atomic mass constant	$u = 1.66 \times 10^{-27} \text{ kg}$

Formulae supplied in the A2 question papers (excluding options formulae)

uniformly accelerated motion	$s = ut + \frac{1}{2}at^2$ $v^2 = u^2 + 2as$
refractive index	$n = \dfrac{1}{\sin c}$ where c = critical angle
capacitors in series	$\dfrac{1}{C} = \dfrac{1}{C_1} + \dfrac{1}{C_2} + \dots$
capacitors in parallel	$C = C_1 + C_2 + \dots$
capacitor discharge	$x = x_0 e^{-t/RC}$
pressure of an ideal gas	$p = \dfrac{1}{3} \dfrac{Nm}{V} <c^2>$
radioactive decay	$x = x_0 e^{-\lambda t}$ $t_{\frac{1}{2}} = \dfrac{0.693}{\lambda}$

Physics formulae *not* supplied in the question paper (options formulae are not included in the list below)

Forces and motion

acceleration	$a = \dfrac{(v - u)}{t}$
density	$\rho = \dfrac{m}{V}$
force	$F = ma$
kinetic energy	$E_K = \frac{1}{2}mv^2$
moment of a force or torque of a couple	$T = Fd$
gravitational potential energy	$\Delta E_P = mg\Delta h$
power	$P = \dfrac{W}{t}$
pressure	$p = \dfrac{F}{A}$

speed $\qquad v = \dfrac{s}{t}$

strain $\qquad \text{strain} = \dfrac{\Delta \ell}{\ell}$

stress $\qquad \text{stress} = \dfrac{F}{A}$

the Young modulus $\qquad E = \dfrac{\text{stress}}{\text{strain}} = \dfrac{F\ell}{A\Delta\ell}$

weight $\qquad W = mg$

work done $\qquad W = Fs$

Electrons and photons

de Broglie equation $\qquad \lambda = \dfrac{h}{mv}$

electric current $\qquad I = \dfrac{\Delta Q}{\Delta t}$

electrical energy $\qquad W = IV\Delta t$

electrical resistance $\qquad R = \dfrac{V}{I}$

force on a current-carrying conductor $\qquad F = BI\ell \sin \theta$

photoelectric effect $\qquad (E_{Kmax} =) \tfrac{1}{2}mv^2{}_{max} = hf - \Phi$

photon energy $\qquad E = hf$

potential difference $\qquad V = \dfrac{W}{Q}, V = \dfrac{P}{I}$

potential divider $\qquad V_1 = \dfrac{V_0 R_1}{(R_1 + R_2)}; V_2 = \dfrac{V_0 R_2}{(R_1 + R_2)}$

power $\qquad P = I^2 R = \dfrac{V^2}{R}$

resistivity $\qquad \rho = \dfrac{RA}{\ell}$

resistors in parallel $\qquad \dfrac{1}{R} = \dfrac{1}{R_1} + \dfrac{1}{R_2} + \dots$

resistors in series $\qquad R = R_1 + R_2 + \dots$

Wave motion

wave speed $\qquad v = f\lambda$

double-slit interference $\qquad \lambda = \dfrac{ax}{D}$

refraction of light:

1. For light travelling at speed c_0 in air (or a vacuum) passing into a transparent substance where its speed is c $\qquad n = \dfrac{\sin i}{\sin r}$ where $n = \dfrac{c_0}{c}$

2. For light travelling from a substance of refractive index n_1 into a substance of refractive index n_2 $\qquad n_1 \sin i = n_2 \sin r$, where $n_1 = \dfrac{c_0}{c_1}$ and $n_2 = \dfrac{c_0}{c_2}$

Forces, fields and energy

activity $\qquad A = \lambda N$

capacitance $\qquad C = \dfrac{Q}{V}$

centripetal acceleration $\qquad a = \dfrac{v^2}{r}$

Coulomb's Law	$F = \dfrac{Q_1 Q_2}{4\pi\varepsilon_0 r^2}$
electric field strength	$E = \dfrac{F}{Q}$
	$E = \dfrac{Q}{4\pi\varepsilon_0 r^2}$
	$E = \dfrac{V}{d}$
energy of a capacitor	$W = \frac{1}{2}QV$
force	$F = \dfrac{\Delta p}{\Delta t}$
gravitational field strength	$g = \dfrac{F}{m}$
	$g = \dfrac{GM}{r^2}$
induced e.m.f.	$V = -N\dfrac{\Delta\Phi}{\Delta t}$
ideal transformer	$\dfrac{V_S}{V_P} = \dfrac{N_S}{N_P} = \dfrac{I_P}{I_S}$
ideal gas equation	$pV = nRT$
mass-energy	$\Delta E = \Delta mc^2$
magnetic flux	$\Phi = BA$
momentum	$p = mv$
Newton's law of gravitation	$F = \dfrac{Gm_1 m_2}{r^2}$
simple harmonic motion	$a = -(2\pi f)^2 x$
	$x = A \sin 2\pi ft, x = A \cos 2\pi ft$
time constant of a CR circuit	$\tau = CR$
thermal energy change	$\Delta Q = mc\Delta\theta$

Glossary

Absolute temperature, T, in kelvins = temperature in °C + 273(.15).

Absolute zero is the temperature at which an object has minimum internal energy.

Activity, A, of a radioactive isotope is the number of nuclei of the isotope that disintegrate per second. The unit of activity is the becquerel (Bq), equal to 1 disintegration per second.

Alpha radiation consists of particles that are each composed of two protons and two neutrons. An alpha (α) particle is emitted by a heavy unstable nucleus which is then less unstable as a result. Alpha radiation is easily absorbed by paper, has a range in air of no more than a few centimetres and is more ionising than beta (β) or gamma (γ) radiation.

Amplitude of oscillations of an oscillating object is its maximum displacement from equilibrium.

Angular displacement, in radians, in time $t = 2\pi ft = \dfrac{2\pi t}{T}$ for an object in uniform circular motion.

Atomic mass unit, u, (correctly referred to as the unified atomic mass constant) is equal to 1.66×10^{-27} kg. It is defined as $\frac{1}{12}$ of the mass of an atom of the carbon isotope $^{12}_{6}$C.

Atomic number, Z, of an atom of an element is the number of protons in the nucleus of the atom. It is also the order number of the element in the Periodic Table.

Avogadro constant, N_A, is defined as the number of atoms in 12 grams of the carbon isotope $^{12}_{6}$C.

Background radioactivity is radioactivity due to radioactive substances which may be in the ground or in building materials or elsewhere in the environment. Background radioactivity is also caused by cosmic radiation.

Beta radiation consists of beta-particles (β) which are electrons emitted by unstable nuclei with too many neutrons compared to protons. Beta radiation is easily absorbed by paper, has a range in air of no more than a few centimetres and is less ionising than alpha (α) radiation and more ionising than gamma (γ) radiation.

Binding energy of a nucleus:
- the work that must be done to separate a nucleus into its constituent neutrons and protons,
- binding energy = mass defect $\times c^2$,
- binding energy/nucleon is greatest for nuclei of mass number 57.

Brownian motion is the random and unpredictable motion of a particle such as a smoke particle and is caused by molecules of the surrounding substance colliding at random with the particle.

Capacitance of a capacitor is defined as the charge stored per unit p.d. The unit of capacitance is the farad (F), equal to 1 coulomb per volt.

For a capacitor of capacitance C at p.d. V, the charge stored, $Q = CV$

Capacitor combination rules

1 **Capacitors in parallel**; combined capacitance
   $C = C_1 + C_2 + C_3 + \ldots$

2 **Capacitors in series**; combined capacitance is given by
   $\dfrac{1}{C} = \dfrac{1}{C_1} + \dfrac{1}{C_2} + \dfrac{1}{C_3} + \ldots$

Capacitor energy; energy stored by the capacitor,
$W = \frac{1}{2}QV = \frac{1}{2}CV^2$

Capacitor discharge through a fixed resistor R;

1 Time constant $= RC$

2 Exponential decrease equation for current or charge or p.d.; $x = x_0 e^{-t/RC}$

Centripetal acceleration:

1 For an object moving at speed v in uniform circular motion, its centripetal acceleration $a = \dfrac{v^2}{r}$ towards the centre of the circle.

2 For a satellite in a circular orbit, its centripetal acceleration $\dfrac{v^2}{r} = g$.

Centripetal force is the resultant force on an object that moves along a circular path. For an object of mass m moving at speed v along a circular path of radius r, the centripetal force $= \dfrac{mv^2}{r}$.

Chain reaction A series of reactions in which each reaction causes a further reaction. In a nuclear reactor, each fission event is due to a neutron colliding with a $^{235}_{92}$U nucleus which splits and releases two or three further neutrons which can go on to produce further fission. A steady chain reaction occurs when one fission neutron on average from each fission event produces a further fission event.

Collisions An **elastic** collision is one in which the total kinetic energy after the collision is the same as before the collision. A **totally inelastic** collision is where the colliding objects stick together.

Coulomb's Law of force between two point charges states that the force is proportional to the product of the charges and inversely proportional to the square of the distance between the charges. For two point charges Q_1 and Q_2 at distance apart r, the force F between the two charges is given by the equation $F = \dfrac{Q_1 Q_2}{4\pi\varepsilon_0 r^2}$, where ε_0 is the absolute permittivity of free space.

Critical mass This is the minimum mass of the fissile isotope (e.g. the uranium isotope $^{235}_{92}U$) in a nuclear reactor necessary to produce a chain reaction. If the mass of the fissile isotope in the reactor is less than the critical mass, a chain reaction does not occur because too many fission neutrons escape from the reactor or are absorbed without fission.

Damped oscillations of an oscillating system are due to the presence of resistive forces due to friction and drag. For a lightly damped system, the amplitude of oscillations decreases gradually. For a heavily damped system displaced from equilibrium then released, the system slowly returns to equilibrium without oscillating. For a critically damped system, the system returns to equilibrium in the least possible time without oscillating.

de Broglie wavelength A particle of matter has a wave-like nature because it can behave as a wave. For example, electrons directed at a thin crystal are diffracted by the crystal. The de Broglie wavelength, λ, of a matter particle depends on its momentum, p, in accordance with de Broglie's equation $\lambda = \dfrac{h}{p} = \dfrac{h}{mv}$

Decay constant, λ is the probability of an individual nucleus decaying per second.

Diffraction is the spreading of waves when they pass through a gap or round an obstacle. X-ray diffraction is used to determine the structure of crystals, metals and long molecules. Electron diffraction and neutron diffraction are also used to probe the structure of materials. High-energy electron scattering is used to determine the diameter of the nucleus.

Efficiency $= \dfrac{\text{useful energy transferred}}{\text{total energy supplied}}$.

Energy to melt a solid (latent heat of fusion) is used to break the bonds that lock the molecules of the solid into fixed positions.

Energy to boil a liquid (latent heat of vaporisation) is used to break the bonds that prevent molecules moving away from each other.

Explosion In an explosion where two objects fly apart, the two objects carry away equal and opposite momentum.

Exponential decrease Exponential change happens when the change of a quantity is proportional to the quantity itself. For an exponential decrease of a quantity x,

$\dfrac{dx}{dt} = -\lambda x$, where λ is referred to as the decay constant. The solution of this equation is $x = x_0 e^{-\lambda t}$, where x_0 is a constant.

Faraday's law of electromagnetic induction states that the induced e.m.f. in a circuit is equal to the rate of change of magnetic flux linkage through the circuit.

For a changing magnetic field in a fixed coil, induced e.m.f. $= -NA\dfrac{\Delta B}{\Delta t}$.

Fission is the splitting of a $^{235}_{92}U$ nucleus or a $^{239}_{92}Pu$ nucleus into two approximately equal fragments. Induced fission is fission caused by an incoming neutron colliding with a $^{235}_{92}U$ nucleus or a $^{239}_{94}Pu$ nucleus.

Force = rate of change of momentum

$= \dfrac{\text{change of momentum}}{\text{time taken}}$

($=$ mass $\times$ acceleration for fixed mass).

Free and forced oscillations
- **Free oscillations** are oscillations where there is no damping and no periodic force acting on the system so the amplitude of the oscillations is constant.
- **Forced oscillations** are oscillations of a system that is subjected to an external periodic force.

Frequency of an oscillating object is the number of cycles of oscillation per second.

Fusion is the fusing together of light nuclei to form a heavier nucleus.

Gravitational potential energy; change of gravitational potential energy, $\Delta E_P = mg\Delta h$.

Gravitational field strength, g, is the force per unit mass on a small test mass placed in the field.
- $g = \dfrac{F}{m}$, where F is the gravitational force on a small mass m.
- At distance r from a point mass M, $g = \dfrac{GM}{r^2}$.
- At or beyond the surface of a sphere of mass M, $g = \dfrac{GM}{r^2}$ where r is the distance to the centre.
- At the surface of a sphere of mass M and radius R, $g_s = \dfrac{GM}{R^2}$.

Half-life, $T_{\frac{1}{2}}$, of a radioactive isotope is the time taken for the mass of the isotope to decrease to half the initial mass. This is the same as the time taken for the number of nuclei of the isotope to decrease to half the initial number.

Ideal gas law, $pV = nRT$, where n is the number of moles of gas, T is the absolute temperature and R is the molar gas constant.

Intensity of radiation at a surface is the radiation energy per second per unit area at normal incidence to the surface. The unit of intensity is $J\,s^{-1}\,m^{-2}$ or $W\,m^{-2}$.

Internal energy of an object is the sum of the random distribution of the kinetic and potential energies of its molecules.

Ionising radiation produces ions in substances it passes through. It destroys cell membranes and damages vital molecules such as DNA directly or indirectly by creating 'free radical' ions which react with vital molecules.

Isotopes of an element are atoms which have the same number of protons in each nucleus but different numbers of neutrons.

Inverse square laws

- **Force**; Newton's law of gravitation and Coulomb's law of force between electric charges are described as inverse square laws because the force between two point objects (masses in the case of gravitation and charge in the case of charges) is inversely proportional to the square of the distance between the two objects. Because the two laws above are inverse square laws, the field strength due to a point mass or a point charge varies with distance according to the inverse of the square of the distance to the point object.

- **Intensity**; The intensity of γ radiation from a point source varies with the inverse of the square of the distance from the source. The same rule applies to radiation from any point source that spreads out equally in all directions and is not absorbed.

Kinetic energy is the energy of a moving object due to its motion. For an object of mass m moving at speed v, its kinetic energy $E_K = \frac{1}{2}mv^2$, provided $v \ll c$ (the speed of light in free space).

Kinetic energy of the molecules of an ideal gas The mean kinetic energy of a molecule of an ideal gas $= \frac{3}{2}kT$, where the Boltzmann constant $k = \dfrac{R}{N_A}$.

Kinetic theory of a gas

- Assumptions; a gas consists of identical point molecules which do not attract one another. The molecules are in continual random motion colliding elastically with each other and with the container.

- It can be shown that the pressure p of N molecules of such a gas in a container of volume V is given by the equation $pV = \frac{1}{3}Nm <c^2>$, where m is the mass of each molecule and $<c^2>$ is the mean square speed of the gas molecules.

- Assuming that the mean kinetic energy of a gas molecule $\frac{1}{2}m <c^2> = \frac{3}{2}kT$, where $k = \dfrac{R}{N_A}$, it can be shown from $pV = \frac{1}{3}N m <c^2>$ that $pV = nRT$ which is the ideal gas law.

Lenz's Law states that the direction of the induced current is always such as to oppose the change that causes the current.

Line of force or a field line of a gravitational field (or electrical field) A line followed by a small mass (or small charge) acted on by no other forces than the force of the field.
Line of force or a field line of magnetic field is the line along which a free north pole would move.

Logarithmic scale This is a scale such that equal intervals correspond to a change by a constant factor or multiple (e.g. $\times 10$).

Logarithms For a number $n = b^p$ where b is the base number, then $p = \log_b n$.
- $\log (nm) = \log n + \log m$ and $\log (n/m) = \log n - \log m$
- $\log (m^p) = p \log m$
- natural logs; for $n = e^p$, then $\ln n = p$.
- base 10 logs; for $n = 10^p$, then $\log_{10} n = p$.

Log graphs

1 For $y = k x^n$, $\log_{10} y = \log_{10} k + n \log_{10} x$; the graph of $\log_{10} y$ (on the vertical axis) against $\log_{10} x$ is therefore a straight line of gradient n with an intercept equal to $\log k$.

2 For $x = x_0 e^{-\lambda t}$, $\ln x = \ln x_0 - \lambda t$; the graph of $\ln x$ (on the vertical axis) against t is a straight line with a gradient equal to $-\lambda$ and a y-intercept equal to $\ln x_0$.

Magnetic flux density is defined as the force per unit length per unit current on a current-carrying conductor at right angles to the field lines. The unit of magnetic flux density B is the tesla (T). B is sometimes referred to as the magnetic field strength.

Magnetic force

- $F = BI\ell \sin \theta$ gives the force F on a current-carrying wire of length ℓ in a uniform magnetic field B at angle θ to the field lines, where I is the current. The direction of the force is given by Fleming's left hand rule where the field direction is the direction of the field component perpendicular to the wire.

- $F = BQv \sin \theta$ gives the force F on a particle of charge Q moving through a uniform magnetic field B at speed v in a direction at angle θ to the field. If the velocity of the charged particle is perpendicular to the field, $F = BQv$. The direction of the force is given by Fleming's left hand rule, provided the current is in the direction that positive charge would flow in.

- $BQv = \dfrac{mv^2}{r}$ gives the radius of the orbit of a charge moving in a direction at right angles to the lines of a magnetic field.

Magnetic flux, $\Phi = B A$ for a uniform magnetic field that is perpendicular to an area A.

Magnetic flux linkage through a coil of N turns $= N\Phi$ $= NBA$ where B is the magnetic flux density perpendicular to area A. The unit of magnetic flux and of flux linkage is the **weber** (Wb), equal to $1\ T\ m^2$ or $1\ V\ s$.

Mass defect of a nucleus is the difference between the mass of the separated nucleons (i.e. protons and neutrons from which the nucleus is composed) and the nucleus

Mean kinetic energy of a molecule in a gas at absolute temperature $T = \frac{3}{2}kT$, where k is the Boltzmann constant $(= \frac{R}{N_A})$.

Mole One mole of a substance consisting of identical particles is the quantity of substance that contains N_A particles of the substance. The **molar mass** of a substance is the mass of one mole.

Momentum is defined as mass × velocity. The unit of momentum is $kg\ m\ s^{-1}$.

Newton's Law of Gravitation; the gravitational force F between two point masses m_1 and m_2 at distance r apart is given by $F = G\ m_1\ m_2/r^2$.

Newton's laws of motion

- **1st Law** An object continues at rest or in uniform motion unless it is acted on by a force.
- **2nd Law** The rate of change of momentum of an object is proportional to the resultant force on it.
- **3rd Law** When two objects interact, they exert equal and opposite forces on one another.

Newton's 2nd Law may be written as $F = \frac{\Delta p}{\Delta t}$, where p is the momentum $(= mv)$ of the object and F is the force in newtons. For constant mass, $\Delta p = m\Delta v$ so $F = \frac{m\Delta v}{\Delta t} = ma$.

Nucleon A neutron or a proton in the nucleus.

Nuclide of an isotope $^A_Z X$ is a nucleus composed of Z protons and $(A - Z)$ neutrons, where Z is the proton number (and also the atomic number of element X) and A is the number of protons and neutrons in a nucleus.

Phase difference, in radians, $= \frac{2\pi\Delta t}{T_P}$, for two objects oscillating with the same time period, T_P, where Δt is the time between successive instants when the two objects are at maximum displacement in the same direction.

Photon Electromagnetic radiation consists of photons. Each photon is a wave packet of electromagnetic radiation. The energy of a photon, $E = hf$, where f is the frequency of the radiation and h is the Planck constant.

Positron A particle of antimatter that is the antiparticle of the electron.

Power = rate of transfer of energy = $\frac{\text{energy transferred}}{\text{time taken}}$.

Principle of Conservation of Energy This states that in any change, the total amount of energy after the change is always equal to the total amount of energy before the change.

Principle of Conservation of Momentum This states that when two or more bodies interact, the total momentum is unchanged, provided no external forces act on the bodies.

Radian 1 radian $= \frac{360}{2\pi}$ degrees.

Renewable energy This is energy from a source that is continually renewed. Examples include hydroelectricity, tidal power, geothermal power, solar power, wave power and wind power.

Resonance The amplitude of vibration of an oscillating system subjected to forced oscillations is largest when the forced oscillations are of the same frequency as the resonant frequency of the system. For resonance of a lightly damped system, the frequency of the periodic force = natural frequency of the oscillating system. At resonance, the system vibrates in phase with the forced oscillations.

Rutherford's α-particle scattering experiment This experiment demonstrated that every atom contains a positively charged nucleus which is much smaller than the atom and where all the positive charge and most of the mass of the atom is located.

Satellite motion A satellite is a small object in orbit round a larger object. For a satellite moving at speed v in a circular orbit of radius r round a planet, its centripetal acceleration, $\frac{v^2}{r} = g$. Substituting $v = \frac{2\pi r}{T}$, where T is its time period, and $g = \frac{GM}{r^2}$, where M is the mass of the planet, it can be shown that $T^2 = \left(\frac{4\pi^2}{GM}\right) r^3$. A satellite in a geostationary orbit is always directly above the same point on the equator. This is because it is in a circular orbit in the same plane as the equator and it has a time period of exactly 24 hours.

Simple harmonic motion An object oscillates in simple harmonic motion if its acceleration is proportional to the displacement of the object from equilibrium and is always directed towards equilibrium.

- The acceleration, a, of an object oscillating in simple harmonic motion is given by the equation $a = -(2\pi f)^2 x$, where x = displacement from equilibrium, and f = frequency of oscillations.
- The solution of this equation depends on the initial conditions. If $x = 0$ and the object is moving in the + direction at time $t = 0$, then $x = A \sin (2\pi ft)$. If the object is at maximum displacement, $+A$, at time $t = 0$, then $x = A \cos (2\pi ft)$.

Specific heat capacity, *c*, of a substance is the energy needed to raise the temperature of 1 kg of the substance by 1 K without change of temperature. The energy needed to raise the temperature of mass *m* of a substance from T_1 to $T_2 = mc\,(T_2 - T_1)$, where *c* is the specific heat capacity of the substance.

Strong nuclear force This is the force that holds the nucleons together. It has a range of about 2–3 fm and is attractive down to distances of about 0.5 fm. Below this distance, it is a repulsive force.

Time period (or period) is the time taken for one complete cycle of oscillations.

Transformer A transformer converts the amplitude of an alternating p.d. to a different value. It consists of two insulated coils, the primary coil and the secondary coil, wound round a soft iron laminated core.
- The transformer rule states that the ratio of the secondary voltage to the primary voltage is equal to the ratio of the number of secondary turns to the number of primary turns.
- For a transformer that is 100% efficient, the output power (= secondary voltage × secondary current) = the input power (= primary voltage × primary current).

Uniform field A region where the field strength is the same in magnitude and direction at every point in the field.
- The electric field between two oppositely charged parallel plates is uniform. The electric field strength $E = \dfrac{V}{d}$, where

V is the p.d. between the plates and *d* is the perpendicular distance between the plates.
- The gravitational field of the Earth is uniform over a region which is small compared to the scale of the Earth.
- The magnetic field inside a solenoid carrying a constant current is uniform.

Wave particle duality
- Matter particles have a wave-like nature as well as a particle-like nature. For example, electrons directed at a thin crystal are diffracted by the crystal. This is wave-like behaviour in contrast with the particle-like behaviour of electrons in a beam which is deflected by a magnetic field. See de Broglie wavelength.
- Photons have a particle-like nature, as shown in the photoelectric effect, as well as a wave-like nature as shown in diffraction experiments.

Work done Work is energy transferred when a force moves its point of application in the direction of the force. The work done *W* by a force *F* when its point of application moves through displacement *s* at angle θ to the direction of the force is given by $W = Fs\cos\theta$.

X-rays Electromagnetic radiation of wavelength less than about 1 nm. X-rays are emitted from an X-ray tube as a result of fast-moving electrons from a heated filament (as the cathode) being stopped on impact with the metal anode. X-rays are ionising and they penetrate matter. Thick lead plates are needed to absorb a beam of X-rays.

Answers to numerical questions

Chapter 1

1.2
1 a 120 J   b 104 J   3 a 2.3 kJ   b (i) 160 J
2 a 1800 m   b 150 kJ   4 b 21 MJ

1.3
1 a 20 J   b 20 J   c 2.5 m
2 a (i) 3.9 J   (ii) 3.9 J, 5.6 m s^{-1}
  b (i) 2.7 J   (ii) 2.7 J, 4.6 m s^{-1}
3 a 1.5 MJ   b (i) 1.5 MJ   (ii) 210 N
4 a (i) 1030 kJ   (ii) 970 kJ

1.4
1 a 500 MW   b 320 MW
2 a (i) 2.4 km   (ii) 84 m, 37 MJ   b 31%
3 a 1.0 MJ   b (i) 0.38 MJ   (ii) 2.0 kN
4 a 3.7 J s^{-1} b 7.4 %

Chapter 2

2.1

1 a (i) $1.2 \times 10^{-18}\,\text{kg m s}^{-1}$ (ii) $0.050\,\text{kg m s}^{-1}$
(iii) $14\,\text{kg m s}^{-1}$
b (i) $6.0\,\text{kg}$ (ii) $20\,\text{m s}^{-1}$

2 a $3.6 \times 10^{5}\,\text{kg m s}^{-1}$ b $60\,\text{s}$

3 a $5.4 \times 10^{6}\,\text{kg m s}^{-1}$ b $45\,\text{s}$

4 a $9.0 \times 10^{3}\,\text{kg m s}^{-1}$
b (i) $-8.4 \times 10^{3}\,\text{kg m s}^{-1}$ (ii) $1.0\,\text{m s}^{-1}$

2.2

1 a $1600\,\text{kg m s}^{-1}$ b $3200\,\text{N}$

2 a $3000\,\text{kg m s}^{-1}$ b $7.5\,\text{kN}$

3 a $4.2 \times 10^{-23}\,\text{kg m s}^{-1}$ b $1.9 \times 10^{-13}\,\text{N}$

4 a $2.1 \times 10^{-23}\,\text{kg m s}^{-1}$ b $9.5 \times 10^{-14}\,\text{N}$

2.3

1 $0.72\,\text{m s}^{-1}$,

2 $0.70\,\text{m s}^{-1}$ in the same direction

3 $0.050\,\text{m s}^{-1}$ in the direction the $1.0\,\text{kg}$ trolley was moving in

4 $-0.63\,\text{m s}^{-1}$ in the opposite direction to its initial direction.

2.4

2 a $9.0\,\text{m s}^{-1}$ in the same direction b $24\,\text{kJ}$

3 a $1.1\,\text{m s}^{-1}$ in the reverse direction b $20\,\text{J}$

4 a (i) $1.0\,\text{m s}^{-1}$

2.5

1 $0.35\,\text{m s}^{-1}$

2 a $0.25\,\text{m s}^{-1}$; the mass of A and X was greater than the mass of B, so B moved away faster.

3 a (i) $0.10\,\text{m s}^{-1}$ (ii) $15\,\text{mJ}$ b $0.19\,\text{m s}^{-1}$

4 a $9.0\,\text{m s}^{-1}$
b (i) $1.1\,\text{J}$ (ii) $81\,\text{J}$

Chapter 3

3.1

1 a $7.3 \times 10^{-5}\,\text{rad}$ b $4.4 \times 10^{-3}\,\text{rad}$ c $0.26\,\text{rad}$

2 a $20\,\text{ms}$ b (i) $0.31\,\text{rad}$ (ii) $310\,\text{rad}$

3 a $470\,\text{m s}^{-1}$ b (i) $0.0042°$ (ii) $7.3 \times 10^{-5}\,\text{rad}$

4 a $7.0\,\text{km s}^{-1}$ b (i) $0.050°$ (ii) $8.7 \times 10^{-4}\,\text{rad}$

3.2

1 a $0.23\,\text{m s}^{-1}$ b (i) $7.9 \times 10^{-4}\,\text{m s}^{-2}$ (ii) $5.1 \times 10^{-2}\,\text{N}$

2 a $0.53\,\text{m s}^{-1}$, $0.66\,\text{m s}^{-2}$ b $9.9 \times 10^{-2}\,\text{N}$

3 a (i) $3.0 \times 10^{4}\,\text{m s}^{-1}$ (ii) $6.0 \times 10^{-3}\,\text{m s}^{-2}$
b (i) $7.9 \times 10^{3}\,\text{m s}^{-1}$ (ii) $5.1 \times 10^{3}\,\text{s}$

4 a $8.4\,\text{m s}^{-1}$ b $88\,\text{m s}^{-2}$ c $175\,\text{N}$

3.3

1 a $6.7\,\text{m s}^{-2}$ b $3.8\,\text{kN}$

2 a $4.1\,\text{m s}^{-2}$ b $3.0\,\text{kN}$

4 a $40\,\text{m s}^{-1}$

3.4

1 a $30\,\text{m s}^{-1}$ b (i) $11.3\,\text{m s}^{-2}$ (ii) $690\,\text{N}$

2 a $25\,\text{m s}^{-1}$ b $20\,\text{m s}^{-2}$ c $2000\,\text{N}$

3 a $13\,\text{m s}^{-1}$ b $13\,\text{m s}^{-2}$ c $240\,\text{N}$

4 $-0.04\,\text{N}$

Chapter 4

4.1

3 a $0.48\,\text{s}$ b $2.1\,\text{Hz}$

4 a $\dfrac{\pi}{2}$ radians b π radians

4.2

1 a $+25\,\text{mm}$, changing direction from up to down
b 0, moving down
c $-25\,\text{mm}$, changing direction from down to up
d 0, moving up

2 a $0.5\,\text{Hz}$ b (i) $-0.25\,\text{m s}^{-2}$ (ii) 0 (iii) $0.25\,\text{m s}^{-2}$

3 a $0.5\,\text{Hz}$ b $-0.32\,\text{m s}^{-2}$

4 a $-32\,\text{mm}$ $0.32\,\text{m s}^{-2}$ b $0, 0$

4.3

1 a $0.33\,\text{Hz}$ b $0.25\,\text{m s}^{-2}$

2 a (i) $12\,\text{mm}$ (ii) $0.63\,\text{Hz}$ b $6.5\,\text{mm}$

3 a $2.1\,\text{Hz}$ b $0.057\,\text{m}$

4 a $3.7\,\text{Hz}$
b (i) $-8.2\,\text{mm}$ towards maximum negative displacement
(ii) $-0.7\,\text{mm}$ towards maximum positive displacement.

4.4

1 a (i) $0.33\,\text{s}$ (ii) $3.1\,\text{Hz}$
b (i) 0 (ii) $-3.7\,\text{m s}^{-2}$ (iii) $-7.5\,\text{m s}^{-2}$

2 a (i) $3.0\,\text{Hz}$ (ii) $0.33\,\text{s}$ b $f_2 < f_1 \therefore m_2 > m_1$

3 a (i) $70\,\text{mm}$ (ii) $21\,\text{N m}^{-1}$ b (ii) $0.53\,\text{s}$

4 a (i) $1.25\,\text{N}$ (ii) $2.5\,\text{m s}^{-2}$ b (ii) $1.1\,\text{Hz}$, $+46\,\text{mm}$

4.5

2 a $60\,\text{N m}^{-1}$ b (i) $7.5 \times 10^{-2}\,\text{J}$ (ii) $7.5 \times 10^{-2}\,\text{J}$

4 a $85\,\text{mm}$ b $44\,\text{mm}$

Chapter 5

5.1

2 a (i) $33\,\text{N}$ (ii) $160\,\text{N}$ b (i) $16\,\text{N kg}^{-1}$
(ii) $4.0\,\text{N kg}^{-1}$

5.2

1 a $1.3 \times 10^{-6}\,\text{N}$ b $5.4\,\text{mm}$

2 a $780\,\text{N}$ b $6.0 \times 10^{24}\,\text{kg}$

3 a $54\,\text{N}$ b $0.24\,\text{N}$

4 a (i) $16.6\,\text{N}$ (ii) $0.2\,\text{N}$
b $16.4\,\text{N}$ towards the centre of the Earth

5.3

1 a $7.35 \times 10^{22}\,\text{kg}$

2 a (i) $68\,\text{N kg}^{-1}$ (ii) $5.9 \times 10^{-3}\,\text{N kg}^{-1}$

3 a $0.028\,\text{N kg}^{-1}$

4 a (ii) $1.7 \times 10^{31}\,\text{kg m}^{-3}$ b (ii) $9.2 \times 10^{15}\,\text{m}$

5.4

2 a $3.4 \times 10^{6}\,\text{m}$ b $3.0\,\text{N kg}^{-1}$ c $5.2 \times 10^{23}\,\text{kg}$

3 b (i) $9.5\,\text{N kg}^{-1}$ (ii) $7.9\,\text{km s}^{-1}$ (iii) $5200\,\text{s}$

4 b (ii) $7100\,\text{s}$

Chapter 6

6.1
2 b (i) 75 nA (ii) 1.9×10^{11}

6.2
1 a 1.4×10^{-3} N **b** 4.0×10^{4} V m^{-1}
2 a (i) negative (ii) 1.3×10^{-7} C
  b (i) 7.3×10^{-3} N (ii) towards the metal surface
3 a (i) 9.0×10^{4} V m^{-1} (ii) 7.2×10^{-14} N **b** 80 mm
4 a 2.9 kV **b** (i) 5.6×10^{-15} N

6.3
1 a 3.7×10^{-11} N **b** 2.6×10^{-10} N
2 a (i) 69 mm (ii) 3.6×10^{-6} N
  b 2.5×10^{-5} N repulsion
3 a 6.1 nC, negative **b** 2.2×10^{-2} N
4 a 2.7 nC, attract **b** 6.2×10^{-3} m, repel

6.4
1 a 5.3×10^{6} V m^{-1} **b** 10 mm
2 a (i) 3.7×10^{8} V m^{-1} (ii) 5.6×10^{-3} N towards Q_1
3 a (i) 4.5×10^{8} V m^{-1} towards Q_2
    (ii) 2.6×10^{8} V m^{-1} away from Q_1
  b (ii) 11 mm from Q_1, 9 mm from Q_2
4 a 4.0×10^{5} V m^{-1} **b** 0.19 m

Chapter 7

7.1
1 a 5.0 μF **b** 2.2 V **c** 9.9 mC
  d 1.4 μF **e** 11 V **f** 3.4 mC
2 a 264 μC **b** 106 s
3 a 27.5 μC **b** 5.5 μF
4 a 910 μC **b** 220 μF **c** 700 μC **d** 7.4 V

7.2
1 a 5.0 μF
  b 2.0 μF; 6.0 μC, 3.0 V; 3.0 μF; 9.0 μC, 3.0 V
2 a (i) 2.4 μF
    (ii) 6.0 μF; 11.0 μC, 1.8 V, 4.0 μF; 11.0 μC, 2.7 V
  b (i) 3.2 μF
    (ii) 4 μF; 14.4 μC, 3.6 V, 10 μF; 9.0 μC, 0.90 V,
      6.0 μF; 5.4 μC, 0.90 V
3 1. All in series 6.0 μF
  2. All in parallel 79 μF
  3. Two in series with the third in parallel, 25 μF, 30 μF,
    54 μF
  4. Two in parallel in series with the third, 9 μF, 16 μF,
    19 μF
4 a 4.9 μF
  b 2 μF; 12 μC, 6.0 V, 4 μF; 17 μC, 4.3 V, 10 μF;
    17 μC, 1.7 V

7.3
1 a 30 μC, 45 μJ **b** 60 μC, 180 μJ
2 a 0.45 C, 2.0 J **b** 10 W
3 2.2 μF; 5.4 μC, 2.5 V, 10 μF; 5.4 μC, 0.5 V
4 a 56 μC, 340 μJ **b** 6.9 μF
  c 8.2 V **d** 4.7 μF; 160 μJ, 2.2 μF; 73 μJ

7.4
1 a (i) 300 μC (ii) 5.0 s
  b (i) 5 s approx (ii) 20 kΩ
2 a (i) 0.61 mC (ii) 0.45 mA **b** 0.23 V, 15 μC
3 a 13 μC, 40 μJ **b** 0.62 V, 0.42 μJ
4 a 0.34 mJ **b** 1.4 s **c** 0.32 mJ

Chapter 8

8.1
1 a 0 **b** 11 mN **c** 22mN
2 b (i) from South to North
3 0.10 N due North at 20° above the horizontal
4 Long sides; 2.7 N on each side perpendicular to the plane
  of the coil and in opposite directions, Short sides; 0

8.2
1 b (i) 1.9×10^{-13} N (ii) 9.6×10^{-14} N
2 3.8×10^{-23} N horizontal due East
4 b (i) 4.4 m s^{-1} (ii) 8.5×10^{-20} N

8.3
1 a (ii) 21 mm **b** 2.8 mT
2 a 4.7 mT **b** 17.5 mm
3 b 1.2 MeV
4 a 8.0×10^{6} C kg^{-1} **b** 1.4×10^{7} C kg^{-1}

Chapter 9

9.1
4 a (i) Vertically downwards (ii) The eastern end

9.2
1 a (i) 1.1 mWb (ii) 2.0 s (iii) 0.54 mV
2 a 1.4 mWb **b** 23 mV
3 a (i) 4.5×10^{-4} m^2 (ii) 1.5(4) mWb
  b (i) 3.1 mWb (ii) 33 mV
4 a 8.0 μWb **b** 40 μV

9.3
2 flux linkage 0, 0, $-BAN$; induced e.m.f. 0, $-\varepsilon_0$, 0
3 a 26 mWb

9.4
3 a 11.5 V **b** (i) 0.26 A (ii) 5.2 A
4 b (i) 17 A (16.7 A to 3 sig. fig.) (ii) 56 kW

Chapter 10

10.2
1 b (i) 273 K (ii) 293 K (iii) 77 K
2 a 328 K **b** 137 kPa

10.3
1 a 23 kJ **b** 535 kJ
2 a 280 s **b** 10.3 MJ
3 a 320 J **b** 130 J kg^{-1} K^{-1}
4 3.2 kW

10.4
2 0.16 kg
3 a 4.2 J s^{-1} **b** 6500 s
4 a 22 J s^{-1} **b** 6.5 kJ

Chapter 11

11.1

1 126 kPa

2 79 kPa

3 0.097 m³

4 b 2.33×10^{-5} m³, 1600 kg m⁻³

11.2

1 a 1.1 moles **b** 109 kPa,

2 a 9.3×10^{-4} moles **b** 2.1×10^{-5} m³

3 b 1.3 kg m⁻³,

4 a 1.2 kg m⁻³ **b** 2.5×10^{22}

11.3

1 b (i) 0.97 moles (ii) 5.3×10^{-26} kg (iii) 7.8×10^{-21} J

2 a 3.3×10^{-27} kg **b** 5.4×10^{-21} J

3 a 7.8×10^{-21} J

4 a (i) 1.48 moles (ii) 4.2×10^{-2} kg

b (i) 7.7×10^{-21} J

Chapter 12

12.1

4 b 3×10^{-14} m

12.2

1 a $^{235}_{92}$U 92, 143, 92; **b** $^{238}_{92}$U 92, 146, 92;

c $^{4}_{2}$He 2, 2, 2; **d** $^{22}_{10}$Ne 10, 12, 10

2 a 3, 7, 0.43 **b** 55, 137, 0.40

c 88, 226, 0.39 **d** 15, 32, 0.47

3 a 9, 6 **b** 4, 1

12.3

2 b (i) 1600 m s⁻¹

3 a (i) 1.3×10^{-11} m

12.4

2 b (i) 56, 98 (ii) 205 MeV

3 b (ii) 5.0 MeV

4 b 17.6 MeV

Chapter 13

13.1

3 a 42 % **b** 58 %

13.2

1 a $^{238}_{92}$U $\rightarrow$ $^{234}_{90}$Th + $^{4}_{2}\alpha$ **b** $^{228}_{90}$Th $\rightarrow$ $^{224}_{88}$Ra + $^{4}_{2}\alpha$

2 a $^{64}_{29}$Cu $\rightarrow$ $^{64}_{30}$Zn + $^{0}_{-1}\beta$ $(+\bar{\nu})$

b $^{32}_{15}$P $\rightarrow$ $^{32}_{16}$S + $^{0}_{-1}\beta$ $(+\bar{\nu})$

3 a $^{213}_{84}$Po, $^{209}_{82}$Pb, $^{209}_{83}$Bi

b (i) 83 p + 130 n (ii) 83 p + 126 n

4 a 3.2 counts per second **b** 160 mm

13.4

1 a 40 s **b** 6 mg

2 a (i) 9.0×10^{14} (ii) $2.2(5) \times 10^{14}$

b (i) 9.0×10^{14} (ii) 15.8×10^{14}

c 1.3×10^{3} J

3 a 19 kBq **b** 2.4 kBq

4 a 4.4×10^{21} **b** 1.1×10^{21} atoms

13.5

1 a 1.0×10^{-6} s⁻¹ **b** 3.9×10^{16}

2 a 6.3×10^{-10} s⁻¹ **b** 20.5 kBq

3 a 2.7×10^{24} **b** (i) 0.65 kg (ii) 1.7×10^{24}

4 a 1.3×10^{-6} s⁻¹ **b** 149 hours

13.6

1 b 1340 years

2 a (i) 730 kBq (ii) 870 kBq (iii) 1.9×10^{-13} kg

4 b (i) 5.2×10^{13} Bq (ii) 3.3 J s⁻¹

Chapter 14

14.1

1 a (i) 0.524 rad (ii) 0.873 rad

(iii) 2.094 rad (iv) 4.014 rad (v) 5.236 rad

b (i) 5.73° (ii) 28.7° (iii) 68.8°

(iv) 143.2° (v) 343.8°

2 a 20 mm, 2.3° **b** (ii) 0.5°

3 a (i) 0.035 (ii) 0.140

4 a (i) 72 mm (ii) 72 mm (iii) 148 mm

b (i) B = 74°, C = 46° (ii) B = 78°, C = 32°

(iii) B = 45°, C = 15°

14.2

1 a $x = 1, y = 3$ **b** $a - 2.4, b = -0.4$ **c** $p = 2, q = 4$

2 a $u = 14$ m s⁻¹, $a = -2.0$ m s⁻² **b** $r = 1.0\ \Omega$, $\varepsilon = 9.0$ V

3 a 0.5 or −3 **b** 1.4 or 5.6 **c** $-\frac{10}{6}$ or 1

4 a $t = -\frac{20}{6}$ or 2 s **b** $R = 1$ or $4\ \Omega$

14.3

1 a (i) 0.477 (ii) 1.176 **b** (i) 1.653 (ii) 0.699

2 a (i) 10.8 dB (ii) 7.0 dB **b** 17.8 dB

3 a $n = 5, k = 3$ **b** $n = 3, k = \frac{1}{2}$ **c** $n = 2, k = 1$

4 a (i) 1.10 (ii) 2.71 **b** (i) 3.81 (ii) 1.61

14.4

1 a (i) 2, 3 (ii) 12, 0.2 **iii** 4, 0.02

b (i) 0.23 s (ii) 3.5 s **iii** 35 s

2 a 11.3 kBq **b** 9.0 kBq **c** 0.38 kBq

3 a (i) 2.20 s (ii) 1.52 s **b** (i) 4.83 V (ii) 1.24 V

4 a (i) 0.14 s (ii) 82 **b** $a = 6.9, b = -5$

Index

Bold page references refer to illustrations, figures or tables.

Acknowledgements

Photograph acknowledgements

The author and publishers are grateful to the following:

Aberdeen University: 12.10a Professor C Henderson; Alamy: 13.14 Brand X Pictures; AEA Technology: 13.23; Ann Ronan Picture Library: 6.15, 13.2; Cambridge Superconducting Centre: 8.1; CEGB: 2.19; Corbis: 1.16 Sygma/Attar Maher; Corel (NT): 3.6, 4.28; Digital Vision (NT): 3.2, 5.1, 5.9, 5.10, 6.10; Dunlop Slazenger: 2.4; Kevin 'Brindle' Briden: 2.20 courtesy of Mike Subritzky; Martyn Chillmaid: 6.4, 6.7, 8.13; Photodisc (NT): 10.1; Science Photolibrary: 12.8, 13.5a, b, 1.1 David Parker & Julian Baum, 8.11 Brookhaven National Laboratory, 9.4 Sheila Terry, 9.9 Brad Lewis, 10.5 Geoff Tompkinson, Science & Society Picture Library: 5.6; Topham Picturepoint: 4.27 Associated Press; UKAEA: 12.4 courtesy of Emilio Segre Visual Archives, 12.22, 13.12a, 13.24;

Picture research by johnbailey@axonimages.com

Cover Photo: Water drop impact by David Parker/Science Photo Library

Every effort has been made to trace all the copyright holders but if any have been overlooked the publisher will be pleased to make the necessary arrangements at the first opportunity.